KATE PHILLIPS is a social development specialist. For over 40 years, she researched, taught and prepared educational material for rights activists, trade unionists, members of parliaments and would-be politicians in the Caribbean, Africa, Asia, the Middle East and Pacific Islands, where she travelled widely. She has a particular interest in women's lives and organisations in Africa. For many years she directed a postgraduate fellowship awarded by the British Foreign and Commonwealth Office and held in the University of Glasgow which brought rights activists from troubled countries in Africa and the Middle East to study in Scotland.

First published 2022

ISBN: 978-1-910022-55-9

The paper used in this book is recyclable. It is made from low
chlorine pulps produced in a low energy, low emission manner
from renewable forests.

Printed and bound by Severnprint Ltd., Gloucester

Typeset in 10.5 point Sabon by Lapiz

Bought & Sold

Scotland, Jamaica and Slavery

KATE PHILLIPS

Luath Press Limited

EDINBURGH

www.luath.co.uk

Contents

Notes on language and money

LANGUAGE. DURING THE period covered by this book, many Scots were adapting their names to an English spelling; at that time, English itself was not completely standardised. Modern Jamaica has retained some original old Scottish spellings for people and places, such as the plantation Argyle, which retains the old spelling, while the place in Scotland is now spelt Argyll. The language used by slaves was evolving, too, with rhythms and constructions from African tongues applied to European words. To help with continuity and for ease of reading, I have standardised some of these spellings, except when quoting letters, documents and voices where the original spelling is more appropriate. When quoting directly from letters, I have therefore kept the writer's own words, complete with their use of capital letters and sometimes random spelling and punctuation.

Money. Jamaica did not have its own currency during the 18th century. Various coins and currencies were in circulation on the island at that time. Pounds were used as the unit of measure for transactions between Europeans and their estates, and sometimes between white men and the black community. Annual salaries for white men were expressed in pounds and often paid in Britain. When Scots talked of pounds, we should assume they were talking of pounds sterling; Scottish pounds were abolished in 1707, though they were still occasionally used for reckoning. There were 240 pence or 20 shillings in a pound. A shilling was therefore worth 12 pence. It is difficult to compare what a pound would buy in England, Jamaica or Scotland, as its value was volatile throughout the century. In 1750, an English pound was worth almost £220 at today's prices, though it bought less in later years. A skilled slave worth £50 to £100 was therefore as valuable as a good second-hand car today. A pistole was a widely used Spanish gold coin, though the word is French. It was the equivalent of almost one English pound. 'Bits' or 'bitts' were the small coins in use in Virginia and Jamaica for day-to-day transactions, such as paying for vegetables and sex. In the first half of the 18th century, slaves were hired to others for two or three bitts a day.

List of illustrations

1. Map of Scotland in 1750.

2. Map of Jamaica in 1749.

3. Kingston Harbour, from above the town. Drawing by James Hakewill from *A Picturesque Tour of the Island of Jamaica* (London: Cox and Baylis, 1823).

4. Simon Taylor's Holland Estate. Drawing by James Hakewill from *A Picturesque Tour of the Island of Jamaica* (London: Cox and Baylis, 1823).

5. List of Pemberton Valley enslaved men and women. Hamilton Family papers. AA/DC17/113 1 January 1756 (reproduced by permission, Ayrshire Council Archives).

6. List of Pemberton Valley enslaved children. Hamilton Family papers. AA/DC17/113 1 January 1756 (reproduced by permission, Ayrshire Council Archives).

7. Trinity Estate, among those captured by Tacky in 1759. Drawing by James Hakewill from *A Picturesque Tour of the Island of Jamaica* (London: Cox and Baylis, 1823).

8. Port Maria showing the sugar works of Frontier Estate also captured by Tacky in 1759. Drawing by James Hakewill from *A Picturesque Tour of the Island of Jamaica* (London: Cox and Baylis, 1823).

9. Golden Vale, home to 500 slaves. Drawing by James Hakewill from *A Picturesque Tour of the Island of Jamaica* (London: Cox and Baylis, 1823).

10. Montego Bay. Drawing by James Hakewill from *A Pic-turesque Tour of the Island of Jamaica* (London: Cox and Baylis, 1823).

11. The sugar harvest, cutting canes. *Ten Views in the Island of Antigua* (London: Thomas Clay, 1823) via British Library, https://unsplash.com/photos/atIgjLlFryg.

12. The sugar harvest, milling the cane. Cut canes had to be crushed in mills which were turned by wind, water or animals. *Ten Views in the Island of Antigua* (London: Thomas Clay, 1823) via British Library, https://unsplash.com/photos/Sh3FPPouOug.

13. Treadmill, Jamaica 1837. Widely used when slaves became apprentices and planters' use of violence was outlawed. Copy-right British Library Board, Tr.148(k).

14. Pamphlet explaining why households should boycott sugar. Printed in Sunderland in 1791.

15. Flogging men and women to instil obedience. Printed for J Hatchard and son, c 1825, Library of Congress Prints and Photographs Division Washington, DC 20540 USA.

Timeline

1660s   Small sugar houses in Glasgow are refining Caribbean sugar.

1707   Act of Union. Scotland joins England and Wales to form Great Britain. Scots sugar trade now protected from piracy and competition by the British navy.

1707   Jamaica becomes a British Colony. Scots take up land in Jamaica.

1728   Maroons (indigenous Jamaicans [Taíno] and escaped slaves) fight British authorities for control of land in Jamaica.

1738   Philosopher Francis Hutcheson publishes *System of Moral Philosophy*, which warns that Scots buying, selling and owning slaves are allowing 'the high prospect of gain' to 'stupefy their consciences'.

1740   After ten years of fighting, Britain is forced to sign peace treaties with the Maroons. Maroon land in Jamaica recognised on condition they return 'runaway slaves'.

1740 Philosopher David Hume publishes his thoughts on Africans: 'I am apt to suspect the negroes to be naturally inferior to whites'.

1744 Jamaican sugar exports now worth £703,000.

1744–8 Britain at war in Europe; French encourage rebellion in Scotland.

1746 Sons of rebel families escape to Jamaica.

1748 Scottish Consortium of Grants, Boyds and Oswalds buy Bunce Island Fort, where Africans are kept like cattle before shipment to colonies.

1752 Royal monopoly over slave trade ends; Scottish merchants and traders invest fortunes in Liverpool, Bristol and Kingston, Jamaica.

1754 Maroon revolt brutally put down.

1760 Tacky, leader of enslaved people, attempts to capture five estates which are brutally reclaimed, but unrest continues for several years.

1762 Jamaican sugar exports now worth £1,003,290.

1765 Merchants invest in industrial-scale sugar refineries on lower Clyde.

1770 James Beattie's thoughts on slavery make him a popular bestselling writer. *An Essay on the Nature and Immutability of Truth* argues that commerce cannot take precedence over justice to fellow human beings. David Hume calls Beattie 'a pretend philosopher'.

1774   Lord Kames argues in *Sketches on the History of Man* that Africans might be an entirely different species.

1775–83   American War of Independence. Britain fears loss of further colonies such as Jamaica.

1776   Martial Law imposed to control continuing and widespread rebellions amongst slaves seeking their freedom.

1787   Society for the Abolition of the Slave Trade formed in England.

1788   Anti-Slavery Committee established in Edinburgh.

1788   Privy Council enquires into nature of slavery.

1789   French Revolution overthrows monarchy, leading to widespread repression in Britain.

1792   Scottish Anti-Slavery Committee sends out 'Address to the people of Scotland', resulting in anti-slavery petitions being sent to Westminster from religious groups all over the country.

1792   Wilberforce tables bill for abolition of the slave trade. Bill derailed when Dundas adds 'gradual' before the word abolition.

1805   Jamaica now has 280,000 slaves; those who die young are replaced by thousands more imports.

1807   Trade in slaves is finally abolished.

1823   Anti-Slavery Campaign revived to work towards the end of the institution of slavery. The Jamaican Assembly refuses to implement the British Government's agreed plan to improve the lives of slaves.

1824   Slaves fight for the implementation of the rights granted to them by the British Government. John Clarke, John Miller and Ben Reynolds, revolutionaries from Argyle Estate, kill themselves and die free rather than be hanged as slaves. Argyle gains symbolic meaning for the slave community.

1826   Questions in British Parliament about perversion of justice in Jamaica during 'recent slave trials'.

1831   Governor of Jamaica reports that despite his efforts to get the Jamaican Assembly to agree upon limited rights for slaves, there is no hope of the Jamaican Assembly approving them.

1831   Jamaica now has 300,000 surviving slaves.

1831–2 In the final revolt, 60,000 enslaved men and women stop work to protest their conditions and demand rights, led by black Baptist deacon Samuel Sharpe. Missionary activity blamed for slave unrest.

1832   Colonial Church Union formed to violently oppose missionary activity in Jamaica. Planters Campbell, Grant, Oswald, McDowel and Napier organise the Trelawny branch.

1834   British Government decrees all slaves over six years old must become 'apprenticed labourers' until 1838.

1834   Compensation of £20 million paid to former slave owners. Apprenticeship abandoned.

Acknowledgements

LET ME BEGIN BY thanking the people of Brighton District, Jamaica who first made me question the idea that the mission to end slavery had righted wrongs done to their country and its people. I also want to thank Roger Thompson in his home-made cabin in the Blue Mountains, who shared his love of preserved fish, oat porridge and so much more from our joint past. I also benefited from many chance conversations and kind encounters which led me on a distressing, complicated, but fascinating journey towards a better understanding of our history. Abey Ina Billow spurred me on with messages from the far north of Kenya, rebuking me for introducing students like him to Glasgow without discussing slavery, an omission I needed to correct. Once I had a first draft, Brenda Graham helped immensely by volunteering to read, comment on and correct my text, and Susan Dalgety offered a crucial suggestion about how to introduce the story. I am indebted to all three of them.

Archivists in Ayrshire, Argyle and Dumfries were most helpful in identifying useful subject matter, in particular Claire Kean in South Ayrshire who directed me towards the Hamilton family papers and the minutes of a great number of local Kirk sessions. Thanks also to Sam Phillips for all his help with the illustrations.

I'm immensely grateful to my editor, Gwyneth Findlay, for making this a much better book by questioning my language, challenging my perspective and sharpening my focus. Finally, my husband Dave deserves a big thank you. He lived with my obsession for a whole year while I struggled to understand the whole story.

Preface:
Freeing our minds

BOB MARLEY SINGS about the painful abuse that enslaved Africans suffered and the damage of slavery which lives to this day, a hangover from events long ago. His songs claim that we cannot properly understand and put right false ideas that we do not acknowledge. He makes a plea to all of us to 'emancipate ourselves' and understand that we need to 'free our minds'.

The Black Lives Matter campaign has rightly drawn attention to the role of prominent Scots in slavery and the way some of these people are still celebrated in our street names and statues. It seems to be the right moment to revisit that period in our history and ask what the people of Scotland thought. How widespread was the belief that 'Black lives' did not particularly matter?

Before Europeans began buying large numbers of enslaved people in Africa, dark-skinned people were simply people. Before the 1700s, when my telling of this story begins, society judged status by wealth and ownership of land. The wealthy were high class; the poor were looked down upon. Those of a different religion were regularly discriminated against, even hated at times, but skin colour was of very little significance. 'Black' and 'white' differences were invented for a particular purpose.

This book uses two small countries, Scotland and Jamaica, to trace the story of how and why many Scots became involved for well over a hundred years in the buying and selling of humans and the crucial change this commerce made to our society, including our understanding of ourselves. As the book explains, the slave trade was vigorously defended by attitudes and beliefs that cascaded down through the generations to produce the long-lasting consequence of widespread racism.

It is worth reminding ourselves about the economic importance of slavery. Although Jamaica is a very small island, throughout the 1700s sugar production by hundreds of thousands of enslaved Africans made the island Britain's most wealthy colony by far. It was worth more than all the tobacco from Virginia, indeed more than the whole produce of North America, to the British economy. Taxes on sugar imports and personal taxes collected from Jamaican slave owners and traders, together with massive transfers of private wealth, were worth many millions to the British economy.

In the 1660s, there were already several sugar refineries on the Clyde in Glasgow. The implementation of English laws principally intended to keep the Spanish and French from 'stealing' England's lucrative overseas trade began to squeeze out the many Scottish merchants. Though subjects of the same king, they were interloping foreigners when it came to trade, unlawfully busy making money in the Caribbean. The 1707 Act of Union which joined Scotland to England specifically addressed this question, giving Scots full rights to trade and settle in the British colonies. The Scots took advantage of this opportunity, becoming major players in and around Jamaica.

In the 18th century, control over enslaved Africans on the lucrative island of Jamaica became very important to Scotland's prosperity. For some idea of how high the stakes were, the legislation which brought slavery in the British colonies to an end included a government payment of the modern equivalent of £2.3 billion (using Bank of England figures) in personal compensation to former slave owners, about 20 per cent of which went to people living in Scotland.

When I set out to write this book, it was not my intention to write a polemic on Black lives in Jamaica. I will leave that to a person for whom racism is lived reality. I could have written an academic text, a 'whole history' packed full of relevant academic references and arguments, but that is not my style, and this is therefore not that kind of book. I began with a simple question: How did so many thousands of educated Scottish Christians become involved in slavery in Jamaica, and how did they justify their lifestyle to themselves and to others? What did Scottish newspapers, popular historians, philosophers and the public think at the time? Did they tell themselves that black lives didn't matter because white people were superior to anyone with a darker skin?

To address this question, I needed first-hand accounts. I needed to go back to the beginning, when Scots first crossed the Atlantic and encountered Africans. I ended up doing a good deal more research than I had anticipated. The question I was trying to pin down was both more harrowing and complicated and the results ultimately more challenging than I had first expected. Fortunately, Scots in the 1700s were literate and opinionated. Our forebears, even in the 1700s, sent letters and instructions back and forth across the Atlantic Ocean. They wrote angrily to the newspapers and argued in Parliament about Jamaica. The place was important enough to Scotland to receive a lot of public attention.

The reason the resulting book is framed quite deliberately as a journey, a story with a beginning, middle and end, is because it is intended as exactly that. My narrative records the many reasons why people from Scotland crossed the Atlantic, the ambitions they had, where those ambitions took them and where that leaves us today. I try to tell it as far as possible through their eyes. In that sense, the story is written from a 'white perspective'. The book ends with the end to slavery, but my research confirmed that the attitudes formed in the time of slavery have undoubtedly been passed down through many generations and remain with us in Scotland today.

The text is informed by wide reading of Black academic sources and writing by people who lived in bondage for much of their lives. For obvious reasons, precious few enslaved Jamaicans left behind written accounts of their lives in the 1700s, though remarkably some did. Wedderburn's recollections of his white father's predatory attitude toward the women he enslaved and his descriptions of his courageous, smuggler granny offer a rare window into their long ago lived experience.[1] Most slave writing, however, was published, and sometimes rather clumsily edited, by white Christians in the United States after slavery was abolished. Though these accounts are very helpful, their time frame and attitudes arose in a more settled society. Scots in the Caribbean Islands were predominantly male, itinerant visitors rather than settler families.

Jamaica had few resident white women and tens of thousands of young, enslaved girls. The result was a society where sex between white men and black women and the sexual abuse of young black girls was widespread.

Letters home to Scotland recorded much about life on the island of Jamaica: recovery from debilitating tropical illnesses, gossip about Scottish neighbours, explanations of how to cook turtles sent as gifts and the delights of eating pineapples. They included details of the birth and health of many Jamaican grandchildren. Family members replied from small towns and landed estates across Scotland expressing hopes for the success of Jamaican enterprises and the safe return of their adventurers. Newly arrived young men wrote to reassure family that they had safely made it, were receiving help from fellow Scots, and hoped to find new positions on the island. Arrangements were made for their children – some white, but mostly children of colour – to be sent home to get a good Scottish education. Successful planters invited friends to visit and view their island lives and arranged regular visits home for themselves.

Some of the language I use to tell this story needs explanation. It was some years before 'white' and 'black' were widely understood categories. I therefore avoid them in the early chapters of the book. Planters used the word 'negro', a word I quote in the text when reporting their speech or views. As I have suggested, 'white' was a category given to Europeans of all classes for political reasons. It came later in the 1700s when the need to keep the enslaved in their place became more strident as some children of colour and skilled slaves were mixing freely in white society. I use the word 'slave' or 'slavery' when I am talking about that system, the institution and the campaigns against it. In doing so, I recognise how hard it is to find words which help us to escape de-humanising ideas and images of enslaved people. I want to rewind, wipe the images and rebuild for a number of reasons. The typical slave cutting and planting cane in the sugar fields was not a black-skinned man with whip marks on his back, though many thousands of such men existed, but a resilient, sexually abused, teenage girl. Enslaved girls thought of themselves as Africans by cultural heritage, and this is the word I mostly use to talk about them. Second and third generation slaves maybe thought of themselves as Jamaican Africans. Scots, by contrast, were 'in Jamaica' but never thought of or referred to themselves as 'Jamaicans'.

In those years, the island had great prestige with which Scots were keen to be associated. Moreover, it was a place that was familiar to many, many Scottish people. When Scots left home for North America, they stayed there, but most of the tens of thousands of young men of all classes and trades who went to Jamaica came back to Scotland. They wrote home regularly. I spent hours in archives with their letters and carefully kept accounts, unwrapping their flimsy, yellowed papers, struggling with the curly flourishes of their script and imagining their journey across the Atlantic all those years ago. I studied the regular orders for nails, hoes, bed sheets, candles, butter and pearl barley. I read the writers' thanks for the presents of pickles, cheese and sauces, safely arrived on the other side of the Atlantic. These letters introduced characters who spoke of bathing in the warm waters of the Caribbean and asking whether the barrel of sugar sent as a present for their grandmother had arrived yet.

Africans might arrive in Jamaica in a wretched state, but they also left homes, familiar foods and loved ones behind. They brought with them plenty of useful African know-how about surviving in a hot climate. Like rural people in Scotland at that time, they knew how to build their own homes and grow their own food. In addition, on arrival they were often trained to became expert masons, carpenters and distillers. In an effort to free the narrative from dominant images, I hesitate to call them 'enslaved' each time they are mentioned, even though they certainly were enslaved, but the word feels dehumanising. They were also struggling to be thinking, feeling, fully human beings. In an effort to restore some of that humanity, I prefer to simply call them 'Africans', 'expert Africans' or 'field workers'. I call them 'slaves' when paraphrasing white thinking, reporting white perspectives and examining official views in order to emphasise that difference.

Scottish place names, smoked herrings in tins, oat porridge and folk with the surname 'Campbell' are obvious signs that Scottish people once lived in Jamaica. Porridge made with ale and sugar is a current staple in the Blue Mountains, a dish which was the centrepiece of Scottish harvest festivals in the 18th century. I had never thought of Scotland and Jamaica as quite so intimately connected. I was surprised to find that four of the six 18th century governors of Jamaica, those who were in charge when the sugar trade was at its height, were proud Scots. These governors received the second highest salary paid to any British colonial official. The post was one of huge influence. The Scots were active in all the Caribbean Islands; in many, they formed a higher proportion of the population than they did in Jamaica, but Jamaica, being the most prosperous, was of much greater importance to Scotland's economy. At the time, it brought more profit to Britain than the much larger colonies of North America.

Shortly after I began my work on Scotland and Jamaica, I made a visit to the island. There I learned that not only Campbell but Thompson, Cameron, Grant and various Mcs and Macs are common Jamaican surnames. Several people I met claimed descent from Scots. I could see superficially that Scotland played a role in shaping modern Jamaica and that the island has undoubtedly influenced Scotland. Jamaicans love preserved fish, and Scots to this day have a sweet tooth. Without sugar from Jamaica, there would have been no Scottish shortbread, marmalade, tablet or boiled sweets. Enslaved Africans were fed from products which never grew in the West Indies and which today's Jamaican residents still have a taste for. But tracking down the more fundamental ways in which the relationship shaped Scotland needed sustained work. Plantation books confirmed that feeding and clothing the enslaved population with barrels of herring, oats and linen cloth were good business opportunities on which many Scottish jobs depended. The cheap imported protein of those days has been passed down through several generations and lives on in modern taste buds. The slave diet of yesterday has become the soul food of today: salt or smoked fish with ackee in Jamaica and ham hock soup with greens in the American South.

Several of the rural shacks in which we slept on our visit to the island were obviously homemade. The plots on which they stood had been handed down from generation to generation on abandoned 'capture land' and settled by squatters. Like many Jamaicans, our hosts might roughly know the history of their homes, but had no documents to prove the little plot on which their home stood belonged to them. When sugar lost the protective taxes it had enjoyed for centuries and workers had to be paid, many European landowners simply walked away, still holding their proof of ownership of the land. The more recent tourist boom has created a potential for profit in the picturesque Blue Mountains, where runaways hid themselves long ago, and on the scraps of provision ground land along the seaside coast, where former slaves made free lives. Squatters are now being confronted by owners who want their land back.

My research uncovered that Jamaica gave Scotland so much more than sugar. Scottish doctors, working on slave ships and sugar estates, practiced the use of quinine for treating malaria and built expertise in tropical medicine. It was in Jamaica that doctors pioneered the widespread use of the live smallpox inoculation that eventually led to better survival rates for Scottish schoolchildren.[2] Scots learned and brought home commercial habits from sugar estates that were later applied to Scottish land management and industry. The profitable business which attracted many to the port of Kingston, the biggest slave trading centre in the Caribbean, was the buying and selling of slaves, which many Scots moved into. They hired hundreds of Scottish seamen and sea captains who risked their lives trading slaves and gained valuable ocean-going navigational expertise in the process. Little real money changed hands in Jamaica. The proceeds of enterprises there were paid into accounts in Glasgow, Ayr or Edinburgh that were used for all financial transactions, including funds to buy shoes and underclothes for mothers and sisters at home.

Estate accounts and ostentatious spending by elite Scots, family wills and eventual compensation for slaves were all testaments to the money made in Jamaica. Some families made enough to be catapulted into a global elite. Since so much has been written about planter families and their estates, I was surprised to find that Scottish traders and merchants were more numerous than planters in Jamaica. Scottish archives brought home to me how many small traders made a living by loading their boats with Scottish produce and crossing to Jamaica, returning with cargoes full of sugar, rum and sometimes cotton from America. This trading brought various degrees of wealth to most of Scotland's coastal towns, such as Inveraray, Ayr, Wigtown, Kirkcudbright, Arbroath, Leith and Dumfries.

Merchant banks in Scotland held the steady flow of profit from the sale of sugar and rum. These banks arranged mortgages for major land and slave purchases to be paid off year by year from Scottish accounts. The most opulent of our merchant families risked their wealth in equipping ships with barter goods for the transatlantic slave trade, establishing trusted kin in each corner of the trade linking Scotland, West Africa and Kingston. They spread their risks by joining funding partnerships for boats venturing from the ports of

Liverpool, London and Bristol. They developed comfortable rooms in which bartering took place, out of sight of the slave holding dungeons and cages on the West African coast. They set up the slave markets in Kingston, Jamaica and stabilised prices by taking bookings for slaves, which were underwritten by guaranteed loans for purchase. They helped to make Kingston the most important hub of the trade, from which the enslaved were transported to America and other Caribbean islands. Scottish families over several generations played a substantial and lucrative role in trafficking the more than six million Africans who were sold into a life of plantation slavery. In the process, they helped to develop the legal and financial pillars of the British Empire and the resulting modern international capitalism. The risks of poor harvests and possible loss of valuable cargoes crossing the Atlantic were protected by a rapidly developing insurance business. Scotland's leading role in banking and insurance therefore owed much to the buying, transportation and sale of enslaved Africans. Vigilance in keeping slaves chained down and locked up on board ships kept insurance risks as low as possible. On the plantations, vigilance and a strong record in extracting hard work and preventing escapes helped bankers to assess risk when granting mortgages.

These are just some of the many reasons why not every Jamaican wants to simply forgive the wrongs done to their people. Exactly how much of Scotland's wealth originated from the sugar and slave trade and all of its associated industries is a matter of debate. It cannot be denied that profits made in Jamaica were transferred to Scotland. This nation therefore bears a significant share of responsibility for the enslavement of Africans, the harm done to the Black population over more than 100 years and Jamaica's post-slavery poverty. There are groups in Jamaica today who say that Scots oppressed them, bled their country dry, got their money out if they could and returned home. If Scotland gets its independence, these Jamaicans want to put a financial figure on that harm and send the bill for reparations.

During the 1700s and 1800s, the columns of our Scottish newspapers took up Jamaican causes and reported the arrival or non-arrival of Jamaican boats in our ports. There were regular reunions in Glasgow where successful ex-Jamaican adventurers drank to their achievements. They fondly recalled their adventures in the sun and toasted continued prosperity to the island that had transformed their lives. So proud were they of the Jamaican connection that they named their Jamaican estates after their Scottish homes and Glasgow's streets after people and places in Jamaica. Those who came home with wealth changed the look of our countryside. They refashioned the land they bought and homes they built in Scotland to look much like the grand plantations they left behind.

For many years, itinerant Scotsmen were preferred as overseers, bookkeepers and managers, experts in cracking the whip over the naked backs of the women and men who laboured on the plantations. At the same time, Scots in Jamaica enjoyed sex, both consensual and abusive, with enslaved women, leaving behind or bringing home a great number of illegitimate children of colour. Initially, the children born to white men with black partners scandalised their

Scottish families, not because they were black, but because they were rather obviously illegitimate. Many Jamaicans have Scottish names. Their claim to being descended from Scots is easier to establish than the authenticity of a surname, as many Jamaicans researching their roots have found. For over 100 years, there was a large, itinerant population of young Scottish men living on the island of Jamaica. Best estimates calculate this population never dipped much below 20,000, but in the late 1700s and early 1800s could have been much higher. They accounted for about a third or perhaps half of Jamaica's white residents. Many only stayed for five to ten years, but new adventurers were found to cross the Atlantic and replace them throughout the whole of the 18th and early 19th centuries. Graves in churchyards in Kirkcudbrightshire record 100 or more such adventurers who died in Jamaica but whose families had taken the trouble to chisel their names on the family headstone.

Diaries, letters and local records of births and wills, as well as Jamaican legislation to control 'mixed-race' offspring, allow us to estimate the resulting progeny of these young men. Scots were probably responsible for a third to a half of the vast numbers of those identified as 'mixed-race' children who were born to enslaved mothers in Jamaica over the years when large numbers of Scots lived there – 30,000 of over 100,000 children would be a rather conservative figure. The British Government required that a census of residents, including enslaved residents, be made from time to time. A figure for these official 'mixed-race' and 'free coloured' individuals is available for some localities. This figure would include only those children whose fathers had the cash to manumit/free them and all those children born into settled enough partnerships for their fathers to register themselves as the white parent. Thomas Thistlewood, one of the diarists used in my story, did this with only one of his several children, his son John.

Children in the census were a small subset of the children born of 'black–white' liaisons over the century. Many of the children of fleeting, coerced or paid sexual encounters, and all of those born to cash-strapped bookkeepers and tradespeople, would not necessarily be included here. These children would grow up enslaved and working in the fields. Their claim to Scots parentage gave them no rights, and a specific parent could not be easily verified. Few children of colour were legitimate, as only free mothers could marry a child's father. Children born to enslaved mothers were owned by whoever owned their mother. Their lighter skin could cause them problems. 'Brown' children were thought to be less capable of hard work, less biddable and therefore troublesome 'field slaves'. Knowing this, and the brutal life in the sugar field, fathers, if they cared at all and had money, found them jobs in or around the great house or paid for an apprenticeship where they might learn a skill. These enslaved children of colour, who were the great majority of those of mixed parentage, had no surnames. They might have known who their father was, they might have used his name, but they did not bear his name legally. Wills of planters show that those children who did have a surname were rarely given their Scottish father's name. In the African community in Jamaica, family life was rarely stable. The bonds of fatherhood were casually broken by the sale and movement of the enslaved or by white men leaving for home, shifting between estates to find better paid work and having great numbers of female partners. Yet African tradition places great importance on lineage, on belonging to a particular man's household. Mothers no doubt told children who their fathers were, but proving paternity would be quite another matter. Christian converts chose a surname; most did not choose the name of their owner, for obvious reasons, even if someone from the estate where they lived was their parent.

To defend their fortunes, Scots helped to build and spread the idea that their 'white race' was morally, intellectually and culturally superior to the 'black race' they controlled. Scottish Members of Parliament, sections of the Scottish Press and many others vigorously and publicly defended this opinion long after slavery was abolished. We have a lot less evidence to help us understand how captured Africans made sense of their lives, how they survived over several generations and did so with more sanity and humanity intact than anyone might imagine. Africans exploited every chink in the planters' armour to hold on to dignity and ingenuity amongst much sadness and degradation. They used what little free time they had to carve out a landed peasant lifestyle, using the plots allotted to them to grow their own food, which gave them cash from sales and helped to shape their Jamaican future. Planters feared and would have loved to curtail these developments, but they dared not disturb the enslaved population's food-growing because they feared revolt, the possibility of which was always present. In the end, Black resistance and the legitimate demand for the rights denied to them, along with the unlawful white response, did eventually bring the system to its knees.

Our close liaison with Jamaica helped to make many Scots wealthy. Jamaican money invested in Glasgow and so many other towns made them the handsome places we know today. From the traders who dealt in slaves and merchant bankers who lent the capital to the pioneering planters who borrowed funds, from the Scottish fishermen and linen weavers who fed and clothed the enslaved to the medical schools that produced doctors and academies which trained boys to take up jobs in accounting, navigation and surveying, the gains were widespread. Those who produced the hoes, chains, candles, timber, water wheels, mills, stills, linen goods, furniture, leather and beef that made the outward journey to the West Indies as well as those who refined the returning sugar and rum were eventually drawn into the political battle over slavery. Many took sides simply to defend their livelihoods, but all of them justified their actions using racist argument and fantasies about white supremacy.

The final benefit, the last chapter in my story, was the vast sum of public money paid to hundreds of slave owners, large and small, as compensation after August 1834, when plantation slavery was finally ended in Britain's colonies. This massive distribution of capital helped to build suburban railways, roads, canals and rental properties in Scotland. It provided some of the funds which underpinned the heavy industries that would make Clydeside famous.

The international cooperation to end slavery, though by no means the only reason why the slave system collapsed, was perhaps the first British example of a modern campaign that united many thousands of people on both sides of the Atlantic in an ethical struggle. Those Scots who relied on biblical truths, all those who believed that 'a man's a man' whatever his colour, had a different vision for their nation. They were the backbone of the movement to abolish slavery, playing crucial roles in both England and Scotland. Nothing quite like this great appeal to hearts and minds had ever been attempted before. Because the abolitionists won the argument and changed perceptions irrevocably, Scotland's view of itself changed too. Eventual acceptance that slavery was incredibly cruel and morally wrong was a judgement on all who took part. New generations were uncomfortable with the levels of violence that had always been needed to enslave people. They rewrote their history to distance themselves from that era and obscure their part in building the system. The proud boast of the Scots in the 1700s – their hard-won wealth earned, as they described it, through a great deal of courage and ingenuity – was carefully hidden from history. The boast was transformed into an account of how enslaved Africans were rescued from slavery by dedicated white Christians.

Bought & Sold places accounts of the better-known history of the abolition campaign in Scotland into the context of the long, hard struggle for freedom from bondage by the enslaved themselves and ferociously cruel resistance to that struggle mounted by Scots in Jamaica. This book includes an account of the development of racist ideas and laws, the use of terror tactics to put down slave revolts and the

Scottish planters' violent attacks on missionaries sent from Scotland, which finally convinced the British Government that the slave system could not be reformed and therefore must be ended.

A powerful longing for a lost heritage and a distrust of white people remained in many Jamaican hearts, with good reason, long after slavery was abolished. People gathered in Augustown on New Year's Eve 1920 to see a man called Alexander Bedward fly back to Africa from a breadfruit tree. Bedward claimed to have been sent by God to lead Jamaicans to their lost home. That people came to watch in great numbers illustrates the fact that Africa was still significant, that it remained somewhere deep in many Jamaican souls. Though Bedward struck a chord with black Jamaicans, the gathering declined to follow him into the tree until he had properly demonstrated that he really could fly. The crowd may have been sceptical about his flying ability, but most would have agreed wholeheartedly with his idea that, as the old slave saying went, 'the devil was in the white man' and should God ever send his only son to earth to save them, Jesus would be black for sure. The authorities were alarmed by such a large gathering of Jamaicans from all over the country. Bedward was arrested for sedition and sent to a mental asylum because lawyers argued he was mad and that it was best not to inflame his followers further.

Scottish culture retained powerful memories too. Scots in Jamaica lived for well over a century with the fear of an uprising amongst the people they enslaved. Ugly, racist views designed to hold down slaves did not end with slavery. The

Edinburgh Evening News carried an article on 13 March 1903 headed 'The Race Problem in the United States' by T Baron Russell about the 'the rapid multiplication of the black races menaces the United States', claiming

> If he remains in the States he will overrun them. America must either exterminate the negro or deport him. The former is out of the question, of course. The alternative course would be difficult and expensive, but is not impossible, and the cost will have to be borne.

The *St Andrews Citizen* of 29 May 1907 explained in a similar vein that 'our brain cells are fixed in number, and black people have far fewer than white'. Churches were divided. The Christian church in southern states of America continued to put out racist propaganda which was accepted by Scottish papers without question. The *Dundee Evening Telegraph* of 2 September 1929 relayed with approval, 'Hidden deeply in the heart of intelligent America lies the dread of the negro problem'.

> Only the other day the clergyman of an episcopal church openly told the negroes present that they could not enter his church again. A touch of the tar brush is now sufficient to exclude men and women from churches.

Deeply embedded racism had day to day consequences. At about the same time that Jamaicans gathered to witness Bedward's proposed flight, officials of the Glasgow branch of the sailors and fireman's union ruled that no coloured man, even a paid-up member of the union (as many were), would be allowed to sail from the city. The memoirs of 'Red Clydeside' leaders at that time, Gallacher, McShane and Shinwell, who was leader of the seaman's union, did not mention the widely reported incident in which Glaswegians stoned and beat up de-mobbed black sailors who were trying to work their passage home after serving Britain in the First World War. On 5 July 1935, *The Scotsman* newspaper reported that George Clark, an engineer, and Wilfred Henry Butcher, an apprentice blacksmith, both 'negroes' from West Africa, appeared in the Sheriff Court at Dumbarton 'charged with being stowaways' on a ship which had arrived into the Clyde from Freetown, Sierra Leone. The men, who spoke excellent English, had stowed away and once the ship was at sea had given themselves up and worked their passage. They were hoping to get to Liverpool to find work. The accused each had a British passport, but the immigration officials in Glasgow were not satisfied that they were British subjects and refused permission for them to remain in the United Kingdom. George Clark told the Sheriff that they had left home because times were bad. Sheriff Burns sent each to prison for 21 days. The Dundee *Courier* of 4 September 1937 reported the death of Rev William H Heard, an 87-year-old African American bishop from Philadelphia. He was identified as the man 'involved in alleged "colour bar" difficulties in Edinburgh last month'. Bishop Heard belonged to the African Methodist Episcopal Church and was one of 500 delegates who attended the World Conference on Faith and Order in Edinburgh in the previous month. At the time, he experienced a fruitless search for somewhere to stay. He was eventually helped by the Archbishop of York, who offered to share his room.

It is noteworthy that people of African heritage never settled in Scotland, the land of many of their fathers, in the numbers they did elsewhere in Britain. This was so despite the fact that the Scottish courts ruled in 1777 that should they step ashore in Scotland, they were instantly free and equal citizens, able to live and work in the country. Still, very few came. Scotland extends a warm welcome to those of Scottish descent from all of the white former British colonies. The diaspora has helped Scotland celebrate what it means to be a Scottish Nation and take pride in Scotland's distinct place in the world. Scots are quick to claim Caledonian descendants in America, Canada, Australia and New Zealand, but not in Jamaica. As far as I know, no representative of the country was invited to Scotland's 'homecoming' for overseas Scots. That there is likely to be a proportionately larger Scottish gene pool in Jamaica than in other former colonies is an uncomfortable truth.[3]

Jamaica is just 145 miles long and 50 miles wide. Though it remains a poor country, this tiny island has a global reputation far beyond its size. It continues to produce many of the world's most powerful athletes and a large body of evocative music. Zachary Macauley, son of the manse in Inveraray, was sent by his father to work in the Jamaican plantations. He later devoted his life to the abolition of slavery and left us a true record of its evils in the hope that this history would never be forgotten. Yet just the other day, in his home town of Inveraray, I picked up a recent publication claiming to be 'history' which claimed Scots had never owned slaves.

Such views should not surprise us. Our historians have carefully obscured the part played by our banks, insurance companies and landed families in enslaving men and women and using them to extract much of the capital which kick-started our development. We clearly have a long way to go toward wholly understanding our past and how it continues to shape the present.[4]

Glasgow City Council recently commissioned research from the University of Glasgow into the city's involvement in Atlantic slavery between c 1603 and 1838. Their comprehensive report uncovers much of the city's hidden history including; profits from the trade, prominent individuals associated with the city who owned or traded in enslaved people, associated manufacturing profits, gifts to the city from the proceeds of slavery and the political involvement of the city in defence of chattel slavery.[5]

CHAPTER I
Seeking a fortune

Not worth a shilling the day he came.[1]

COLUMBUS DISCOVERED LAND on the far side of the Atlantic in 1492. There followed a long period in which the major European nations fought each other over who would control what we now know as North America and the Caribbean Islands. The English won Jamaica from the Spanish in 1655 and began to settle people there. At this time, the Scots were farmers and sea-going traders. Settlers on the other side of the ocean, in the islands and America, needed many things: nails and hinges, hoes and saws, barrels and blankets, candles and quill pens for writing home. Scottish traders were keen to supply them. A bit of enterprise and lots of courage were needed in order to make the six-week ocean crossing, but money could be made by loading up a small boat with goods to sell and making a return journey with the products of the fertile soil on the far side of the Atlantic. In the year 1707, when Scotland joined England to form Great Britain, Scotland ensured that the union agreement explicitly recognised its participation in England's colonial trade. Through the Act of Union, Scotland gained the protection of the British tariff system, and her ships the protection of the British navy and the Navigation Acts, which kept out rival traders. Merchants calculated that an investment of £1,000 could be tripled over a couple of voyages to buy West Indian sugar. They were quick to exploit this possibility. The merchants in Scotland's many ports wasted no time. By the end of the 18th century, there were 100 ships from the Clyde, employing over 1,000 sailors, trading across the Atlantic.

1707 was also the year when Jamaica became a full British colony, and the British government began looking for new residents. For the next 50 years, Scots used their new status as British citizens to arrive or send their sons to take up British Government offers of cheap land in Jamaica. Our story of Scotland and Jamaica begins with these early settlers and Scottish workers, many of whom arrived in the early to mid 1700s.

The island of Jamaica is not much bigger than the county of Argyll in Scotland, and it is much more mountainous. Scots who arrived in the 18th century cleared and cultivated land in Westmorland in the south-west corner of the island. Dugald Malcolm of Kilmartin, Argyll, was a junior landlord of the Argyll clan. He arrived in 1752 with several workers from home; men who could clear land, cut stone and shape wood for building. Letters home to Scotland are proof of a great exodus of young Scots like him from all over Argyll, Ayrshire, Inverness and the North East throughout the 18th century. Malcolm had been a transatlantic trader; he already knew Jamaica. He had also raised hardy black cattle on family land in Scotland. When he bought land in Jamaica, he began with something familiar: cattle raising.

In the 1640s, an Englishman called Drax studied Spanish sugar making and made some sugar production experiments of his own. The techniques for crushing canes and using copper cauldrons to boil and crystallise the juice took several attempts to master. The £5 per hundredweight he received for his harvest was four times the price of any other known crop. Drax's heirs to this day are enjoying the fortune he made. A cursory look at the history of Scotland's better off families gives some idea of the kind of 'white gold rush' mentality that overtook many of their sons in the mid-1700s. Most of those who joined the rush to Jamaica could not buy land outright. Scotland's landed gentry had little spare capital to invest in the first half of the century, but rapid returns from planting sugar changed that. The Scots were quite accustomed to borrowing money. They regularly pawned chunks of their estates to provide dowries for their daughters, or to get through a lean harvest. Their sons would borrow from the Kirk poor box to pay their travel to and from university. And as Adam Smith taught generations of Scottish students, there was nothing wrong with borrowing money, provided they knew the difference between productive and unproductive expenditure and knew how to calculate it. Estimates vary, but by 1785, about 9,000 Scots were working on or owning land in Jamaica; larger holdings employed one or two estate managers and more lowly bookkeepers.

The well-connected Dugald Malcolm borrowed to expand. He bought land and purchased many enslaved Africans so that he could move into the much more lucrative business of sugar growing. It was a risky investment. Sugar production was a complex process about which the Scots knew little, except that sugar of good quality sold in Clyde ports for a lot of money. Men like Malcolm and Peter Campbell initially hired expert enslaved Africans from established estates to run the sugar processing at harvest time. The early years of the sugar venture of young Peter Campbell and his brother, who were neighbours of the Malcolms in Argyll and Jamaica, were hit by poor weather. Peter wrote home from Fish River in Westmorland to Archibald Campbell in Knockbury, Argyll in 1732, explaining that it was 'out of my power to pay you any remittances' this year.[2] He was hoping that his benefactor 'did not want your money for a year or two more... as we are but young settlers' and promising 'that next year my brother James and I shall be able to pay you off'. Income from an average-size sugar estate could be affected by droughts and hurricanes, but in a good season could produce an income of as much as £3,000. By comparison, the Earl of Marr's huge aristocratic land holdings in Scotland, confiscated in 1745, made £1,678; the Stirling family of Kier collected £1,296 in rents before they lost some of their land.

Scottish parents who could afford it paid for their sons to take secondary school classes in commercial, technical and useful subjects. Apart from posts as Kirk ministers, an option not particularly attractive to many young men in the early 1700s, there was a lack of respectable employment for the sons of better off families. Medicine and the law provided a few openings. Travelling, trading, and the buying and selling of goods – commerce, however lowly – was one of the few areas where money might be made. By mid-century, boys in Inveraray, Dumfries or Ayr could be enrolled in arithmetic for bookkeeping, geometry for technical drawing and mapping, and astronomy for navigation. They also learned a great deal of respect for property and hard work. As businesses grew, planters wrote home to find such young men to organise the estate work, order supplies and keep good records. The duties of a junior manager involved supervising and measuring the tasks of the field workers, ensuring they rose early, continued until late and did not slacken in between. These managers of enslaved workers had the somewhat euphemistic title of 'bookkeeper'. Planters like Dugald Malcolm found these bookkeepers through family networks, as rural Scotland had an excess of young men with a good education looking for opportunities. Bookkeeping for a family friend in a lucrative business across the sea was an attractive adventure for many, and possibly the only chance these young men would get to secure their own future. Most of them hoped to return home a bit richer.

In Jamaica, a young man might start out on £40 or £50 per year with board. This was more than a skilled tradesman in Glasgow could earn, and probably sounded more enticing than spending hours at a desk, bookkeeping in a Glasgow counting house. Boats regularly visited the harbours and loch side jetties of Scotland's coast, picking up mostly teenage lads who were willing to take a chance and were rash enough to sign away a few years of their lives to pay their passage or were able to borrow their fare. Estates recruited other skilled men from home, such as distillers to make rum from the leftovers of the sugar crystallising process. They bought iron hoops and paid the passage across the Atlantic for coopers to make the barrels in which they shipped their produce. Family at home often asked their Jamaican cousins to look for openings. Colin Campbell had been asked about a position for the grandchild of his old nursemaid. He wrote to his cousin at home;

> I shall be glad to see her Grand Child if you think he's capable of doing anything for himself, and free of Vice I can be of some service... Distiller Dugald proposes a trip home. He's now worth over £1,000 sterling tho' not worth a Shilling the Day he came to me... I can put that young Fellow in the same way.[3]

In several parts of Scotland, loyalties between tenants and clan chiefs were already being overtaken by more commercial ideas. After 1737 when John Campbell, the second Duke of Argyll, was installed in Inveraray, he set about modernising his estate, replacing the mutual responsibilities of clan with profitable rents. Shared farms let to groups of sub-tenants who lived and worked together were being swept away. Larger parcels of land were now auctioned directly on the open market for the use of one tenant. In Kirkcudbright, the Hamiltons' tenants were breaking down the walls he had put up to enclose black cattle and protesting against the removal of 'good and sufficient tenants' like themselves. Across Scotland, the landed class was creating a pool of footloose workers searching for opportunities. Not all of them mourned the loss of the old clan ties. A better educated generation possibly welcomed the freedom to work for a wage and embrace new pastures. Stockmen and ploughmen increasingly bartered for their wages at hiring fairs. Many carpenters, stonemasons, blacksmiths and weavers sold their services and products as independent artisans. There was nothing new about young Scotsmen travelling abroad. Clan leaders had supplied mercenary armies for popes and the crowned heads of Europe for centuries. The Duke of Argyll was now paying the passage to Jamaica for adventurous youngsters from the county. As the Argyll carpenter John McVicar wrote home in 1806, he had made £200 in that year, had bought a slave boy and was teaching him the building trade. 'The height of my ambition is to be able to purchase a small farm in Argyle', he proudly informed his family.[4]

Some of the first recorded settlers in Jamaica were Scots. Archibald Campbell, a military man, was amongst those who attempted to establish a Scottish colony in modern-day Panama, a venture known as the 'Darien Project'. Like many such ventures, it failed, yet Archibald refused to return home; instead, he married a widow with land in the south-west of Jamaica. His land at Black River, an inlet on the rocky coast, can be seen on the boat journey around the south coast from Kingston. Over the succeeding years, he lent funds to fellow Campbells and enticed his kin in Argyll to develop virgin land in Westmorland and the neighbouring county of Hanover for cattle farming and sugar estates. The colonel's headstone declared that because of his 'extreme generosity and assistance', 'many are possessed of opulent fortunes'.[5]

Thomas Thistlewood was an Englishman from Lincolnshire. In 1750, when he was in his late 20s, he sought out West Indian traders in their London coffee house, hoping to find a job in Jamaica. He was given a letter of introduction and a name in Westmorland. He crossed the Atlantic to try his luck, settled in Westmorland and stayed there until he died in 1786. Throughout his Jamaican life, he kept a diary recording the main events of his own life and incidentally the lives of his neighbours, most of whom happened to be Scottish. His diary provides one of the few glimpses we have of the day-to-day lives of Scots in Jamaica in the middle of the 18th century.

In 1752, Thistlewood recorded that 22 young men had arrived on the latest boat to dock in the little local port of Savanna la Mar. Mr Cope, his sugar planter employer, who hailed from Strathbogie in Aberdeenshire, reported that 20 of the newly arrived were Scots. These young men would walk around the countryside looking for their kinsmen, who were easily identified by their estate names; Dundee and Argyle, Minard and Culloden. If they passed by Thistlewood's home, he thought he would invite them in for refreshment. He said it was a lonely life being the only white man living with dozens of slaves. Like many of his generation with an education, he was a sociable man interested in new inventions and the application of science to life. He was a free thinker and an avid reader of moral philosophy. On hearing of a boat arrival, Thistlewood would ride into town to pick up the latest gossip and look out for the books and seeds he had ordered from merchants in London for his horticultural experiments.

By the mid-18th century, the volume of commercial traffic between Scotland and the West Indies was such that in addition to the many merchant boats, packet sailings with regular departures and advertised rates left from both the Clyde and the Forth. They carried letters, parcels, commercial documents and lightweight cargo to and from the islands. These were small boats for crossing the Atlantic, maybe 60 feet long and under 20 feet wide, with a crew of nine or ten. The boats had a fire for cooking and carried live hogs and chickens to be slaughtered and eaten on the six- to eight-week journey. Their fresh water was shipped in barrels, which often tasted of the molasses or tobacco they had transported on a previous crossing. The boats had limited space for a few passengers. Even for the wealthy with their own cabin, the conditions were quite primitive.

A vivid picture of life on board a Jamaican packet boat, providing a regular service to and fro across the Atlantic, has been preserved in Janet Schaw's letters. In October 1774, she left from her home in St Andrews Square in Edinburgh to board a packet boat in Leith.[6] Her little party of five could afford to charter the boat to make the Atlantic journey. Her brother was taking up a position as a customs officer in Virginia. She was accompanying two young Scottish relatives who were returning to family in the West Indies after several years of Scottish schooling. She described her cabin, 'the state room', as just over five feet long, with enough width for three people to lie down. She and her 18-year-old cousin were squeezed into narrow beds. Her maid slept on the floor between them, where she was sometimes soaked by waves flowing over the prow once they hit the Atlantic swell. Her brother Alexander boarded the boat with his East Indian manservant called 'black Robert'. At nightfall, just before departure, a black slave called Ovid was hustled on board in a spiked metal collar and chains. He belonged to the boat owner, a Scot who had recently returned home from the West Indies. This man owned several slaves, whom he was sending back to the islands to be sold. Janet, having surveyed the boat's poor accommodation and contemplated what they were paying for it, wrote of the chained man, 'whatever crime he had committed, he behaved much worthier than his scoundrel of a master'.[7]

On their first morning at sea they were woken by a cock crowing, followed by the pecking of hens on the deck above their heads. They were all feeling sea sick. Black Robert was called in to make tea. 'To be certain my Lady', he replied. Perhaps the cockerel had crowed his last, since Robert returned with the 'the most charming chicken broth that ever comforted a sick stomach'. They could not keep warm, 'the air is bitter beyond expression with the addition of the constant ragling rain', Janet recorded. As they rounded the north of Scotland, a family group appeared from the depths of the boat. Unbeknown to Janet, they had been confined below the hatches because of rough weather. They 'gaze[d] fondly' in 'silent sorrow' as Orkney came into view.[8] For generations, they informed Janet, they were farm tenants there, but had been driven out by rent rises way beyond what could reasonably be earned from the land. Ruined by their landlord, they had sold several years of their working lives to the ship's captain in exchange for their passage. He would sell these working years again, at a profit, in the West Indies. During the crossing, their one little chest of belongings was ruined by storms, leaving them without candles and with very little food for the journey.

Janet's letters record 'a vessel so deeply loaded' that the deck was 'within inches of the water'. During storms, waves poured into their cabin 'like a deluge often wetting our bed clothes as they burst over the half door'. 'The vessel which was one moment mounted to the clouds... descended with such violence' as made her 'tremble for half a minute with the shock'. Nine hogsheads of drinking water, the hen coops and poultry, the cooking utensils, a barrel of fine pickled tongues and half a dozen hams were all washed overboard. When the boat broached, the 'sea chests, chairs, stools and pewter plates' all came tumbling on top of the travellers. The tea kettle was saved, and whilst the family surveyed their cuts and bruises, the faithful servant Robert made tea. They still had potatoes, onions, oats and herrings, but would be on short rations for the rest of the journey. They congratulated themselves that they had saved the beef, too, until the two sharks which had been following the boat discovered the beef had been hung overboard in the salt water to keep it fresh; they seized it. The travellers had their revenge, catching the sharks, viciously chopping off their heads before they could bite anyone and eating them. The travellers tried several times to catch a turtle to eke out their reduced rations, but without much success. When calmer weather returned, they had the pleasure of playing cards on deck.[9]

Sharing the space in steerage with the Orkney emigrants were a cooper, a blacksmith, his wife and two tailors. Janet, her niece and her brother lifted the spirits of this motley group of migrants by singing 'Lochaber Nae Maer' and 'Haeven preserve my bonny Scotch laddie' accompanied by the harpsichord and a flute that they had somehow squeezed on board.[10]

The tradesmen sharing Janet's journey had probably answered an advertisement such as this example from the *Caledonian Mercury* on Thursday 22 June 1749:

> The good Ship the *Snow Adventure*, Capt. John Smith Commander, is to sail from Clyde to Jamaica upon the 10th Day of July next, and is to take in Goods and Passengers, for whom the Master has very good Accommodation. He will also take Servants, any Tradesmen, who incline to hire themselves, to whom he will give all reasonable encouragement. Any Persons who have a mind to hire themselves for Servants, may apply to Capt. Hugh Maclauchlan or William Macgowan Merchants in Glasgow, or to John Watterston to be found at the Laigh Coffee-house in Edinburgh.[11]

We can suppose that the young Scottish arrivals which Mr Cope mentioned to Thomas Thistlewood would have travelled in similar cramped conditions to the Orkney passengers.

They probably stepped ashore to stretch their legs, after weeks at sea, at the ship's first port of call in Kingston and would no doubt have sampled one of its many taverns. Being less urbane than Janet Schaw, who was already acquainted with the high-class fashion for black servants, they would have met muscular, black-skinned Africans with tightly coiled hair, the overwhelming majority of Jamaica's residents, perhaps for the first time.

From Kingston, they would re-board their boat to sail west along the southern shores of the island. At first sight, the rocky coastline, with its pretty sandy bays, narrow fertile plain and vast high mountains rising up behind, might have been somewhat reminiscent of their Scottish home. But as they stepped ashore at Savanna la Mar, the sights, sounds and smells which greeted them would be entirely foreign. They also saw enslaved girls carrying their masters' vast array of farm produce in baskets on their heads: cabbages, broccoli, peas and beans, asparagus, oranges, bananas and pawpaws, fish and all kinds of wild fowls. This abundance of fresh food would have been a welcome sight after their ship's supply of biscuits, oats, turnip and salt herring.

The black girls themselves might have been just as fascinating. Small Calvinistic communities in Scotland would be unlikely to have exposed these unmarried men to bare-legged, flimsily dressed, bold girls like these. Each would be exposing more female flesh than these young men would have seen in their lives. The slave girls would return the white men's curiosity. Young black women in Jamaica had an intimate knowledge of white men. Some girls were sent to meet ships in the harbour and earn money for their masters by prostitution.

Since the English seized the island of Jamaica, it had become the wealthiest of all the West Indian islands; by the 1750s, the most productive. Of the 45,775 tons of sugar imported by the mother country, 20,400 tons were produced here. Jamaica had a rapidly growing population of 18,000 people who were classed as 'white', about 7,000 former slaves who had bought their freedom who were referred to as 'free black' and many children of mixed parentage referred to as 'coloured', and 170,000 enslaved Africans. Most of these Africans were recent arrivals, captured somewhere on the African continent and trafficked to the island.

Calvinism may have hitherto curtailed the sexual adventures of the latest arrivals, but it would have ensured they had a good Scottish education. A typical sugar estate was a complex establishment: a labour camp with more than a hundred captive workers – often many more – a cattle farm with beasts to turn mills and produce manure for fertiliser, a tree felling operation with carpenters to build fences and chop wood for the boiler fires and, during sugar harvest, a factory to crush sugar cane, crystallise the juice and pack it into barrels for shipping. The planters and farmers of Westmorland had managers for the whole operation, known as attorneys and overseers, assisted by junior bookkeepers. Reading and letter-writing skills were required in order to send for supplies, record the workers' rations and ensure accurate production figures and slave numbers were sent to the local tax office. Young Scots, with their education and Presbyterian work ethic, were much preferred for these posts. The recent arrivals into Savanna la Mar from Scotland were carrying letters written by relatives or influential family friends back home testifying to their honesty, good education and hard-working nature. If the young men picked up a newspaper in Kingston, they might have noted the paid adverts offering rewards for the return of runaways, including slaves. They might have been experienced in keeping accounts, but they must also have wondered how they would be able to manage such charges.

A publication by William Daniel in Jamaica listed runaway slaves and indentured servants each week.[12] For the week ending 29 June 1754, the list included:

> From Harbour Head Plantation belonging to William Beckford Esq at St Thomas in the East:
>
> An indented servant named William Broxup, by trade a Carpenter, about five feet 4 inches high and has got the Yaws... Whoever will apprehend the above mentioned servant will deliver him to Mr James Fogo at the estate, to Peter Russell Esq in Kingston or Mr Richard Lewing in Spanish shall receive two pistoles reward. NB He arrived in this Island in March 1750, in the Pompey, Capt. England, and came from Enfield, near London.
>
> From Rock Fort:

A Negro Man, named Bristol, belonging to John and Edward Foord; he is a lusty Fellow well known in and about this Town. Kingston, June 18, 1754... one pistole reward.

From the Brigantine 'William and Mary', William Gerrard Master, now lying at Corbett's Wharfe:

An indentured servant named William Walker, born in Scotland a lusty well-set Fellow, about five Feet ten Inches high, of a ruddy Complexion, pretty much marked with the Small Pox... two pistoles reward.

Taken up at my Plantation at Black River, a Negro Fellow without Name or Mark, he says he has been Run-Away above six Years, and has lived in the Woods all that time; he can give no further account of himself... Whoever owns the said Fellow, and will apply to Dominick Lopdell, may have him paying the charges.

From John Ross:

A Tall, slender Creole Negro Man, named Guy, without any Mark, formerly the Property of William Wanning; and is known by having the Care of said Wanning's House at Cow-Bay... two Pistoles and all Charges paid.

Some of the 'runaways' listed here are 'indentured' Scots. William Walker mentioned above and the Orkney travellers on board the Jamaican packet with Janet Schaw were indentured. They had promised to work for a set period of years for a particular master in return for their passage to Jamaica, with the possibility of a bonus or a small plot of land at the end of their service.

The county of Westmorland that surrounds the port of Savanna la Mar is a hilly place of fertile river valleys, coastal plain and swamp. There were over 40 estates of 1,000 acres or more in the 1750s and many smaller ones. Westmorland was a well-developed community with a volunteer militia – towns in Scotland had militia at the time. In Jamaica, this was organised amongst local planters and called out to protect white residents from unruly slaves and foreign invasions. Black slaves could also join the militia as foot soldiers. An elected white council held magistrates' courts to keep order amongst the residents. There were shopkeepers, lawyers and teachers living in the town. Dancing and music teachers advertised classes that taught favoured mixed race girls to learn the kind of arts which might win them white husbands. There was no church to be seen, but carpenters' workshops, a tailor who made up the latest fashions, bakers, cook shops and several taverns were open for business. The place was unexpectedly sophisticated and possibly more highly developed than some of the communities the Scottish immigrants left behind.

The young men now arrived from Scotland were no doubt confident in locating some of their clansmen to house them while they looked for positions. As an Archibald Cameron from Lochaber wrote to his anxious family,

I was lucky enough to meet Archy Torncastle and
John Cameron a brother of Stronse on my Arrival.
John desired me to make his house my home. I very
thankfully Accept his offer. Mr Gair the Gentleman I was recommended to by Doctor Gair was
vastly Kind to me. Used all his Endeavours to get
me provided.[13]

The previously mentioned Malcolm family, who came from
Argyll, called both their modest cattle farm and more ambitious first sugar venture 'Argyle'. The family eventually bought
11 estates in Jamaica and used their newfound capital to
massively expand and improve their holdings back home in
mid-Argyll. In early 1746, a further wave of Scottish incomers arrived: Stuart loyalists who lost at the battle of Culloden
and as a consequence suffered confiscation of all or some of
their Scottish estates. Many branches of the Grant clan of the
North East and the Stirlings of Kier were amongst them. The
Wedderburns and junior branches of the Drummond family
were also followers of Bonnie Prince Charlie. All were intent
on restoring their fortunes in Jamaica. For the next 100 years,
such families would join the large class of transatlantic Scots,
with several generations of younger sons moving backwards
and forwards across the Atlantic, looking after the family
businesses and living part of their lives in Jamaica.

The island had enough Campbells to continue the old tradi-
tion of naming them by their estates, such as Campbell of Black
River, Campbell of Fish River and Campbell of Orange Bay.
Dunbars, Lyons, McLeans, MacDonalds and Macphersons are

some of the many Scottish names in Jamaican parish records. Registers of wills and tax returns give an idea of money made, families established and whether these incomers ever returned home. Macpherson became a Member of the Jamaican Assembly; his family members were still there in 1821, when three grandsons and two granddaughters born to a slave woman were freed on payment of £70 each to the Government. Duncan Robertson of Larbert was an Edinburgh-educated doctor who also served as a Jamaican Assembly member. He bought a small farm in Westmorland and eventually retired to Harley St in London. A Scottish Kerr family owned the Three Mile River sugar plantation in the same county, expanding later to the Moor Park estate in St James and Dundee estate in nearby Hanover. The will of a John Drummond, of Drummond Lodge, a surgeon educated in Edinburgh and Fellow of the Royal Society, describes a Jamaican family of African proportions, five slave 'wives' with whom he fathered a great many children. Most of these men were middle-sized farmers in Thomas Thistlewood's day, owners of less than a thousand acres and fewer than a hundred slaves. Maps made by the early surveyors of the island, who were, incidentally, mostly products of Scottish schools, record places such as Fort William and Glasgow, and estates called Balindean, Auchterhouse and Glen Islay.[14]

Better off Scots learned classics but in addition took classes in all kinds of practical subjects. This technically savvy generation of young men had a range of useful skills and a sense of adventure. As they crossed the Atlantic, Janet Schaw's brother, Alexander, was keen to practice his navigational skills. He was disdainful of their older ship's captain and 'suspects the Captain's calculations' since, according to Alexander, 'he has no education to fit him to command a ship'. Alexander worked with one of the younger sailors to keep a careful daily log. They consulted the set of 22 maps Alexander has brought on board, and won their bet with the captain that they could better predict the ship's whereabouts than he could.[15]

Scotland's three medical schools produced eight out of ten of Britain's doctors throughout the 1700s, far in excess of the numbers which could be absorbed at home. Scottish universities became the prime producers of doctors, who took up posts in the plantations in the West Indies. Many of them were little more than teenagers when they started work. Three Wedderburn brothers arrived in Westmorland post-Culloden. Like some of the Scottish 'doctors' working in Jamaica in the first half of the century, they were not actually the product of a Scottish medical school at all but learned the trade from someone in Jamaica who was. The Wedderburn brothers made a good living by treating planters with bouts of gonorrhoea and inoculating slaves against smallpox. Paying to try to cure the pests and yaws which made Africans too sick to cut cane was worthwhile for their owners. The Wedderburn 'doctors' went on to acquire around 17,000 acres and many hundreds of slaves in Jamaica, enough riches to reclaim the family land lost at Culloden.

Thistlewood was one of the Dr Wedderburn's patients. Unlike the doctor, Thistlewood did not manage to make a fortune, but he did very well for himself. Without the kin networks of his Scottish neighbours, he did not have the merchant contacts to borrow the kind of money needed to make a start in the sugar business. Instead, in 1767, he borrowed from a Spaniard. Using the reputation of his Scottish employer, Mr Cope, as a bank guarantee, he bought 160 acres and some men and women to work this land. Much of his estate was swampland, on which he kept livestock and shot wild fowl. Thistlewood grew vegetables and flowers, which his slaves marketed. He arranged to supply stores and taverns in the town of Savanna la Mar. By the 1760s he owned 30 slaves, contracting them to work on local estates at harvest time. From this labour contracting, the business of growing and selling vegetables, and the marketing of logs and fish, he made a modest living. Though not wealthy by Jamaican standards, he had an income of around £1,000 per year.* In Jamaica, it was enough to establish himself as an educated and congenial member of the community. He loaned out a growing library of books to neighbours. Though not of their class, he sometimes mixed with members of the 'thousand acre' sugar plantocracy. He was accepted amongst them. His enslaved housekeeper and sexual partner, Phibah, was an excellent cook, and with his fish, fowls and fresh vegetables, he could put on a good feast. He regularly invited his neighbours, sometimes the wealthier ones, who were happy to accept and enjoy his hospitality.

---

* Equivalent to over £100,000 in today's purchasing power.

Though Scots in Jamaica longed for home, they did not miss the Scottish weather, as John Campbell wrote in 1747:

> I am fixed in my resolution to come home next Spring... I am resolved to lay my bones in my native Country... Shall expect you'd provid a Good warm house, you may be assured that I'll provide a good Store of Jamaican rum. God grant us a joy-full meeting.[16]

The more ambitious Scottish incomers changed the Jamaican landscape. They brought water down from the mountains for irrigation and built wind and water mills to crush their sugar canes. Those who were lucky rapidly built up a healthy Scottish bank balance. They returned to Scotland as much more wealthy men.

CHAPTER 2
The planters

Pemberton Valley often disappoints us.[1]

HUGH HAMILTON AND his brother ROBERT were sons of a former town treasurer and merchant from Ayr. They were some of the earliest Scots crossing the Atlantic to sell goods in Jamaica. Cutting cane was gruelling work. It was discovered early on that an African slave could work in the Caribbean sunshine and was quick to master the techniques of sugar production. A slave bought in Africa could be sold for much more in the Caribbean. Arriving in the 1730s, the Hamiltons began buying African slaves in Kingston and trafficking them on to North America and the Spanish Colonies. They shipped sugar and rum back to London and Glasgow and took Madeira wine, tallow candles, ironware and mosquito nets to the West Indies. In 1734, Robert met and married a widow with land on the island and became co-owner of two Jamaican plantations. One of them, Pemberton Valley, was over 1,000 acres in St Mary's parish, close to Jamaica's north coast.

By 1738, Robert was already putting away money to fund his return to Scotland. As he put it, he was intending to have 'a good share of my money fix'd in Scotland'. He disliked Jamaica with its 'unhappy climate'.[2] He was also anxious to begin the new life of landed status he had arranged for himself in Scotland. Most Scottish planters returned home as soon as possible to enjoy their newfound wealth, leaving the day-to-day management of their estates to others. Robert did not make it back to his beloved Ayrshire until 1744 because war broke out between Britain and Spain in 1739. Naval hostilities in the Caribbean made travel home with his wife and daughters too risky to contemplate. The family eventually set up home at Bourtreehill in Ayrshire.

When Robert returned, he was minded to sell the Jamaican estate. He did not find a suitable buyer, and the family joined the hundreds of transatlantic Scots who for several generations had friends and relatives living on both sides of the Atlantic, with some family members travelling regularly to look after the family's farming, financial and trading concerns in Jamaica and sending trusted young men to spend a few years overseeing day-to-day management.

On his return, Robert sent an overseer, Mr Stirling, to manage the estate. Managers like Mr Stirling were tasked to extract as much as possible from the slave workforce and spend as little as they could to meet slaves' needs, thus ensuring the maximum income for a family at home. They submitted regular reports on the slaves, the work completed and reasons for any expenditure. Important decisions were made by a local Jamaican attorney who visited from time to time to supervise. He received six per cent of estate turnover, £60 for every £1,000 worth of produce sold. His responsibilities were set out in Jamaican law; to keep and submit account of 'the quantity of sugar, rum and molasses' produced, 'to buy and sell land and slaves' and deal with 'merchants and shippers' on an owner's behalf.[3] Though overseers could order supplies from Scotland, owners had overall control of the estate bank account in places such as Glasgow or Ayr and kept a careful eye on spending. The vast majority of attorneys and overseers managing Jamaica's hundreds of estates were said to be Scottish. Their work ethic, together with their technical and accounting skills, made them particularly well-fitted for managing a complex operation like a sugar estate.

Mr Stirling made a detailed estate plan with named pieces (fields) so that he could discuss work details with the family in Ayrshire. In 1745, he reported that two workers had died, a woman and a boy, and problems with runaways, particularly with three men. He advised the Hamiltons to 'ship' these three, who were constantly troublesome, selling them on and buying in new ones. Under pressure to raise production, he tried hard to persuade the Hamiltons that they needed 20 or 30 more 'Negroes' to ensure that they had enough labour to hoe and manure the whole of their land. But the Hamiltons' attorney, Mr Adam, would not approve such expenditure without the Hamilton family's permission. The Hamiltons paid the passage of a copper smith to Jamaica to do much-needed repairs to their copper stills at a cost of almost £6 in 1746, but the surviving accounts show no record of the purchase of more Africans.

The pressure to raise production and the lack of adequate manpower therefore remained. Robert's wife and her sister each had a stake in the estate. His wife died not long after their return to Scotland. Her sister was dependent on the estate income and thought it should be making more money than it was. The Hamiltons may have been finding their elite lifestyle at home more expensive than they imagined. Returning planters expected to live extravagantly. This involved land, a fine home with luxurious furnishings, lots of entertaining, a cellar stocked with good imported wine and women wearing the latest fashions. Returning planters and merchants with money from Jamaica used their cash to impress and secure a place amongst the landed elite. This was particularly important to Robert, who had daughters for whom he eventually secured marriages with young men from Scotland's very best families.* Bills have survived for the purchase of the finest silk, picked out by their friend Lady Grant in London, for a Miss Hamilton's wedding suit in 1755. In 1762, they spent £88 servicing and refitting their coach with the best leather upholstery. We need to multiply these figures by one hundred or more to get a rough idea of their value in today's prices.

Robert wrote to a doctor friend in October 1747,

> Pemberton Valley often disappoints us, and I must Say it is one Estate that has hitherto been most ungrateful considering what has been laid upon it, however I am hopeful it will now begin to raise business, tho, by the by it is what I cannot perswade my Sister-In-Law to believe, for which indeed I cannot much blame her, as she has been so often disappointed in the expectations she has reason to entertain of it.[4]

---

* One of them married into the Oswald slave trading family.

They still wanted to sell. To get the family money invested in Pemberton Valley back to Scotland, they would need a fellow Scot to complete the sale on their side of the Atlantic. In the meantime, Mr Stirling had returned home, and Robert's nephew John had been sent to attempt to squeeze a bit more profit from the estate. John arrived in 1756 and reported that the estate had been left 'in a miserable condition' by his predecessor. There had been a hurricane, they needed a new roof on the boiling house, they were cutting shingles (wooden tiles) to re-roof the sugar curing house and 45 acres of land still needed to be cleared and planted. He had the place valued and was told 'it would take time and money to get it back into good order'. This would not please the family in Scotland. What was more, according to John, the previous manager had let the slaves get out of hand. Apparently 'he listened to the negroes' about the running of the estate. It had taken John some time 'and a good deal of trouble' to break the slaves of their bad habits. Rather than buying more slaves, he reported that, with good management, he should be able to get more work out of the ones they had. He hoped to get every piece of land planted to grow the family's income.

Most of a planter's money was invested in slaves; they were the estate's most expensive asset. Planters borrowed to buy slaves. British law explicitly stated that a slave owner could use this human property as security when taking out a loan to buy land or new slaves to work it. Planters who did this were under pressure for rapid returns to pay off mortgages by improving the harvest. They transferred this financial pressure to estate managers, who made sure the mortgaged workforce put in exceedingly long hours to plant as much, and harvest as much, as any human being possibly could.

Pemberton Valley was a comparatively small estate with 90 males (48 working men, 11 working boys, 16 infant boys, 12 old and poorly men, and three rebels to be shipped) and 59 females (28 working women, seven working girls, 12 infant girls, and 12 old and poorly women); 149 slaves altogether. The nearby Holland Park, later owned and in the 1750s managed by one of the Scottish Taylor family, was a much bigger operation. It had two water mills and a windmill, 400 field slaves, 22 enslaved carpenters, 15 enslaved masons, 100 mules and 100 head of cattle.

Sugar making was an agricultural process, but it was also a quasi-industrial one. Pemberton Valley had mills to crush the sugar canes, mills which must be kept turning during the harvest. A good manager would note the amount of fertiliser from the lime kilns applied to the cane fields and the amount of cattle dung being used. Pemberton Valley imported oak staves from Virginia to be shaped into barrels. The necessary tools – axes, saws, chisels and hammers – had to be kept in good condition and under close supervision. The slave system was brutal and absentee planters were uncaring about the humanity they exploited, but the process of management was sophisticated and enlightened in the sense that it applied the latest science to production. Scotland had few enterprises as large and complex as a Jamaican sugar estate.

John Hamilton ordered cloth to be made into clothing for his slaves. It would come from flax grown on Scottish farms and woven into a rough linen. One slave wrote that it was so rough that you could scratch your back by shrugging your shoulders. West Africans loved bright clothes and sometimes dyed the dull cloth with home-grown indigo, using techniques common in West Africa, before cutting and stitching it. They invented the first blue jeans.

Mr Stirling had ensured the slaves were always fed by supplementing what they grew themselves with estate-grown corn, yams and plantains. John Hamilton fed the slaves some necessary protein. He sent for smoked fish, caught by Scottish fishermen and gutted and smoked by their wives. Slave clothing and food, along with all the necessary tools, were all shipped from Scotland to Jamaica. The returning sugar crop and rum, which paid the bills, were sold by merchants and refined in Greenock or Rothesay on the Clyde. Scottish agents insured the risky sea journey. By the late 1700s, tens of thousands of Scottish jobs depended on this trade with Jamaica; 15,000 were involved in the herring industry alone – not all supplying Jamaica's 170,000 slaves, but a large part of an industry sustaining highland crofters was also sustaining Africans in Jamaica.

White Jamaicans were ostentatiously class conscious. John Hamilton ordered the sorts of luxury items a man of his station expected. A little Madeira and Indian tea, some salt beef, and rounds of Scottish cheese and pickles, though cheese did not survive well in the Jamaican climate. Peter Campbell of Fish River thanked his Argyll family for a gift of cheeses, but explained it was so bad on arrival that he 'had to distribute it to the Negroes'. John Campbell of Orange Bay thanked the family in Kilberry for a gift of sweet meats, pickles, jellies and some ketchup made by an aunt from mushrooms picked below the castle and oysters available on the Argyll shore.[5]

Janet Schaw described in her letters a simple West Indian breakfast of locally grown coffee and imported tea, breads, ham, eggs and pineapple marmalade. She also enthused over a rather grand West Indian dinner with many dishes laid out in rows. These included turtle soup and freshly baked turtle.

> Many kinds of fish served with hot pepper and lime, including king fish in a rich sauce. The meats served with pickles include guinea fowl, turkey and pigeons. There is mutton shipped live from New England and freshly slaughtered. Next come fruit tarts, a cheese cake with cocoanut, several puddings and jellies.[6]

It was not just visions of feasts and recipes for sauces that made it home to Scotland. Young men managing estates ensured new ideas flowed back and forth across the Atlantic. The distillers of Scottish whisky no doubt originally informed distillation of rum in Jamaica. In the 1820s, the transatlantic Shand family had a commercial distillery at Fettercairn using their experience of making rum on the family plantations in Jamaica. John Campbell of Orange Bay drew views of the plantation using a camera obscura and urged the family to show them to the Duke of Argyll if they were passing the castle in Inveraray. He asked the family to find out about a newly patented invention, 'White's Air Machine', which could pump cool fresh air and looked decorative enough to be a piece of household furniture.

Estates built water mills fed by elegant aqueducts carrying river water down from the mountains. They tried out various kinds of waterwheels. They dug small canals for crop transport, with floodgates, weirs and reservoirs for controlled irrigation. They surveyed their land; they drew the first maps of the island. They experimented with plants from all over the world and animal breeding. A young man with an education had a blank canvas on which to test all the science he had learned. He could send for skilled masons and carpenters, brick makers and distillers, and in time he had access to the essential capital with which to fund his ideas. Letters home discussed projected improvements. Diagrams and maps were sent in packet boats. Campbell of Orange Bay asked the family to find and send a mason 'qualified in all kinds of arches'. The man selected would need to be 'a good draftsman', because he had 'all kinds of whimsies in my head' which he 'should like to see on paper' before he 'engaged further in them'.[7] He wanted the man to have a look at Captain Robert Fairlies' Lime Kiln in Greenock before he travelled to check in 'what manner it is made'.[8] Campbell said he had 'seven good negroes' that this skilled man would teach. The man should therefore bring sufficient trowels, hammers, sieves and a book on making arches with him.[9]

On arrival in Jamaica, new African members of the labour force were inoculated against smallpox and checked by doctors who mostly hailed from Scotland. Various methods of mass smallpox inoculation were used on slaves, then applied successfully to school children in Scotland, long before Jenner launched a vaccination programme in the 1790s. In 1760, Douglas Clarke, son of a black slave educated in Scotland by a white father, took out a patent for an improved steam-powered sugar mill, three years before Watt's better-known and improved steam engine was patented.[10] Successful transatlantic entrepreneurship changed the business habits of returning planter families. They bought landed estates all over the country, where they applied more rigorous accounting and management procedures, in many cases exchanging a system of farm rents for gangs of labourers working on controlled schedules. Their sons often took these methods out to Britain's colonies or invested the family fortune in industry, where they appointed skilled managers who took responsibility for the production process, kept accounts and developed rigid labour regimes, helping to shape the modern factory system in Scotland.

John Hamilton's task on Pemberton Valley estate was rather mundane: he had to whip the captive workforce into shape. To get all of the family land hoed and planted without extra workers would only be achieved by force. The African workforce faced threats and punishments if they did not complete the heavy daily work load he had planned for them. White men controlled but also feared their workforce. They were vastly outnumbered by their African women and men. They recognised the dangers of black solidarity and that slaves could be fiercely loyal to each other. Owners hoped to sow division by buying Africans from different language groups and giving out extra rewards to some but not to others. There is little evidence that their efforts worked; the bonds between black captives confined far from home were not usually broken by a few extra rations. Thomas Thistlewood recorded being attacked by a group of black men. As they tried to drown him in the river, he was relieved to spot a little group of his own Africans approaching, but they walked on, ignoring his pleas for help. He escaped by the skin of his teeth with the assistance of his most trusted slave, Lincoln, but even Lincoln was not prepared to give evidence about the attack to any court. His attackers got away with attempted murder, and Thistlewood took no revenge against his slaves who had left him to die. On reflection, he knew he was asking the impossible; some lines could not be crossed.

Planters used a branding iron to mark ownership. The first slave code of 1696 strictly and severely punished runaway slaves.

> If a planter had a Negroe who was always running
> away, he [wa]s allowed to fit him with an iron yoke

that had three long hooks projecting from it to hinder future escapes.[11] These iron collars were still in use over 100 years later, and as Janet Schaw saw, on occasion, even in Edinburgh. A slave owner was free to do whatever he liked with his slaves; they were his property recognised in law. He was allowed to rape or beat them. The law allowed no more than 39 lashes of the whip, but there was no way of checking excessive violence. Slaves were barred from giving evidence against a white man and would be punished with death for striking one.

Escapes were a real possibility. Runaway communities in the impenetrable Blue Mountains offered an alternative to captivity. Planters were vulnerable, paying mortgages on slaves or using them to secure loans to buy more or to pay off family debts. Slaves were a commodity that planters could not afford to lose. But slaves were also an expensive investment that had to make returns. Lashing with whips forced the captives to work inhumanly hard to produce enough for the attorney's percentage, the overseer's living, the slave doctor's fees, taxes, tools, food and clothing, and still leave enough to support their owner's gracious living on the other side of the Atlantic. The landed class learned lessons in the West Indies about how to extract the maximum from both the land and the workers. Output per person was estimated to be much higher in Jamaica than anywhere else in the world, including the North American colonies, England and Wales. As one slave account observed:

> The devil was in the Englishman, that he makes
> everything work. He makes the Negro work, the
> horse work, and the wind work.[12]

Scottish managers like John Hamilton had a reputation for harsh discipline. Those who had visited other parts of the West Indies reported that French and Spanish slaves were more contented and better workers than those under British rule. According to former slave and British abolitionist Olaudah Equiano (1745–97), they 'were better treated, had more holidays, and looked better than those in English islands'.[13] The

Governor of Jamaica, John Dalling (1772–81), agreed that African slaves were 'under much better regulations among them than with us'.[14]

Planter households depended on slave cooks and washerwomen for their home comforts. A paternalistic affection or professional respect might sometimes blur, but never removed the strictures of ownership and an obsessive drive to make money. Mastery over a group of imprisoned men and women was ultimately maintained by violence. Thistlewood thought himself enlightened, but recorded whipping two-thirds of the men and half of the women slaves, even pregnant women, in his first year as a bookkeeper in Jamaica. Later, when he bought his own slaves, if particularly annoyed, he rubbed salt and hot peppers into the cuts his whip made and locked them up without food in a prison he kept for that purpose. He sometimes punished them by hanging them up by their hands. Thistlewood's actions would not have been judged extreme by his friends and neighbours. Overt, public violence was intended to fill enslaved people with fear. Terror tactics were normalised and defended as a necessary way to manage slaves.

Surviving children of Thistlewood's women slaves, even some of his own progeny, represented a growth of his assets and appeared in his carefully kept accounts. Once little children started to work, weeding or tending goats, he recorded their labour and set a market value on the child.

Despite these one-sided calculations, black–white affection was also possible. Thistlewood had a long-term relationship with his slave cook, Phibah, who was owned by his neighbour, Mrs Cope. Thistlewood therefore paid Mrs Cope for Phibah's hire. This rental payment for his 'wife' appeared as an outgoing expense in his accounts. We do not know whether Mrs Cope kept a profit and loss account, but all of Phibah's children, including one fathered by Thistlewood and another by Mrs Cope's stepson, belonged to her and should certainly appear on her quarterly tax return, as her capital gain would transfer a little more income to government. The power difference did not wholly prevent Phibah and Thistlewood caring for each other; they remained together for more than 30 years.

Field slaves worked continuously for at least 12 hours each day, six days a week, digging, planting and cutting sugar cane. Men like John Hamilton would think long hours were normal, as rural life in Scotland at that time was also one of unrelenting manual work. Farm servants worked in all weathers, beginning at five in the morning and continuing until darkness fell. In larger farms, the labour force was disciplined like a military regiment with hierarchies, rules, strict working hours and barrack-like living quarters. In Jamaica, the slaves' rhythmic, militaristic work pace was enforced by overseers' whips. Each slave moved with machine-like precision, in step with their fellow slaves. During the two-hour meal break at midday, they were responsible for lighter tasks such as collecting grass to be carried back to feed the master's mules and other livestock.

Owners and managers in the West Indies took for granted the master–slave relationship. They were accustomed to brutality before they arrived on a plantation. Their ideas about managing others were formed commanding soldiers in foreign wars, whipping sailors at sea and packing trading boats with slaves. Whilst the life of a worker in Scotland was in no way comparable to the excesses of slave masters, these were cruel times. The old and the sick in Scotland might be given charity, but parishes usually denied help to healthy poor people. A regime of hard work was thought to improve the morals of those not working, whatever the cause of their idleness. Kirk sessions were entitled to put the poor and their children to work in return for their keep. Children found begging might be removed from their parents altogether. As towns in Scotland expanded, there was intense anger amongst the unemployed in places like Paisley when industries suffered a downturn. Help for the many destitute families was rarely forthcoming, lest these lower classes get used to indolence. Church records from Maybole in Ayrshire from the 1790s show a family of six, with all of the children working, described as 'living comfortably', 'without burdening the public', surviving on seven shillings a week or just over a pound a month.[15] From this they could buy only bread, salt, a little tea and sugar, one or two candles, soap and some thread to mend their clothes. They presumably grew a few potatoes and a little cabbage if they had access to a garden. Landowner–tenant relations were harsh; until 1747, a Scottish landowner had the right to legally judge and punish his tenants. In the latter part of the century, Scottish law was implemented by courts made up of the landed. Scottish newspapers regularly reported on workers found guilty of 'breaking a contract' by arriving late or going home before time and who had been fined or sent to prison.

There were published manuals about organising slave work schedules and dividing the workforce into groups. Estate managers created approximate ratios of working people to carts and cattle, and ratios of workers to land pieces. They surveyed, mapped and subdivided the plantation by rows of bamboo, then estimated the number of rows per piece and plants per row. From this, the managers worked out the numbers of men and women needed to plant or harvest each part, along with the number of hours it would take to complete the task. Overseers kept up the pace of the work to realise the manager's plan; in this way, production was maximised.

John Hamilton would inform the family at home of his overall production goals. It was a brutal regime only limited by the human capacity to work. Demanding the greatest possible quantity of sugar and rum in the short run had an impact on profitability in the longer term, as both soil and slaves were rapidly worn out. The Hamiltons, especially Robert's sister-in-law, seem to have had unreasonable expectations of what the enslaved workers at Pemberton Valley would be able to achieve.

The Taylor family (originally Tailyour) became fabulously wealthy transatlantic Scots, but they did not start out that way. Several sons travelled to Jamaica in the 1720s. One of them, John, was a merchant and slave trader who married the daughter of a West Indian merchant in Glasgow, called McCall. They made enough to send their son Simon to Eton. Simon Taylor (1740–1813) returned to Jamaica and used his father's name and capital to borrow excessively and buy large numbers of slaves and estates. He gained experience in managing other people's plantations and eventually combined this with his legal education to act as an attorney. As such, he was entitled to a percentage share of estate income – attorneys for large numbers of absentee planters like Taylor built themselves huge and regular income. Simon advised estate owners to be wary of

> pushing your Negroes too much and killing them,
> which I am sure will not be for your advantage.[16]

'They are not steel or iron', he wrote. He advised planters that 'extra Negroes' would pay for themselves 'by the greater quantity of sugar you will make'. He advised one of his planters to 'buy sixteen people each year' on credit to replace those who were worn out. More slaves would keep sugar mills turning day and night. During the sugar crop there was no time for rest; according to Simon, 'the poor wretches do not get above 5 or at most 6 hours (rest) out of 24'. Perhaps he was betraying self-interest in recommending annual slave purchases; Simon's other business, which I will come to in chapter 5, was arranging loans for buying slaves.

It has been estimated that field slaves worked 4,000 hours per year – three or four times the hours of a modern factory worker. It seems unlikely that John Hamilton would write home to the already disappointed Robert advising him not to expect too much of the Pemberton Valley slaves. John was already under pressure from the family to extract as much work as possible from all of the women and men under his control. He would also benefit from an increased harvest, since he was both attorney and overseer; each extra hogshead of sugar shipped became a little more personal income for him. His African workers could do little to appease John's drive to extract every penny from both land and the workers, but slaves drew their own conclusions:

> When black man tief,* him tief half a bit (two-pence farthing); when backra tief, him tief whole estate.[17]

---

* Jamaican patwah. Africans brought the rhythms and structure of their mother tongues to English to create a whole new way of expressing yourself: backra = white boss, tief = thief.

CHAPTER 3

The enslaved men and women

10 pounds of fish... a good serge suit and hat once a year.[1]

MOST DESCRIPTIONS OF THE lives of slaves were written by white observers. Janet Schaw recorded what she had heard from friends in the West Indies. She wrote of different kinds of Africans depending on the places they came from. Some she described as 'brutes only fit for labour in the fields' whilst others made 'faithful, handy servants'.[2] Abolitionists, on the other hand, collected the worst excesses of slave owners and stressed slave passivity, powerlessness and a childlike ignorance. Their accounts were written to arouse pity and disgust amongst good Christians. While it was important for anti-slavery activists to record truths about brutality in the lives of captive Africans, we should not overlook the skills, ingenuity and resilience of African women and men forced to labour in the islands.

The Edinburgh observer of Jamaican life, James Stewart, left us a description of a slave village in the early 1800s:

> 50 or more cottages with a living room and one
> or two bedrooms, furnished with table, chairs
> or stools, maybe a cupboard big enough to put
> away a few wooden bowls and calabashes, a

household water jar and wooden mortar for
pounding Indian corn.[3]

I should also note the skills that travelled with the Africans to Jamaica. They made coiled pots called 'Yabbas' to
keep water cool, as well as pestles and mortars. They also
wove baskets and mats, thatched their roofs and repaired
the mud walls of their houses. Their wooden beds and cup-
boards were probably made by the estate carpenters. The little houses, James Stewart said, were surrounded by a plot of
ground, shaded by fruit trees, where family members were
buried 'with gravestones erected to mark their passing'. This
last mention of marked graves beside the home reminds us
that these men and women were struggling to preserve some
dignity and family bonds in a situation which respected neither. A man, woman or child could be sold to live elsewhere
at any time. Scottish planters were quick to point out that a
slave's home was a good deal more comfortable than some
of the earth floored hovels that Scottish peasants shared
with their animals. While this observation might be true, we
need to remain sceptical about white accounts written for
white readers.

Men like Stewart were distanced from and mostly
blind to life in a slave village, and we have limited records
from slaves themselves. Stewart stressed that slaves were
happy and smiling, wearing 'very gay apparel' when going
to dances:

> the men in broad-cloth coats, fency waistcoats,
> and nankeen or jean trowsers, and the women in
> white or fancy muslin gowns, beaver or silk hats,
> and a variety of expensive jewellery.[4]

If his account bears any semblance to reality, it sounds as if slaves had retained a West African dress sense. How much more of African tastes, beliefs and ceremony survived in the slave village, we cannot now know. Before they were transported, these Africans were perhaps poets or iron smelters, healers or cloth weavers, brewers or wise men. All this was brutally stripped from them. In Africa, different groups would have had clear rules about women and men's roles, which fathers and sons were musicians, what a man must exchange for a wife in marriage and what her duties were. Stewart suggested that within the slave compound, people lived by their own rules and senior men kept order. On many estates, he said,

> the headmen erect themselves into a sort of bench
> of justice, which sits and decides, privately, and
> without the knowledge of the whites, on all dis-
> putes and complaints of their fellow-slaves.[5]

It would be interesting to know whether these courts worked by African ideas of right and wrong or followed those of their white masters. The word 'privately' suggests to me they had their own way of doing things. African music, stories and dress all survived in Jamaica, and probably much more besides.

Sometime in 1754, John Hamilton sent a list to the family in Ayrshire of all those labouring at Pemberton Valley, detailing each of their jobs and fitness for work. The family at home and probably their bankers would want to know the number and health of their stock of slaves. Such lists showing regular updates from Jamaica can be found in Scottish archives. Because such papers were prepared for official purposes, they were carefully preserved. Pemberton Valley was a small slave community of 149 slaves altogether. The only unusual feature was the predominance of men; women were more numerous on most estates. The Hamiltons held 48 adult males, 28 adult women and 18 working children aged from around five or six to 13 or 14 as slaves. Of the adults, 24 were too old or unfit for work. It seems likely that John Hamilton was managing this labour force alone. A household of more white men would certainly have employed more household help than appeared in his account.

In 1754, there were obvious tensions on the estate. John was attempting to get a good deal more effort and hours from the workforce. Three men, Charles, Jasper and Cuffie, who were described as 'stout and able', had recently been shipped to Honduras.[6] They had been suspected of plotting an escape or possibly organising 'an insurrection'. The mountains that loomed up behind the estate were regularly patrolled with vicious dogs trained to sniff out and attack Africans. The threat of attack by dogs was enough to deter most bids for freedom.

The law would have allowed the Hamiltons to hang these three men, but they preferred to sell any troublemakers on to the Spanish colonies in order to recoup their costs in buying the men. A skilled and healthy male slave would be worth over £100. A slave was a costly piece of property to be bought and sold or rented out. Dozens of slave lists survive to tell us of jobs done and prices paid.[7] Love between men and women – their pain, anger and occasional good times – was rarely recorded anywhere. One supposes John kept Charles, Jasper and Cuffie in collar and chains before they were shipped. He was, after all, trying to restore control. Would he have had the humanity to let them say goodbye to their wives? If so, did Charles' wife dry her tears and kill one of her hogs for a wake on the Saturday night to give him and his comrades a good send off, as Thomas Thistlewood records in his diary? Did the head boilers donate some of their extra rum ration for a party? Which of the men on John Hamilton's list played a homemade banjo and which one beat the drums? Did some of the younger women from the field workers, Lily, Fiba, Sabena, Hannah and Ibo Sarah, find the energy to dance until dawn? Did the older folks, such as Flora, Judith, Delia, Chloe and Mumbo, lead the final sad songs which captured what was in their hearts but not on their faces as they contemplated their final goodbyes to the three 'stout and able' members of the Pemberton Valley community? As William Prescott, a former slave, wrote,

> they will remember that we were sold, but not that
> we were strong. They will remember that we were
> bought but not that we were brave.[8]

It is very unlikely that John Hamilton allowed any drumming, dancing, feasting or drinking in the slave village.

The Hamilton family were experienced people traffickers, capable of packing chained humans into boats and, as John put it in one of his letters home, giving them the 'shocking punishments they deserve' if they tried to escape.[9] The Hamilton family's hearts were hardened against the humanity of Africans.

The Jamaican sugar plantation produced most of its essentials in house. Timber came from hillside woodlands, limestone for building and fertiliser was excavated and burnt in kilns. Some, but not all, estates grew back-up food crops for slave rations in dry seasons, such as corn, plantains and yams. These were grown on those bits of the estate unsuitable for sugar. Livestock were raised to transport heavy goods and provide manure.

Slave drivers were normally promoted from amongst the slave group to crack the whip over their fellow workers. Top of the list of Pemberton Valley labourers were two drivers, London and Zoell.[10] Drivers like these were part of the system, rewarded for their loyalty in carrying out the commands of a white master. James Stewart thought that when an African was promoted to this kind of senior position,

> he considers himself as then belonging to a superior caste; but, like too many of his white prototypes, he is prone to exercise but little moderation in his new office, to domineer with a high hand... He himself has been domineered over by a driver, or head-man; it is now his turn to domineer over others.[11]

John Hamilton's drivers would whip the 'field gang' to keep up the pace of their labour each day and be called upon to punish the workforce under John's direction. If John had to go into town, or was invited to ride over for a ceilidh with neighbouring planters, London and Zoell would be left in charge. These African drivers must also have been managing much of the day-to-day work. They would be paid well and called bookkeepers if they were white and literate, but using slaves in this role was much cheaper.

Next on John Hamilton's list came the head boilers, Primus and Cupid, and assistant boiler, Wiltshire. These men were the family's most valuable assets, experts at turning cane into sugar. The family fortune was literally in their hands. Pemberton sugar would have an established reputation to maintain in the markets on the Clyde. Poor sugar fetched only half the price of an established 'brand'. Some estates hired out their boilers and assistants. Thistlewood reported that 'a negro man... came to Egypt boiling house from mr bernard senior at mint estate', 'he is a famous boiler'.[12] Thistlewood gave the man a large tip and two bottles of rum because he was so pleased with his work, and he rewarded the man's assistants 'with 14 bitts worth of bread and sailfish'. Loyal and valuable men like these should be treated well, according to Drax, the man who developed the first British sugar plantations and left his influential instructions for would-be planters. He suggested that 'excellent slaves and overseers with responsibilities' be given

> an extra 10 pounds of fish for their families, as well as a good serge suit and hat once a year.[13]

Some Scottish estates bought 'Kilmarnock Bonnets' (similar to Tam o' Shanters) for such men. These closely resemble the iconic beret Che Guevara wore. London and Zoell would, as Drax suggested, be better fed and dressed than other slaves, with suits and hats to denote their status.

Next in importance to estate profits were the two rum makers, Eugene and Andrew, who had mastered the complexities of distilling alcohol. Below them on the list were several strong armed sawyers of wood: English Cuffee, Diptford, Doctor, Tom and Richmond. Presumably, wood was cut from the mountainside portion of the estate to use for the boiler fires and lime kilns, as well as fencing. The sawyers chosen to work at the margins of the estate were presumably the more trusted of the group. Two skilled carpenters, Brutus and Bob, worked with the wood cut by Eugene and Andrew.

These carpenters probably built beds and stools for their neighbours on their weekly day off. One wonders what kind of designs they favoured, the traditional three-legged African stool or something four-legged and European. There were also two skilled coopers, Basnet's Cato and Cajo, who made and mended the barrels in which the sugar and rum were shipped. The Hamiltons likely imported Virginian oak staves and Scottish metal hoops for barrel making.

Two men, Little Scipio and Ayr, had the task of looking after the cattle. There was a team of six mule men, one of whom, Primus, was described as the 'head muleman'. James Stewart suggested that 'along with... great strength and hardiness', 'the mule of the West Indies has a perverseness and stubbornness very difficult to subdue' but 'the negroes... have a wonderful knack in managing them'.[14] Fellow feeling for those who are tired and overworked might be the secret of the mule man's success. In addition, Pemberton Valley had a rope maker, Quartious, expected to turn out 30 metres of rope a day, and Burford, who looked after sick slaves. Most of these tasks – cutting wood, boiling sugar, distilling rum, stoking fires and controlling mules – were thought to be unsuitable for women.

Twelve men were listed as unfit, possibly old; some of these were kept busy as watchmen and rat catchers. Two did what was described as 'fine trimming' (probably weeding), one was described simply as 'a boy'. It has often been asserted that slaves thwarted their owners by refusing to work. Some of the group sound as if they were not working hard enough for John Hamilton's liking. English Coffie and Hercules were not unfit but were listed as 'lazy'; presumably they were on a go-slow. A man by the name of Bristol, who was also fit, was described as 'entirely useless'; perhaps he was on persistent strike, or he may have fallen into such a deep depression that he was totally detached from reality. One wonders how many beatings, how many lashes of the whip, these three had endured. It is likely that they were eventually shipped to the Spanish colonies.

Of the 90 African men and boys maintained on the estate, only 26 were available to plant and cut cane in the field. Eighteen boys and girls were also listed as workers, helping all day with cattle and lighter field work. All the Pemberton slaves were listed by name, and so were the cattle and mules. Slaves and cattle had similar names, for example, cows were called Fanny and Quasheba, and steers had names such as Harry, Ben and Toby. Only the mules were listed with a date, giving us some idea of their age.

Plantation children were more fortunate than some. Mary Prince, who freed herself by making the journey to Britain, described working in salt ponds as a youngster up to her knees in water from 4.00am until late at night, eating soup made from boiled corn and becoming covered in salt blisters on her feet and legs after standing in salt water for hours and hours.

Because these Africans were listed by their skills and in work groups, John obscured their family relationships. Some of the men and women on this list would have cared for each other for years and considered themselves man and wife. They would have been loving mothers and fathers to some of the 18 boys and girls, too. There were 59 women altogether, but only 28 were fit adults. This imbalance was a source of disgruntlement amongst the slaves. Mr Stirling, the previous estate manager, reported complaints from the men that the estate had not enough women to go round; they wanted the Hamiltons to buy some young females. Both Scots and Africans came from cultures where family and clan were strong bonds, but sugar making had no respect for human affections. The men's desire for more partners was of no interest to the family in Scotland.

Managers usually chose one or two sexual partners amongst the women slaves. Three of the boys under six were of mixed race, called Thornton, Harry and James. There was one mixed-race little girl, too, named Margaret. These were probably the previous manager's children, although Mr Stirling, who had returned to Scotland, did not appear to have any interest in them. Even if he did, the annual salary he earned from the Hamiltons for managing the estate would be nowhere near enough to free these Scottish children.

Of the women slaves, Sydney the cook came first on John Hamilton's list. She would have known how to bake bread, cakes and pastries, make marmalade, kill, pluck and roast fowls and cover them in appropriate sauces. She would have kept the larder well-stocked, attended to the salted meats and bacon, and ensured the household did not run out of fresh vegetables and fruit. She could probably have produced a passable haggis for special occasions and black pudding whenever a hog was slaughtered. Janet Schaw certainly enjoyed both on board a boat to Virginia. Enslaved in a Scottish household, Sydney could no doubt have made a good Scotch broth. John Hamilton's shopping lists regularly contained plenty of barley, split peas and pease brose to be sent from Scotland. Another woman, Marjory, washed and pressed his clothes. On his arrival in Jamaica, he sent for a new mattress, feather pillows, cloth to renew the mosquito nets and thread to mend the sheets. Marjory would have probably completed these tasks as well.

Rose was described as 'in the great house', where John Hamilton lived. A great house was furnished with all the comforts of the day: a dining room which could be laid out with china and silverware to impress visitors and a comfortable drawing room with sofas, carpet and armchairs. Beside his bed he probably had a table, wash stand, a chamber chair with pot and a looking glass. Most masters had a black mistress. The previously mentioned old Etonian and Scottish Attorney, Simon Taylor at Holland Park, managed several properties. He had women and children at almost every one of them, according to his Holland Park housekeeper and long-term partner.

It is not clear whether Rose was 'in the house' to polish the silver and empty the chamber pot or as John Hamilton's sexual partner. It would have been quite normal for Rose to do both. A woman called Lady took care of fowls, and Daphne looked after his hogs with the help of 'old Abba'. Mary Anne and Diana were described as 'very lazy'; presumably they were regularly whipped by London and Zoell for refusing to work hard enough. By describing three of the men and two of the women as 'lazy' and 'entirely useless', John recognised that though he owned these slaves, they were successfully defying him. He could get little or no useful work out of these brave souls. An additional category includes 12 more women who were described as unfit and several as 'entirely useless', probably women who were bought and settled on the estate long before Mr Stirling took over. Such women would have become field workers in their early teens; if they had survived ten to 20 years' hard labour, they would be completely worn out.

This left 25 women available for heavy field work. Given the shortage of women, one cannot help wondering whether London and Zoell used their power and status to allow sexual abuse of the young women in the field or whether they offered the women a little fatherly protection. Hopefully enough African village rules survived in the Pemberton Valley community to ensure that teenage girls were protected from abuse whilst working in the fields.

Three things stand out from John Hamilton's account of his workforce. Firstly, although we might suppose that men were doing the heavy work in the fields, stripped to the waist and whipped to keep up the pace of cutting cane and digging, there were as many women amongst the field workers. Pemberton Valley was one of many estates, including Holland Park, which had more women than men in the fields. More men were trafficked into Jamaica each year, about two men to every one woman. Half of these male slaves would have been trained in Jamaica by local tradesmen or skilled men brought to Jamaica for the purpose. Once they arrived on an estate, men often did more specialised and less physically exhausting work. Women endured heavy digging and cutting work and became rapidly worn out. This is borne out by John Hamilton's 12 women who were not ill but described as unfit or 'entirely useless'. The old and feeble were turned out of some estates to fend for themselves. This was common enough that the Jamaican Assembly attempted to outlaw the practice. However, those who did no work were not usually entitled to any estate rations. The Hamiltons appeared to allow worn-out men and women to stay.

Secondly, although masters attempted to convince themselves that Africans were 'brutish', about a third of Pemberton Valley's captives were highly skilled and working at a specialised task. Together, these men and women possessed all the know-how to run a profitable agricultural production process and fashionable household. As already noted, Jamaica had the highest productivity in the world in the late 1700s. And according to Janet Schaw, slaves also worked for themselves on their day off. They would have earned personal money by making, building, sewing and fixing things for white neighbours, charging a little less than the master would have hired them for. Personal money, though it would never buy their freedom, would have given Pemberton's captive workers the chance of a little dignity. In addition to playing their part in producing Pemberton's lucrative exports, the Africans built, furnished and repaired their own houses, grew most of their own food and kept white households supplied with fresh fruit, butcher meat, eggs, fish and vegetables sold in local markets.

Thirdly, very few children were born into slavery in Jamaica, which the very small numbers of surviving slave children on plantation accounts confirm. Though Virginians bought slaves, they did not buy them in such vast numbers as the Jamaican planters, who drove slaves hard and quickly wore them out. Virginians were reputed to encourage slave partnerships in order to create new generations of enslaved workers. In Jamaica, more than any other island, enslaved people were forced to work so hard that they died young and had few offspring. They were also subject to a carefully restricted feeding regime that gave the slaves just enough protein to keep them working and no more. Exhausted, undernourished workers were less likely to run away, but they died young and worn out. About half of Jamaica's enslaved women were childless. Of the 59 women on Pemberton estate, 12 were probably past child-bearing age and seven were under 14. On a Jamaican estate, having 16 boys and 12 girls under six was a healthy, even unusual, number of children. What the slave lists do not do is group people by family. We cannot see who ensured these little slave children survived or which of the women on the slave list risked punishment for spending too long feeding them in the field. While John Hamilton criticised much of his predecessor Mr Stirling's approach, Stirling must have fed the women slaves well and not overworked them. From family letters, we know that the Hamiltons were slow to spend money on fish rations. Mr Stirling therefore prioritised the planting of supplementary food such as potatoes and sweet corn over planting more canes to increase sugar production. The survival rates of babies also indicate that he allowed mothers time to feed their babies in the fields. Compared to other plantations, young slaves survived and thrived under Mr Stirling's regime. For example, the Worthy Park plantation had 240 women, most of whom worked in the fields. Over more than ten years, 124 of these women got pregnant and 89 gave birth, but only 19 had children growing up on the estate – just one more than Pemberton, which had far fewer women.

Periods, pregnancy and suckling infants were all interruptions to rapid returns in the sugar business. At harvest time, field work was particularly long and heavy. The harvest took place in the dry season when garden plots would produce little food. On many estates, young women field workers must have experienced the normal response of the female body to stress, overwork, little nutrition and loss of weight: amenorrhea, a pause in monthly periods. Given the impossible conditions under which slaves raised their children, it would not have been surprising if girls welcomed their lack of fertility.

Household slaves with access to food and a lighter work load had many more children. A woman called Minny (1770–1825) lived on the Mesopotamia estate in Westmorland. Like Rose at Pemberton Valley, she worked in the great house. Minny bore her first child at the age of 13, a second at 15, then had five more mixed-race babies and seven black ones, making 14 children in total. The lack of babies born on sugar estates was taken up by critics of the slave system who said it was caused by underfeeding and overwork. Propagandists for the system argued that on the contrary, African women were not natural mothers. Janet Schaw recorded her views. She heard when visiting the Scotsman Colonel Martin on his plantation in Antigua:

> [t]his one of the oldest families in the island, has for many generations enjoyed great power and riches... living on their Estates, which are cultivated to the height by a large troop of healthy Negroes, who cheerfully perform the labour Imposed upon them by the kind and beneficent master... He told me he had not bought a slave for upwards of twenty years... there were no less than fifty-two wenches who were pregnant. These slaves born on the spot and used to the Climate are by far the most valuable.[15]

The secret of all this fecundity on the estate, according to the colonel, was that his 'wenches' were 'well fed'.

Women could not be whipped into line with babies tied to their backs. Little ones were normally left in the slave village or laid down in the field whilst their mothers worked. There was no time to feed them regularly. Men were mostly punished for defiance and aggression, pregnant women for not keeping up with the pace of field work and mothers for spending too long feeding little ones. When questioned about the lack of babies on an estate, planters usually responded that African women were not natural mothers. I suspect this word 'natural' was an oblique reference to their lack of periods.

Since 1735, slaves could

> carry about and sell many provisions, fruits, fresh
> milk and other small stock of all kinds

provided they had a ticket from their master that authorised them to leave the plantation.[16] We do not quite know exactly when it was established that a slave owner would buy only salt fish, smoked herrings and other cheap proteins to feed his slaves. By law, Sundays and sometimes Saturday afternoons (outside the months of sugar crop harvest from January to April, when slaves might work both day and night) were set aside for slaves to work on growing their own provisions. These weekend market gardening businesses fed not only the slave population, but much of the white population too. Pemberton Valley's household slaves such as Marjory, Rose, Lady and Daphne would have more time and energy for their farms on weekends. Lady and Daphne probably had plenty of fowls and hogs of their own, as well as raising them for John Hamilton's table. On the other hand, the field women were probably too exhausted at the end of the working week to produce much in the way of provisions for themselves. The greatest problems which arose from slaves growing their own food arose in the months of January to April, which were often very dry. In some years, when there was little food to be bought and food import prices rose, some slaves undoubtedly starved. When the heavy cane-cutting months coincided with food scarcity, records show that many came close to starving.

The planter found this system of slave food production attractive. Merchants in Glasgow advanced supplies to estates and sold the estate's sugar crop. From the sugar profits, the merchant subtracted a bill for the provisions shipped. This monopoly was an obvious recipe for inflated food bills. Oat growers on the east coast of Scotland complained bitterly of merchants in Glasgow raking in profit by buying oats for two pounds a hundredweight and selling them to the West Indies for seven pounds a hundredweight. Any planter would be pleased to avoid such inflated bills.

White men had little idea what to grow in the hot climate, unlike the Africans who arrived with skills in cultivating tropical soils and an understanding of tropical plants. As more good land was given over to sugar, more food needed to be purchased. This necessity created an opportunity for the African population. White households bought their fresh supplies from slaves in the neighbourhood. Africans walked to their grounds and local markets, growing, selling and keeping the profits from their sales. Edwards, the Jamaica commentator, wrote in 1793 that provision grounds were a universal system to which slaves 'were so attached' that it was recognised as 'dangerous to interfere with it'.[17] Slave owners compensated slaves if it became necessary to move their gardens. They tolerated these slave businesses partly because they provided much-needed fresh food, but also because they rooted slaves to the neighbourhood. By growing familiar foods in traditional ways, the African population became a little more reconciled to life in Jamaica. Provision grounds allowed some dignity and control for a woman or man deprived of both. However, significant amounts of cash in slave hands troubled the Jamaican authorities. The African population was so successful in raising livestock such as turkeys, cattle and pigs, that the island government eventually placed restrictions on slaves producing the more valuable kinds of animals.

Black women in Jamaica were ill-treated and horribly abused, but they were also great survivors. More men than women were imported every year, yet near equal numbers survived. Women have some natural advantages: they live longer, girl babies survive better and during the years when the slave trade was threatened, planters imported more young women in order to grow their own slave population. Despite the greater burden of field work, women generally survived rather better than men did. Throughout the 18th century, girls with rural skills arrived from Africa. They would be accustomed to working all day, carrying water, digging with hoes and planting. In their African communities, farming skills were of great value to a girl's birth family and much more important to a future husband and his kin than her looks, important enough for cattle and goats to be exchanged for her at the time of marriage. In most cultures in Africa, men never participated in family farming tasks; cultivating family food was women's work. Women arriving from Africa brought expertise in vegetable cultivation. Many used their provision grounds to earn money.

Thistlewood's 'slave wife' made regular appearances in his diaries. Though not typical, her day-to-day existence allows us some insights into black women's lives. She belonged to Maria Dorrill (later Mrs Cope), whose father was Thistlewood's initial employer. When we first meet Phibah in Thistlewood's writing, she is an accomplished household cook and possibly a bit younger than Thistlewood's 29 years. He said that she knew African folk law and remedies. Because she had a sister who lived nearby, Phibah was thought to be a Creole, that is, born locally. However, she and her sister could just as easily have arrived together and been separated from their mother at the slave auction in Kingston by a buyer who had no use for two young girls. Perhaps she was sold cheaply to neighbourhood planters from a small boat at one of the jetties along the Westmorland coast. Phibah and her sister were perhaps two of the thousands of little girls captured and transported, then separated from their parents throughout the 18th century. The adult Maria refused to sell 'her Phibah', although Phibah would have commanded a good price. Thistlewood pleaded to buy her, again and again, during the 36 years when Phibah was his 'wife'. Maria agreed only to rent Phibah to him for £18 per annum.

Perhaps Phibah was of sentimental value to Maria Dorrill. She was certainly trusted, on visiting terms with local white women and given much freedom to move around. Possibly she had been a nanny and companion to Maria, and had previously accompanied Maria as little girl on her visits to neighbouring households. When Thistlewood met Phibah, Maria was a teenager who had recently married the much older and rapacious Scotsman, Mr Cope, who inherited the family plantation through the marriage upon the death of Maria's father. Phibah was the cook at the family's sugar plantation. Phibah's daughter Coobah belonged to Maria too, but we have no idea who her father was. Coobah worked in the Cope household as Maria's personal maid. Both Phibah and her teenage daughter had babies fathered by Mr Cope and by his son from a previous marriage.

African children grew up fast, washing clothes, cooking food and helping to grow vegetables. Jamaica was probably not so different in this respect. Young girls like Phibah and her sister would have started work at six years old. Phibah, if she was born in Jamaica, would have accompanied her mother to their provision ground at weekends, helping to carry a basket of produce to the market and to haggle a good price for their vegetables with cooks and housekeepers sent from the local 'great houses'. In Africa, a man inherited land and a woman gained access to land through marriage.

She dug, planted and cooked for her family's survival. Her future rested on being able to make the most of this opportunity. In most traditions, she would feed the family, cook for her husband, then market and save any money earned from the garden produce as her own to use. Husbands might plead for some of a wife's cash, but women had a right to spend or save this money as they wished. In Jamaica, planters often paired up their slaves as they saw fit and allotted couples joint provision grounds. I suspect that the rules for a couple in Jamaica were African rules. Whatever the quality of the relationship, if he was her sexual partner, she did most of the garden work and gained some control over her life in the process.

Phibah, her sister and their friends had learned this lesson. Phibah cooked remarkable banquets for wealthy planters on special occasions, and other women came into the house to tailor and make dresses. We must assume that their masters rented them out for fees on these occasions, but they also used their skills to earn for themselves on their days off. In addition, they all sold garden provisions and livestock. In the year 1772, Thistlewood recorded that Phibah earned just over £10 18s from sewing, cooking and selling the watermelons she had grown. It is clear from his account that the money Phibah earned was not her owner's or her sexual partner's. Phibah and friends also dealt in horses and butcher meat. Phibah, we read, sold a filly for £5 13s 9d. In 1778, Franke sold a horse for £12 and a filly for £6. Vine sold a horse around the same time for £17. In 1781, Thistlewood bought a sow from his slave Abba.

Damsel killed her 50lb hog and sold a leg of it to Thistlewood and the rest in 12 smaller pieces for ten pence per pound. Thistlewood also bought pork from Franke. He also tells us that she killed one of her heifers as a feast for a leaving party when her 'husband' was being taken away to America. African rules of household management appeared to have survived, and women defended what was rightly theirs. This would explain the sometimes relatively large amounts of cash in women's hands. Estate workers, bookkeepers and white artisans were always short of ready cash because their employers were reluctant to draw money from their banks at home to pay them. In his first year in Jamaica, Phibah lent Thistlewood £10 in cash and regular sums thereafter. In 1769, he recorded his return of £27 2s 6d borrowed from three women slaves, Phibah, Franke and Egypt estate's Lucy. His wage was only £50 per year with board at the time. Thistlewood sent only women to market the imported goods and home-grown produce on which his livelihood depended. They were trusted with his money. Thistlewood recorded that he had advanced credit to some of his female slaves to acquire imported goods, such as ribbons, nails and combs, for their own petty trading businesses. His men were sometimes sent out to sell his fish, fowls and seeds, but he regularly punished them for suspected dishonesty. When the favoured slave Lincoln went out to sell Thistlewood's seeds, Jenny, who was said to be 'teaching him the art of higglering', accompanied him.[18]

These slave women had money and goods. We might compare these incomes with the wages of farm servants in Scotland at the time. There, a family with working children might get around £12 a year between them, less if they were given land on which to grow food. A woman servant living in a house where she was fed might have earned as little as £3–4 a year. A schoolmaster earned around £30 with a school house and could charge a bit more for extra tuition.*

The sexual rules in 18th century Jamaica were crude but simple. For the white man, they were derived from property law. A planter or overseer was entitled to sex with his slaves since they were his property, but he might give a small tip or gift, as Thistlewood sometimes did. A man having sex with someone else's slaves had to pay a market price. For an attractive young woman, this could be higher than a day's field work. According to Thistlewood, Mr McDonald paid Thistlewood's slave Eve six bitts for sex, which was two or three days' hire for a field slave. Mr Cope ordered the slave Tom to fetch the young girl Beck. Mr Cope could order Beck to come to bed with him whether she liked it or not, because he owned her. Indeed, enslaved women were beaten for refusing their owners' sexual demands. The possibility of such demands was one reason why Thistlewood did not like his long-term partner Phibah, whom he rented but did not own, visiting her owner's house in the evening. The pimping out of slaves was commonplace; women slaves were bought with an eye to this dual purpose. Young virgins and big-breasted, handsome girls fetched a higher price in the African slave markets. Mr Collgrave, the man who agreed to introduce Thistlewood to

---

* See my notes on money.

planter friends in Jamaica, lectured him on the importance of hard work and honesty. Thistlewood later said that he had discovered Collgrave

> used to buy clothes for Negro girls if they are handsome... they were to give him a half of what they got from any white person.[19]

One suspects Thistlewood did something similar, because without fail, he recorded every single penny the girls received for sex at the neighbourhood parties he held with his friends, a number he could surely only be confident of if he collected the money.

Itinerant overseers were often lonely for something more akin to a relationship. Men attempting longer-term liaisons did not have things all their own way; even Thistlewood's Phibah cheated with African men now and then. Enslaved girls in this situation, though by no means in control, were not entirely powerless. They gave and withdrew affection, sulked and demanded favours from their lovers. In exchange for being a man's special partner, they received presents of clothing, money and household goods. When Thistlewood arrived in Jamaica, Vineyard cattle farm's Phibah (not Egypt estate Phibah, with whom he eventually lived) offered to cook local foods for him to taste. He took this food sampling rather seriously, carefully recording his opinion; plantain tart, he wrote, was 'just like apple pie'; green corn *dokunnu* he observed to be 'very good'; star apples he did not like, but various tasty treats made of pea flour and corn he liked very much.[20] African tradition dictated that the man with several wives slept with the one that had cooked for him at sundown. Looked at from Phibah's view, was all this late evening food tasting a simple kindness to the new overseer, or did she hope to entice him into looking after her? Yet Thistlewood overlooked Phibah and took up with a girl called Jenny. He showered Jenny with beads, money, cloth and a pretty blue coat. He took back the coat when he suspected her of cheating, but left her his small collection of household goods and was sad to part from her when he moved on to Egypt estate. Thistlewood relates how Samuel Mathews hired Dido to live with him, and Thomas Fewkes fell out with Lydde and burnt the coat he gave her. Maria's husband Mr Cope seemed to have a passion for Little Bimber. The new teenage arrival Crookshanks had a noisy quarrel with Mirtilla, cried over her being sold to another estate, consoled himself with Bess and eventually rented Mirtilla from her owner for £20 per year. He loaned her to Mr Cope as a field worker at two bits per day to defray some of the rental cost, but she claimed to be too ill (Thistlewood thought she was pregnant) to stoop to doing field work!

James Wedderburn, one of the three Scottish doctor brothers already mentioned, had at least two families with slave women and a white family with the heiress he married on his return to Scotland. Robert, his son, worked his way to London and wrote a bitter account of his father's treatment of his slave mother Rosanna. Robert Wedderburn's story introduces us to the horrors of women's lives, but also to their unbowed resistance. According to Robert, his father used all of his female property for sex as and when he pleased. James Wedderburn took a fancy to Rosanna at the house of a neighbour and bought her to be his housekeeper and sexual partner. She was not as enthusiastic a partner as he had hoped. When she became pregnant with Robert, Wedderburn sent the enslaved Rosanna back to her former owner. Once he was born, the little boy lived with his mother. James bought his son's freedom. When Rosanna was again sold, she didn't take Robert with her; she preserved his freedom by sending him away to his grandmother 'Talkee Aimee'.

Robert later published his story, which was widely read and quoted by abolitionists. He described Aimee as an ill-treated old slave in her 70s at the time she was looking after him, but he also recognised her as an independent trader with her own funds.[21] One commentator implied that she was a garrulous old woman, hence the name 'Talkee'. I interpret her nickname 'Talkee' as one given to her by people she dealt with who knew she could talk a person into accepting her price for goods and into parting with their money. Before the 1830s, direct trade with Britain's European competitors and their colonies was illegal, but of course American, French and Spanish goods were regularly smuggled into Kingston. Aimee was owned by a smuggler. She kept his store and was his agent, disposing of all his smuggled goods. Robert recorded her dealing in fancy clothes, cheese, china, milk and gingerbread. She found buyers, knew the value of his goods and drove a hard bargain. She had obviously driven a similar hard bargain with her owner, because she made 12.5 per cent for herself on all his goods that she sold. According to Robert, Talkee Aimee took him to see his father to ask the Scotsman for a contribution to his son's upbringing and education, for which she got only abuse. Aimee bravely stood her ground and called the wealthy planter 'a mean Scotch rascal' to 'desert his own flesh and blood'. She declared that she had raised Robert so far and would continue to do so without any paltry assistance from him. She made the money to educate her grandson in the rough underworld around the docklands of Kingston. She taught him well, and would be proud that he travelled Britain talking to groups about the evils of slavery, especially the abuse of women slaves like his mother and grandmother.

CHAPTER 4
A different kind of brethren

I was not remarkable for that cold Virtue, Chastity, but indiscriminately... gave rather too great a latitude to a dissipated train of whoring.[1]

DURING THE 1700s when Scottish people were becoming more familiar with Jamaica, lives were ruled by literal interpretations of the bible taught by the Church of Scotland. The reformation in England replaced allegiance to the Pope with a mild protestant version of the Christian religion. Though extra-marital sex was discouraged, it was of no great importance. But in Scotland, the Kirk was both judge and jury in cases of sexual wrong-doing, and it decreed that sexual morality was of the utmost importance. In each little parish, once or twice a month, the Kirk session met to pursue its mission to wipe out the scandal of 'anti-nuptial fornication', sex amongst the unmarried. Prying eyes saw young men and women meeting in the woods, couples dancing in suspicious ways, widows receiving male visitors and servants found in bed together. All were thoroughly investigated. Neighbours were called to relate what they had seen: the touching, the looking, where and how long men and women were alone. They asked if it was long enough for 'carnal dealings' to have taken place. Pregnant girls blamed partners. Both had to 'appear before the congregation to be rebuked for their sins'. Unable or unwilling to accuse the gentry, whose sins in this regard might be well-known, the Kirk contented itself with keeping lesser mortals under close surveillance. Small-town and rural Scots were, by and large, God-fearing and supportive of the Kirk's view of sin. They did not have much choice; in order to move from one parish and live in another, certificates of good behaviour were required from the Kirk, and these had the force of law.[2]

Things were not so different in the city of Edinburgh. David Hume may have been respected across Europe as an enlightened philosopher, but he was popularly known in his home city as an affront to a God-fearing nation. The good folk of Edinburgh were scandalised when free-thinking Hume pronounced his scepticism about the existence of God. Such views ensured he was barred from public office in a university, lest he corrupt the young with his ungodly ideas. In response to reports that he was on his death bed and the gates of hell were awaiting him in August 1776, a great crowd gathered outside his home, anxiously awaiting news that he had retracted his heretical stance. Hume was to disappoint them. He slipped away gently, a sceptic to the last. His good friend Adam Smith had a successful career as Professor of Logic and Moral Philosophy at the University of Glasgow. He possibly agreed with Hume, but had the good sense not to put his doubts on paper lest they be used against him. Nevertheless, Smith helped to drive Glasgow University away from literal interpretations of the Bible and the study of classics, which were still the mainstay of Oxford and Cambridge Universities, towards commerce, medicine and engineering. Smith himself developed courses in understanding market price mechanisms and the efficient use of capital. These were useful in the eyes of the West Indian merchants of Glasgow, useful enough to persuade them to invest a portion of their considerable fortunes in a university education for their sons. This was the deeply Christian yet pragmatic home that emigrant Scots left behind to help to shape a new world.

Emigration figures show that families leaving Scotland tended to travel as indentured servants with a long-term goal of finding land to settle in North America. Scottish families who made their lives there played their part in building the God-fearing southern states. The Jamaican sugar economy tempted young men of every class and skill: tradesmen such as blacksmiths, coopers, wheelwrights and millwrights, and those with building skills such as masons and carpenters, most of whom passed on their skills to enslaved Africans before they returned home. Every estate mapped out its boundaries, inoculated its work force and kept accurate account books, creating openings for surveyors, surgeons, overseers and bookkeepers. By the late 1770s, Scottish Atlantic traders were more numerous in the ports of Jamaica than all of the doctors, bookkeepers, surveyors and landowners put together. Estimates vary, but in the latter part of the century, around 9,000 Scots were involved in managing Jamaican estates. Ship rosters show that from the 1630s onwards, nine out of ten immigrants into Jamaica were men between 15 and 24 years of age. Using Scottish names on shipping lists, it has been estimated that between 1750 and 1800, more than 20,000 young male passengers came and went on regular crossings. In addition, large numbers crossed on smaller trading boats from all over Scotland. On an island not much larger than Argyll, this was a huge gathering of young, single men. Only a minority came from Glasgow and Edinburgh; most left from the north of Scotland, particularly Aberdeen, Inverness, Ross-shire, Stonehaven and Banff. In the west, the largest numbers came from Ayrshire. In Virginia, only one in three residents were slaves, while in Jamaica, nine out of every ten people were captives, more than half of them women. Whatever skills newcomers had and whatever tasks lay ahead, young Scotsmen who were looking for work on plantations would be expected to help police these labour camps of slaves. They would be isolated and vastly outnumbered by black women and men. Amusements and entertainments were few, but both sex and rum were freely available. Far away from the constraints of the Kirk, they indulged in both. To find work, make friends or borrow cash, new arrivals had to be accepted by the old Jamaican hands. They were drawn to adopt the elders' ethos. A different kind of orthodoxy reigned amongst them. Young men bonded by drinking and 'wenching' together, to use the euphemistic phrase of the time. Drinking sessions were a step towards acceptance by other men from all classes. In Jamaica, men were introduced to a very different way of life from the one they had left behind.

Planters in Westmorland undoubtedly drank to excess. High rewards and high risks encouraged a hedonistic lifestyle.

Extra-strong rum was made in house and issued as part of a man's rations, which white men of all classes enjoyed generous quantities. They used it as a pick-me-up in the morning, mixed it with coconut water and lime to make a cooling drink on hot afternoons and shared a bottle in the evening whenever they had the company of other men. Slaves were also supplied with rum rations from time to time. In addition, vast amount of all kinds of alcohol were imported. Gallons of beer, tens of thousands of pounds worth of port and Madeira, as well as crates of French and Italian wines, were all shipped across the Atlantic. Janet Schaw, writing from Antigua to her friends in Edinburgh, reported on the habits of the wealthy:

> The drink which I have seen everywhere is Punch, Madeira, Port, Claret... in some places they have also Burgundy. Bristol beer and porter you will constantly find. But they have not as yet been able to have Champaign as the heat makes it fly too much.[3]

Successful West Indian merchants in Glasgow relived those drinking days of their youth for many years afterwards, mixing bowls of Jamaica rum punch and celebrating their mutual success with toasts to the good old days.

Zachary Macauley (1768–1838) was the son of the minister of Inveraray, Argyll, one of 12 children. At 14, his respectable family found him a bookkeeping post in a merchant house in Glasgow. Amid concerns about his fondness for the drinking dens of the city, Archibald Campbell, one of his father's clan contacts (already mentioned as resident in Black River but originating from Argyll), talked Zachary's father into packing his son off to new opportunities in Jamaica. Zachary arrived to the island with letters from Sir Archibald. 'Not one of them procured me' even an 'invitation', he later wrote.[4]

> Without money, or a single friend to whom I could turn for assistance, the vision presented to me rapidly receded.

He eventually obtained work as a bookkeeper, which was, according to his letters home,

> laborious, irksome and degrading to a degree of which I could have formed no previous conception, and which none can imagine fully who have not, like me, experienced the vexatious, tyrannical and pitiless conduct of the Jamaican overseer. I had no choice under the circumstances between doing... [the work] or starving... [I] was exposed to the sight and practice of severities over others... which made my blood run cold... [But] the die was cast there was no retreating, I should gladly have returned but I had not the means,

and neither had his father.

> I resolved to get rid of my squeamishness, as a thing which was very inconvenient... Picture me in

a field of canes amidst cursing and bawling, maybe one hundred of the sable race, the noise of the whip resounding on their shoulders and cries of the poor wretches.

Looking back in later life, Macauley wrote that he became 'callous and indifferent' and 'began to like my situation'. He admitted that he had adopted,

the grossly vulgar manners, and practices which disgrace almost every rank in the West Indies... my habits and dispositions were now fundamentally the same. The most degrading servitude to the worst of masters.[5]

New arrivals like Macauley faced grave risks. Many white immigrants as well as Africans died in their first few years on the Island. It was said that the island and its climate were unhealthy, yet this seems unlikely in any physical sense. Jamaica has fertile soil where a variety of fruit and vegetables were grown all year round, even in the 1700s. It has rivers, streams and springs pouring clean water down from the mountains. John Campbell of Orange Bay, writing home to his family in Argyll, proclaimed it the 'finest climate in the world for an old man' and encouraged his father in Minard 'to come for a course of tepid bathing' which would be of 'inexpressible benefit'.[6] Perhaps a more important danger to health was the melting pot of peoples, each bringing diseases from their particular parts of the world and passing them to others who had yet to build any resistance. Africans brought deadly yellow fever, dysentery and malarial mosquitos, while Europeans passed on venereal diseases, influenza and smallpox. White immigrants, moving rapidly from plantation to plantation, seeking better money, were exposed to dozens of different groups of Africans. Wedderburn, who had years of experience treating illness amongst the local planters and overseers, formed the view, after some years observing white lives, that the dangers from contagious tropical diseases were exaggerated while drunkenness and endemic gonorrhoea were the major killers of Europeans.

White men and slaves suffered constantly from re-occurring venereal diseases, which were treated with mercury, a cure that was probably just as dangerous. Contemporary accounts confirm that sex with multiple partners was commonplace. Men blamed the weather and bad women for their immorality. Young men about to set sail for the Caribbean were warned against the effects of a hot climate on a man's sexual appetite. One young Scotsman was given advice on surviving the climate and its effects from a friend, an old Jamaica hand,

> I would point out the great danger of promiscuous intercourse with the female Sex... one half of the young men who go abroad are destroyed by the disease contracted from bad women, or by the mercury injudiciously taken to cure it.[7]

Despite such warnings, the novelty of controlling young women with whom they could indulge in any amount of sex, at no cost and without the disapproval of others or shame on their part, was probably sufficient to explain men's excessive sexual behaviours. As Robert Graham, a son of Gartmore and Ardoch estates in central Scotland, wrote to friend in 1760, the availability of so many young women suited him well:

> I was not remarkable for that cold Virtue, Chastity, but indiscrimately... gave rather too great a latitude to a dissipated train of whoring, the consequence of which I now dayly see before me in a motely variegated race of different complexions.[8]

More than ten times the number of children of colour were born in Jamaica than were born in North America. Official figures represent only children born in more or less settled relationships, children registered by their fathers or owners. These were a small subset of all the children born from white sex with black slaves. On Mesopotamia estate in Western Jamaica, where the previously mentioned teenage Minny worked in the great house, eight white men fathered 43 children with 23 slave mothers. All of these children remained enslaved. Thistlewood had a child, John, in his long-term relationship with Phibah, and his friend and employer Mr Cope had a young wife, but they also invited each other to sex and drinking parties that resulted in slave children they barely acknowledged. One of the 'perks' of an often lonely existence cracking a whip over dozens of slaves, was that at least half of them were young females. When ordering slaves from African depots, buyers often stipulated the sort of females they liked; not surprisingly, the size and shape of breasts was spelt out. Handsome young women cost more too. Whatever had been believed in Scotland about fornication, illegitimacy and irregular marriage, all went unremarked upon in Jamaica. Few disapproved, and colonial law did not recognise a sexual offence against one's own property. Presented with the opportunity, and stripped of the social restraints which governed behaviour at home in Scotland, men abused, raped and sometimes formed more kindly relationships amongst the many women they controlled. Thomas Thistlewood's diary reveals a white community openly engaged in multiple sexual encounters with captive females. He tells of parties which ended with each man demanding a slave woman to take to bed,

> mr cope and mr stephen coppige come and stayed all night, mr cope had silvia mr coppice had egypt susannah gave her 6 bitts she pissed the bed.[9]

On another night,

> mr cope had coobah mr coppice wanted little mimber but mimber wouldn't go to him and egypt susannah was roughly taken to him in her stead.

As Talkee Aimee's grandson, the anti-slave campaigner Robert Wedderburn would later write,

> My father ranged through the whole of his household for his own lewd purposes for they being his

> property cost nothing extra; and if any one proved
> with child – why it was an acquisition which might
> one day fetch something in the market.[10]

Janet Schaw excused the wealthy men around her, saving her outrage for the unmarried black girls and their illegitimate offspring whose lifestyles violated her Scottish standards of propriety. Her letters reflected the excuses she had been given. She complained to friend at home in Scotland,

> Every unmarried white man... has his black or his
> brown mistress, with whom he lives openly; and of
> so little consequence is this thought, that his white
> female friends and relations think it no breach of
> decorum to visit his house, partake of his hospi-
> tality, fondle his children, and converse with his
> housekeeper... these wenches become licentious
> and insolent.[11]

She found her countrymen's sexual behaviour unacceptable, but viewed it as an unfortunate result of the temptation presented by 'licentious and insolent' enslaved women. She, like Lady Maria Nugent, the Governor's, wife thought that the situation could only be rectified by reforming these 'insolent' women and promoting Christian marriage amongst them. As Lady Maria Nugent put it,

> if religion, decency, and good order, were estab-
> lished among the negroes; if they could be prevailed

upon to marry; and if our white men would but set them a little better example... they would... render the necessity of the Slave Trade out of the question, provided their masters were attentive to their morals, and established matrimony among them; but white men of all descriptions, married or single, live in a state of licentiousness with their female slaves.[12]

Her comments reflected a growing sentiment in Britain that morality and family life should be established by promoting Christian marriage and that this would result in responsible women raising many more children. She added a story she had heard from a Mr Shirley, a Member of the Jamaican Assembly, who had advised one of his slaves to marry. The African replied,

Hi, Massa, you telly me marry one wife, which is no good! You no tinky I see you buckra no content wid one, two, tree, or four wifes.

James Stewart, from Edinburgh, wrote in his account of life in Jamaica,

It is probable that nineteen-twentieths of the white males have their brown or black mistresses, either free or otherwise, by whom they generally have children. The male part of this population may be divided into three classes – namely, the offspring of men of fortune and station (some of the most distinguished in the island have families in this class), who are sent to Great Britain to be liberally educated, and are destined to inherit independent fortunes – the offspring of men in moderate circumstances, who generally give them a plain education, and leave the bulk of their property among them at their death – and, lastly, the offspring of men who either have not the means or the inclination to provide for them. This last is probably the most numerous class.[13]

As James Stewart noted, men having sex with black women accepted varying degrees of responsibility for their children of colour, who were known as mulattos. Wills were often the way that those at home learned of the existence of an extensive number of brown relatives in Jamaica, the partners and children of their family member. That some Scotsmen had caring long-term relationships with young African women, despite the huge power differences between them, is borne out by the numbers who left most of their property and sometimes loving messages for the offspring of these unions.[14] Such wills used the euphemistic word 'reputed' or 'natural' rather than illegitimate when describing sons and daughters of these long-term partnerships. James Blair, a member of a family of merchants of Glasgow who had property in the Parish of Saint Elizabeth in the County of Cornwall in Jamaica, made a will in August 1835. His clothing and personal effects were left to a woman of colour named Elizabeth Pennycook. His estate was to be shared between a dozen children including 'Elizabeth', his 'reputed' daughter by 'Margaret Blair', and their other children named as Thomas, William, David, James, Eliza, Henry, Robert and Isabella, and also his 'reputed' children by a woman called Ann Cook, now residing on Mount Zion, named Agnes, Mary and Horatius.

James Hutcheson belonged to a trading family in Ayr; his Jamaican relatives were also extensive. His will left some of his wealth and use of a piece of land during her lifetime to, 'Peggy Powell, a free woman of colour', by whom he had two children. During her lifetime she was to receive,

> £50 per annum and the further sum of £10 per annum to be expended in keeping up the furniture and mending the fences against trespasses. She was to be given a piece of meat when a goat, sheep or hog was slaughtered by the overseer. She would also be allowed a woman to wash for her and to keep a mare and two cows on his land at Friendship pen.

His sons by Peggy had the surname Robinson. To them he left,

> William Robinson, born 06/12/1801, £1,000, and to her second son who is to be named Henry Robinson one other sum of £1,000 Jamaican currency when they attain the age of 21 years.[15] My executors to see that William and Henry Robinson are decently educated in England and brought up to some trade that they may get an honest living,

and charge my estate with the amount of such expenses. I also recommend these boys to the care of my son Augustus F Robinson particularly, and to my daughter Mary Robinson who will upon the survival of maturer years be convinced that they have as infants themselves been highly protected and affectionately treated by a loving father.

In addition he was leaving,

Jane Collingwood, a free woman of colour, 25 acres of land near Lynn Hill which she has now in possession and the [?] here unto annexed during the term of her natural life and it is my will that the same may be open and planted and that a decent house be kept in repair for her, chargeable to my estate. Also to her, two Negroes to be purchased by my executors. And she having any children of my body begotten I then bequeath the aforesaid 25 acres to him or her after her decease, and they to be treated in like manner as my before mentioned two children, giving to each of them £1,000 Jamaican currency at age 21 years.

Furthermore Elizabeth Hunt of Manchester, a free woman of colour, £200 until the youngest of my reputed children, Jean Hutchison, Eleanor Hutchison, Margaret Hutchison, David Hutchison, Charlotte Hutchison and James Hutchison attain 21 years. They are to receive £100 each at the time of my death, then £200, then £1000 each when they attain 21 years. A comfortable dwelling house is to be erected and furnished on Coffee Grove for Miss Hunt and her children, and they are to have to services of 8 slaves. Interest is to be paid annually as aforesaid to such of my reputed children hereinafter or as may be residing in Great Britain or Ireland.

Each of the three mothers of his ten children were free women; no doubt he bought their freedom. He particularly favoured Elizabeth Hunt's children, to these children of colour he gave his family name. Since all ten children are described as 'reputed', they are all illegitimate. Hutcheson obviously never married Elizabeth, Peggy or Jane. He clearly wished and expected that at least some of these Jamaican children would be educated or given some training. If so, he left instructions that they should be educated in England, away from his relatives in Ayrshire. Perhaps he recognised that the family and the strictly religious community in Ayrshire could not be expected to welcome so many illegitimate children. But Hutcheson hoped and expected that some of these children would settle in Britain. His commitment to their future is laudable, and his message which says he is a 'loving father' was not unusual. This distribution of his vast family fortune would no doubt have disappointed any relatives he might have in Ayrshire. His will, like many others, might have been open to dispute.

Jamaican attorney Malcolm Laing looked after the estate of William Perrin in the mid-1700s. He therefore had the task of sorting out William Perrin's affairs when he died. In Jamaica, Perrin had a 'housekeeper' called Elizabeth Fickle living with him when he died. He also had a wife in London. Laing wrote to Perrin's London wife after his death to offer some sympathy about the amount of wealth he had left his mistress Elizabeth. He stressed in his letter that Elizabeth Fickle had 'Served [William] faithfully and was about him during his Sickness and at his last moments'. Elizabeth may have only served as Perrin's nurse, but such language was generally code for a mistress, especially as Perrin left Elizabeth so much property. In his will of 1758, he gave her 10 slaves, a plot of land in Kingston, money with which to build a house upon it, 20 acres of plantation land in St Andrews, his residence in Vere parish and a £50 annuity for life.

Loved by their fathers or not, in the eyes of many in Scotland these children were illegitimate, fathered by men involved in sinful liaisons. That immoral women should be rewarded so handsomely was shocking. As James Stewart noted, almost all of the men in Jamaica had brown or black mistresses by whom they generally had children; it had become a settled way of life. But in a country like Scotland, where religious leaders were intent on preventing sex amongst the unmarried and men and women spending time alone was thought to be a temptation to sin, the behaviour of these women and their menfolk was outrageous. In Scotland at the time, an unmarried pregnant girl would be stood on a stool in front of the assembled community week after week to be rebuked until she repented her sins, then was fined for her licentious behaviour. Black women's availability was blamed by white visitors to Jamaica for leading white men astray. Black girls had no choice in these sexual encounters, yet they were seen as the sinful party. Christians at home in Scotland agreed with Lady Nugent's suggestion that a civilising programme was needed to ensure religion, decency and good order were established amongst 'the negroes'. They decided that slaves needed to be taught Christian family values, to understand the importance of chastity and to marry only one wife. Only then could it be expected that white men would behave decently. Christianity could ensure sexual morality was established. For all those men in Jamaica with several black mistresses, and for all those of promiscuous character and predatory sexual appetites such as Robert Graham, Lady Nugent's wishes that Christians arrive in the island to teach a new sexual code to slave women was a most unwelcome thought. Such men would fight to maintain their right to do as they liked with the women and girls they owned and accept no interference between them and their property.

CHAPTER 5
Scottish traders

There is one trade by much the most beneficial
of any carried on from Europe to the British
West Indies.[1]

SKIPPER DUNCAN, AS he was known to his relatives in Argyll, had a trading base in Rothesay on the Clyde. He regularly sailed between Britain and Jamaica, where his uncle James Campbell had a sugar plantation at Salem in Hanover. Skipper Duncan not only shipped his uncle's sugar and rum, but also carried family letters, gifts from home and all the other supplies needed by his planter relatives. Duncan regularly sent the family letters about his seafaring adventures. These tales eventually arrived by boat to his kin living along the Scottish coast. In August 1748, he wrote,

> No doubt you have heard of my Double Misfortune. At Latt. of 47 and about 15 Deg west from England we met with a Most Severe Gale in which we lost our rudder which had likes to have proved fattal to us all, for the Rudder By going torn away tore the Rudder Irons from the ships bottom, drawing all the Large Nails with it. The ship then all of a Sudden Made an immense deal of water Insomuch that we

could hardly keep her free with both pumps working Constantly. In this condition we continued for six
days (I having only nine hands). With me to work at
the rate of a ship of 800 tons, the Master being sick
in his cabin and several of our people dying, some
we Burried having hove a good part of our Cargoes
overboard to lighten the ship... we were luckily taken
up by a french Letter of Marque Ship bound for the
West Indies... our ship having at the time 4 feet of
water in her hold they abandoned the Ship.[2]

As skipper Duncan suggests, Atlantic trading was not for the
faint hearted. But Scots in the Caribbean and North America were bound by the Navigation Acts to buy their supplies
and sell their crops in Britain. By the turn of the 19th century,
around 100 boats were crossing the Atlantic from the Clyde
alone, employing almost 2,000 seamen and carrying around
£700,000 worth of Scottish goods.[3] Experiments with sugar
and whisky stills in Glasgow led to a thriving market for Scottish rum stills in Jamaica, worth well over £12,000. A number
of ironworks in Argyll and at Carron and on the banks of the
Kelvin made profits from the sale of thousands of plantation
hoes, hinges and barrel hoops. This trade in iron goods from
Scotland to the colonies was worth well over £33,000. Linen
became Scotland's most important manufacturing industry and
Osnaburgh* slave cloth its biggest export. Between 1746 and
the 1790s, output of linen doubled by volume and increased
fourfold in value. It is estimated that work in linen supported

---

* A rough linen cloth distributed to slaves to make their clothes.

40,000 male weavers and 170,000 women and children in small towns, transforming places like Forfar. Schools were opened to supply the trade with girls who could spin and boys who were skilled weavers.

About the year 1745 or 1746 the manufactory of Osnaburgh was introduced here, which from very small beginnings has grown into a great trade, and has become the staple of the place; and the happy influence of which, particularly of late years, is visible in the amazing increase of population and wealth, and the consequent improvement of every thing... the trade increased so rapidly, that, before the year 1750, there were upwards of 140 looms going in Forfar, and at present there are between 400 and 500... Manufacturers are just now giving from 15s to 20s for working the piece of ten dozen of yards, which a man of good execution will accomplish in nearly as many days; and a man working his own web, has been known to produce 18 such pieces by his own hands in the space of 19 weeks. This however is allowed by all to be extraordinary, though it shows what sobriety and diligence may do... The trade and wealth of Forfar having increased so rapidly since the year 1745, this must naturally be supposed to have produced great alterations in the appearance of the place and the manners of its inhabitants. Accordingly their

> buildings, their experience of living, and their dress
> are almost totally changed since that period,

the Reverend Mr John Bruce of Forfar reported in the First Statistical Accounts in 1791.[4]

It took about 18 months from planting canes to harvesting sugar. Once the sugar was crystallised and packed into barrels, it then spent several weeks at sea. Landlords in Scotland were used to receiving rent payments in farm produce. Scottish merchants adopted a similar system. A planter opened an account in a Glasgow merchant bank, lived on credit while his sugar was growing, then paid his debts in rum and sugar, which these merchant bankers refined and sold. The little sugar refineries working in Glasgow in 1600s moved down river. The population of Greenock on the lower Clyde, where industrial sugar refineries were built, was 2,000 in 1700 and 17,500 by 1801 as the sugar buying and refining business massively expanded. Less well-off members of families in Scotland were helped by their Jamaican relatives. Peter Campbell of Fish River paid his old father's medical bills in Argyll and bought his sister Molly new underclothes from the Fish River account in Glasgow. Campbell of Orange Bay paid funeral expenses for a relative, the passage for his mother and sister to visit him, and a gardener to be sent to Jamaica with seeds and tools. Embarrassed by his lack of good silver on his sideboard, Campbell of Orange Bay arranged with his merchants to fund the shipping of the family china, linen, books, watch, rings, candlesticks, wine labels and fine lace from the house in Minard. They were all to be packed into strong boxes. He gave strict instruction that the goods must be insured for at least £400, that the key to the strong boxes be sent separately, and that his precious things must not be put on a Loch Fyne boat, as this would be too risky.

By 1729, wealthier Scots were replacing a glass of ale or tot of whisky in the morning with sweet tea. Brigadier William Mackintosh, Laird of Borlum (1658–1743), Scottish soldier and a leader of the Jacobite rising, reported that people used to ask whether you had drunk your 'morning draft'.[5] Now they enquired about you having 'your tea'. The fashion for sugary tea drinking spread, until even the weavers of Forfar were claiming they had tea kettles by 1745. Over the century, a Scottish taste for all things sweet led to shortbread, jam on bread, fruit cakes and buns with sugar toppings to eat with tea. In Jamaica, they were rapidly expanding estates to keep up with demand. Easy credit encouraged planters to replace any remaining paid workers with slaves, who could be forced to work day and night during the sugar harvest and once bought were available for life.

Human trafficking became absolutely essential to sugar profits. A slave bought for very little in Africa could be sold for £50 or more by the middle of the century. Scottish merchants were well aware of this demand for workers. As early as 1705, the Covenanters' champion, John Spruel, was looking for partners for a trading voyage to the 'negroe coast'. He suggested locally made cloth, scissors and knives could be traded for Africans and that Glasgow plaids and bonnets might be suitable gifts for the African princes who dealt in human cargo. On realising how profitable the trade could be, the Stuart kings who ruled both countries in the 1600s had granted themselves a monopoly on the selling of humans to their colonies. However, there were many interlopers because the trade was difficult to police. Slaving ships left from ports in Scotland throughout the 1600s and 1700s. Scottish merchants regularly petitioned the royals to be allowed to trade legally, but it was not until 1752 that legislation reorganised the trade and gave Scottish traders legitimate access. At this time, 20 or more boats were regularly trading from the Clyde. The last of these, the *Juba*, left in 1766. About 5,000 people are thought to have been shipped by these boats; there are records of 1,000 people being trafficked by Montrose boats and boats leaving from Leith. Many more would have been bought in the Kingston market and shipped by Scottish traders to the Spanish colonies and the American mainland throughout the century.

Until copies of the popular coloured cloth from India, which was traded in West Africa for humans, were made in cotton factories in Britain, all of the cloth used in trading for slaves had to be bought from the East India Company monopoly and import tax paid on it. The resulting high prices for equipping a slave trading boat could be evaded by loading the ships from the Isle of Man. Ships could then sail along the southern coast of Scotland to pick up a doctor and crew. This explains why so many doctors, ship's captains and traders who travelled to or were stationed on the African coast came from Dumfries and Galloway region in the south of Scotland. It also explains why ship owners the Tod brothers came from the unlikely town of Moffat, Samuel McDowal from Wigtown and Henry Clarke from Dumfries. All of them made fortunes as slave traders and eventually in trading from Liverpool. Samuel McDowal is recorded as making 45 voyages from the city. As the demand for sugar rose and merchant profits soared, the supply of slaves became a crucial issue. In the second half of the 18th century, the number of sugar estates and the sugar output of Jamaica both doubled. Scottish planters, sugar refiners, those who supplied all the farm and sugar boiling equipment, and the household items bought by planters were all at risk should the supply of slave labour falter. Most importantly, bank loans to planters were threatened should there be any disruption of the traffic in human labour, which produced the sugar on which it all depended.

Merchants pocketed a percentage on loans, took a percentage on the island produce bought and sold, and made a bit more from sending out supplies. The money made on the Scottish side of the Atlantic was lent back to planters. The system was expensive for Scots in Jamaica. They put up with the arrangement because it ensured all their money was transferred safely home. They rarely had to risk transfers of cash in small boats on the high seas. The largest of these money-lending, sugar-buying sellers of overpriced supplies built great reputations in Glasgow and smaller towns like Ayr and gave their names to their handsome streets. Once planters had committed themselves to mortgages to expand their business, they worried about enough slaves arriving in time for the harvest, and so did their bankers. When human trafficking was opened up to the market, small Scottish concerns could no longer compete. Wealthy merchant bankers in Scotland, intent on protecting their loans, stepped in and used their capital to control a considerable portion of the trade in England, Africa and Jamaica. At the beginning of the 18th century, the number of slaves in Jamaica was around 45,000; it rose to 75,000 by 1730, passed the 100,000 mark in the 1740s and by 1805 stood at over 280,000 survivors from the many more who had arrived in Kingston and since died. The value of sugar, molasses and rum exports from Jamaica rose from £237,000 to £703,000 by 1744, then as high as £1,003,290 in 1762. Slaving became a specialised, high risk, global trade. Tens of thousands in capital, a vast fortune, was needed to equip a boat. Merchant bankers intent on increasing the supply of slaves to the West Indies were determined to cut out as much risk as possible. Bringing together a group with capital in a joint venture with experienced English merchants was one way for Scots to enter the trafficking trade on a larger scale.

Wealthy men who lived in the islands would offer to guarantee a loan for a planter up to a certain fixed figure. Knowing what he could spend, the planter would then approach one of the merchant houses in Kingston who took orders for slaves. These orders were passed on to the slave trading arm, the partners in British ports. Once the list of slaves ordered was large enough to finance a trip, these partners would borrow tens of thousands of pounds to equip ships and set off for Africa, knowing they had guaranteed buyers when their ships docked in Jamaica. Bills for the subsequent buying of slaves in the Kingston market were settled harvest-by-harvest from planter accounts at home. Consequently, Scottish banks and merchant houses had a lot of capital lent out for slave purchases, slave ships and the goods carried in them. Because they were profiting from constant slave replacement, they had absolutely no financial interest in reducing demand by ensuring slaves were well-fed, survived for long periods or able to reproduce. On the contrary, by squeezing planter profits hard, banks and merchant houses could ensure slaves were driven as hard as possible, creating a rapid turnover of slaves: slaves lived short lives and replacements were constantly needed. As the century progressed, they took much of the risk out of the business for Scots by ensuring demand for loans and a steady sale of captive African workers. During the 18th century, the enterprising and seriously Christian country of Scotland was becoming a country with a lot of banking capital lent directly for slave purchases and many livelihoods involved in the wider slave economy. Expanding commerce with the colonies was a national success story that came at the cost of becoming more entwined with buying and selling humans. At the same time, the middle class of educated city dwellers was becoming better informed about Africa and more enlightened in its approach to ethical questions. The free-thinking University of Glasgow professor Francis Hutcheson (1694–1746), no doubt aware of the buying and selling of humans carried out by boats based on the Clyde, had already noted the paradox in his *System of Moral Philosophy* in 1738:

> Strange that in any nation where a sense of liberty prevails, and where the Christian religion is professed, custom and the high prospect of gain can so stupefy the conscience of men, and all sense of natural justice that they can hear such computations made about the value of their fellow men and their liberty, without abhorrence and indignation.[6]

Almost nine out of ten British doctors graduated from Edinburgh, Aberdeen or Glasgow. It is not therefore surprising that towards the latter part of the 18th century, when slave ships attempted to stem losses by carrying doctors, almost half of ships' surgeons sailing from Liverpool were trained in Scotland. However, the title 'doctor' did not indicate maturity; James Irving was a teenager of about 16 when he wrote home, before he set sail on his first voyage, to assure his mother and father at the bakers shop in Langholm that,

> I eat in the cabin and have a good coat [cot?], bed blankets and quilt, and I sleep very well. I get £4 per month plus head money, if we only bury 6 slaves. My couzin will receive £100 and £50 bounty. If we bury 9 slaves my cousin will receive £50 and I £25. I don't expect we will be out more than 12 mths altho my couzin says 10 months.[7]

An older doctor, Thomas Trotter from Melrose, gave evidence to Parliament against the trade. He took a job as a doctor for slaves after being discharged from the navy. He made one voyage to Africa and vowed to never make another, turning down the chance of promotion and the considerable rewards available to a ship's captain. Twenty per cent of Liverpool slave ship captains were recruited from the doctors and experienced merchant seamen north of the border.[8]

The Portuguese and Spaniards had transported Africans to their colonial plantations in Brazil and Mexico for centuries. A culture of slaving was established in many parts of Europe long before West Indian sugar planters wanted slave labour. They had set up a structure with holding forts and island prisons, referred to as 'factories', along the African coast, from which captured humans were collected. From these warehouses, boats could be quickly supplied, cutting the number of weeks at sea, risks of piracy, illness or mutiny, and reducing the amount of food carried to feed captives and crew. A group of resident traders in these forts arranged bartering meetings with African headmen along the banks of the major rivers. In the 17th and early 18th centuries, when the supply of slaves to British colonies began, woollen and cotton cloth, metal bars and copper, amber and glass beads, cowrie shells, weapons, gunpowder, tobacco and barrels of rum were popular items of exchange. In 1682, the British Royal African Company exported 10,000 iron bars per year, mostly bought from Sweden and Germany. Before traders could get a look at any of the Africans on offer, they had to display samples of all of their barter goods. Ships heading down to Africa from Bristol or Liverpool were floating emporiums of internationally traded goods. African slave dealers were knowledgeable and had precise requirements. Different sorts and qualities of metals were required for smelting. They already had beads and indigo dyed cloth in Africa, but Venetian glass beads, Indian cottons and heavy silks were highly prized. Between 1766 and 1770, the purchase and sale of £39,000 worth of Venetian glass beads to Africa-bound ships in the port of Liverpool appear on the books of Davenports, a major slave trader. African dealers preferred the multi-coloured, heavily embossed cotton cloth of the type manufactured in India, and later copied in Lancashire specifically for the West African trade. African traders were connoisseurs of distilled spirits and had particular tastes in tobacco. Three guns in exchange for a slave was the going rate in the second half of 18th century. Three hundred thousand European guns were exported this way, a considerable market for the gun makers of Birmingham. Satisfying these desires and wants of the African traders was the only way for Europeans to access the most strongest Africans.

Fraud was reported amongst European traders, including faulty guns, half-filled bottles of liquor and ships sailing off without paying. Well-founded evidence given to The House of Commons Select Committee on the Slave Trade exposed some fearsome practices, all corroborated by many witnesses.[9] Ships' captains advanced goods to encourage the seizing of local people. Local headmen were given weapons and alcohol in return for a promise to come back with suitable men and women. Armed locals went out at night and brought back villagers who were then locked up at the factory. Evidence was provided of 'different kinds of chains' and

> an instrument of wood an inch in diameter and about five inches long which was thrust into the mouth and tied in place

to prevent 'captives crying out when transported at night'.[10] One naive youngster, now in chains, told a ship's doctor he had been tricked by his own curiosity. He was asked by a local man if he had ever seen a ship and accompanied the man to see one. Children were separated from parents. A Dr Trotter gave evidence to Parliament that many little boys and girls on board slave ships sometimes played a game called 'slave taking' or 'bush fighting', acting out their capture and being subdued. Canoes were reported coming alongside slave ships at night to hand over captives who were paid for in cutlasses and muskets. A Mr Kiernan told the House of Commons Committee of lying in wait in a village and seizing whoever they could. A Mr Dalrymple told of 3,000 Africans seized by setting fire to their villages and catching those escaping.[11] Residents along the African coast never went unarmed when slave vessels were around, in case they were seized. Sir George Young said he had purchased a beautiful infant boy for a bottle of wine because he was about to be tossed overboard when the traders could not find a buyer. A captain of a Liverpool trading ship had a girl as a 'temporary mistress', and instead of sending her back, he took her away with him. A Mr Marsh, who ran a slave collection point on the West African coast where slaves were bought from African traders and imprisoned whilst waiting for European buyers to arrive along the coast, was reputed to have said that he did not bother himself with how the slaves were obtained so long as he 'had purchased them fairly'.

Slaves were displayed, examined and shipped naked. The ship's captain made the final choice, guided by detailed requirements relayed from prospective buyers in the colonies. 'Nothing shorter than five foot seven inches', 'the blacker the better' and 'no women with hanging down breasts' were some of the prejudices of West Indian planters.[12] The captives were put through a small gymnastic routine, in pairs, to demonstrate their working parts. The ship's doctor made an intimate examination of mouth, teeth and sexual organs. Broken teeth, signs of disease and any with small penises were rejected. Those chosen were branded with a hot iron and loaded onto the boat. Six witnesses to the Commons Select Committee confirmed that most were in state of 'extreme distress and despair', many were 'making a howling melancholy noise, expressing extreme anguish'. This was especially true of the women, some of whom were subject to hysterical fits. During the voyage, many would dream in the night that they were at home and on waking in captivity would howl uncontrollably. Prisoners were chained and packed in tight rows. Buckets were provided as latrines, but climbing over the tightly packed bodies whilst still chained to others meant that it was not unusual for a prisoner to be forced to lay in excrement. Women were sometimes unchained in order to be used and abused by the crew. Under parliamentary questioning, traders claimed that once out of sight of their African home, when the desire to jump overboard had passed, a well-managed ship might give prisoners regular exercise, wash and scrub the hold with vinegar and distribute two meals a day. Crews bought rice, yams and beans on the African coast to feed their prisoners. Evidence presented to the Select Committee showed that when men and women were brought up for air and food, they were chained to rings on the deck. After meals, captives were whipped with a cat o' nine tails, which was justified for 'health reasons' to make the prisoners jump about. A Mr Falconbridge estimated the space per person was not so roomy as a coffin. As a ship's doctor, he had to go below and, as he explained, after five minutes his shirt was wet as if dipped in water. When the shutters over the air gratings were closed in bad weather, people's cries of 'we cannot breathe, we are dying' were heard. Dysentery and overheating were thought to be the main causes of death on board.

The Select Committee asked witnesses if the prisoners on board slave ships sang, as traders claimed they had witnessed. 'They sang songs of sorrow', was the reply, 'songs of their wretched situation and of returning home'. On average, 20 per cent of the kidnapped Africans died during the crossing. From the merchants' perspective, this cut profit margins down to ten or 15 per cent of their investment. Keeping a doctor on board and making bonus payments to captains for each delivered slave did not do much to help improve survival rates. Around 20 per cent of sailors did not return home from the slave voyages either. Their bodies had no defence against African viruses and bacterial infections brought on board and forced to fester in the tightly packed, inhumane holds.

By 1785, eight out of ten trafficking ships sailed from Liverpool; almost 2,000 set off to buy slaves in the 20 years before the traffic was outlawed in 1807. The port had an advantage; it was close to the English districts where coloured cloth, guns and other goods for the West African market were now made. The consortia which funded the trade were wealthy, respected citizens. Most ships' captains worked their way up from a lower class. They were mainly local, from Lancashire and the Isle of Man, but about one in four was Scottish. Ships carried a surgeon even before it became compulsory to do so. Scottish surgeons experienced with treating slaves were often promoted to captain. The youngest captain to sail from Liverpool was Thomas Mullion, a 20-year-old Scot. He left the port on 6 June 1797 in command of the *Amacree,* which picked up 363 slaves. His boat was owned by William Harper and Robert Brade. The second ship he commanded was the *Kingsmill*, which carried 510 slaves, one of the largest in the trade. The *Kingsmill* was owned by the linen merchants Hamlet Mullion, William Lenox and Co. Hamlet Mullion had been a slave ship captain for five years and may have been Thomas's older brother. A captain's basic pay was under £100 per voyage. To encourage good management and safe delivery of slaves, captains were rewarded with 'privilege slaves' and commissions, which was where the real money was made. A Captain Wright made over £155 on his seven 'privilege slaves', over £192 from his 2 per cent commission on delivery to West Indies, and a further coast commission which came to £360 for the slave barter on the West Coast of Africa.[13] Robert Bostock, captain of the *Bloom* that carried 307 slaves to the Caribbean in 1784, received over £224 for seven privilege slaves, £192 for a 2 per cent commission, and a coast commission of over £360. As well as guiding their ship across the oceans, a captain had to have expertise in African and Caribbean markets, an understanding of maritime and tropical diseases, and above all, the ability to maintain discipline aboard vessels with up to 70 crew and hundreds of human cargo. Captains were also at risk of picking up tropical infections when they went ashore to stock up on provisions and negotiate for slaves. Returning to his home town of Hawick, Scotland, in 1803, a 23-year-old captain, Mr Swanson, 'took ill and died, either from a previously contracted virulent fever, or from delirium tremens'.[14] Alcoholism was another great risk over months spent at sea.

Captives offered for sale were said to be prisoners of war, collateral from fighting between African tribes. Buying already captive people was a more palatable story, often relayed in defence of the business. Supporters of the slave trade argued that the captives were better off in the West Indies cutting cane than they were in their home countries. It may have looked that way to anyone who saw the miserable pens and dungeons on the African coast, where many hundreds of humans were kept like animals waiting for buyers.

European traders passed their time in Africa in more comfortable surroundings. Bunce Island in the Sierra Leone river estuary had been a British holding fort for the Royal African Company. In 1748, it was sold to a Scottish consortium made up of Sir Alexander Grant, John Boyd and son, and the Glasgow merchant family, the Oswalds. The Boyds and Oswalds prided themselves on their good taste. Both families owned fabulous collections of European art. In keeping with their refined style, they furnished a 'cool and convenient gallery' for the traders, and armed the fort with guns facing out to sea to protect the waiting ships and cargoes from interlopers.[15] To amuse traders while they waited, there was a golf course with African caddies dressed in kilts made in Glasgow. The place was managed by a James Aird and 30 or 40 Scottish clerks and their assistants, most of them the owner's relatives.

Once small Scottish trafficking concerns could no longer compete, Scottish merchants joined ventures with experienced English traders to stabilise the supply of Africans. Others established themselves in ports, where experienced crews and supply lines of specialised goods for barter with West Africa were already set up. Scottish bankers needed no introduction in these ports; they had an established reputation for funding planters to buy slaves. The Scottish merchant house Anderson & Co entered the trade in Bristol to become one of the five big slaving companies operating there. Between 1762 and 1805, they sent out at least 82 vessels which transported around

26,000 slaves. John Fowler and his brother Andrew, wealthy planters in Jamaica and natives of Ross and Cromarty, were business partners of another important Bristol slave trader, James Rogers.

When the Todd brothers and Samuel McDowal moved from the south coast of Scotland to Liverpool to grow their business, they were not alone. Between 1752 and 1807, vessels owned or chartered by the Scottish Shaw & Co made at least 87 voyages from Liverpool carrying close to 30,000 Africans. In the 1760s, when slave trading was thrown open to the market, committees of traders in the main British ports began to invest to reorganise and control the trade to ensure a constant supply of captive workers. Archibald Dalzel (1740–1811), son of a carpenter from Kirkliston, who had experienced the trade at close quarters and having begun as a doctor to the trafficking business on the West African coast, was appointed to a new post. His accumulated knowledge of slave requirements and relationships with headmen and tribal leaders led to his appointment by the Committee of Merchants to manage and maintain its slave depots along the coast. A grand title, Governor of Dahomey (modern-day Ghana), came with the job. This title was a misnomer in many ways, since at the time, Britain was a visiting trader with no jurisdiction over anything but a few slave forts.

Planter families avoided any risk of a labour shortage and increased their wealth, by getting involved in buying and selling African slave labour on a massive scale. The Scots amongst them put their capital together to fund new ventures. The previously noted Grant family from the east of Scotland were typical of the many who graduated into the business. As already noted, they became partners in the purchase of Bunce Island in the river in modern-day Sierra Leone. Twenty years before their venture into capturing Africans, a son of the Grant family appears in Jamaican records. Arrivals for 1721 list a young man called Grant, a 'Practitioner in Physick and Chiurgery' trained in Edinburgh.[16] By 1730, he had acquired 300 acres in the parish of St Elizabeth, and some doctor cousins had joined him. He also became a Jamaican trader by jointly leasing a storehouse with Peter Beckford (the man with children by 13 women, according to Thomas Thistlewood's gossip). From their store, the men sold supplies to neighbouring planters. By 1739, there was a further venture into a London based business making loans to Jamaican planters for slave purchases, employing Grant family members. Between 1752 and 1768 the family bought many sugar estates in Jamaica, but also invested in Scottish land around Elgin and Nairn. They established themselves as a leading Scottish transatlantic family of planters, merchants and slavers. In 1761, the serving Baron became a Member of Parliament for Inverness, from which position he defended the slavers' cause. The total value of his property when he died was £61,000, a staggering amount in those days.

Many who started out as small traders used their profits to move into the profitable shipping of human cargo. In 1740, the well-educated John Harvie left Scotland for Barbados. Family connections in East Lothian led to an opportunity to act as tutor to a planter family in the island. John did not teach for long. Three years later, he began importing linen and calico from Scotland to clothe slaves, and he was joined in the business by his brothers, William and Alexander. A start-up loan and the necessary business guarantees came from the English financiers Lascelles & Maxwell. The Harvie brothers got help from the Scottish partner Maxwell, another Barbados adventurer and family friend. George Maxwell left the island in 1743 and used his Scottish connections to become a partner in a number of joint trading ventures. Maxwell was a partner in a Lascelles venture to place a group of ships just offshore in West Africa for the storage and rapid loading of slaves. This arrangement was popularly known as the 'floating factory'. George's father had been a planter who made a good marriage into the East Lothian gentry. The East Lothian Maxwells in turn had connections with the Lascelles. By this chain of friendships, the Harvie brothers were able to supply manufactured goods, using loans from Lascelles & Maxwell, in return for sending cargoes of sugar and rum back to Clydeside for refinement. Within a few years, they had their eye on more lucrative trading possibilities. Alexander Harvie wrote in 1746,

> There is one trade by much the most beneficial of any carried on from Europe to the British West Indies and that is the trade to the coast of Africa for slaves by which the people of Liverpool have enriched themselves.[17]

John and Alexander travelled to Jamaica to explore possibil-ities, leaving William to manage their business in Barbados. Maxwell had big plans for the Harvie brothers. Jamaica was now a significant distribution centre for human trafficking. Regular shipments arrived and were sold on to buyers around the Caribbean. With George Maxwell's help, within three years, the brothers were dealing in few dry goods and had moved fully into the Jamaican slave importing business. Just as the free market in slaves was opening up in 1753, George arranged credit of £20,000 through his Lascelles partners to underwrite the Harvie brothers' entry into the trade. With these funds, they were able to guarantee loans to slave buyers in Barbados and Jamaica, enter partnerships in Bristol and Liverpool for the hire of ships and crews, and fill them with the specialised goods needed for bartering on the African coast. George Max-well went to Liverpool to find business for them and helped to introduce the Harvie brothers to the port's slave traders. Eight shipments of slaves from West Africa to Jamaica followed quite rapidly. The Harvie family firm expanded rapidly, perhaps too rapidly. They made many more voyages shipping thousands of slaves; however, they went bankrupt in 1777. By this time, the brothers had amassed 20,430 acres of Jamaican property worth £87,000, which the courts handed over to George Max-well's English partners, the Lascelles banking family.

We know little about most of the hundreds of Scottish trading ventures apart from brief records of their voyages, numbers of humans shipped and profits made. But the Taylor family (originally Tailyour) preserved a vast array of family papers and letters that allow us to look into their thoughts and feelings about the way they earned their fortune. The family first appear in Jamaican records when several sons travelled to Jamaica in the 1720s. One previously mentioned brother, John, was a merchant and slave trader who married the daughter of a West Indian merchant in Glasgow, McCall, whose son Simon Taylor (1740–1813) was the man with a favourite slave girl on every estate. Simon was a great risk taker. He returned to Jamaica and used his father's capital to borrow heavily and build the number of family estates to 12. He also acted as attorney for many absentee proprietors. His most ambitious purchase was the grand Holland Park estate; the repayments for this amounted to £10,000 every year for six years and £5,000 for eight years thereafter. His letters describe the impossibility of predicting the estate's sugar income, the disasters caused by floods and droughts, his sleepless nights when the crops were inundated with little black flies, his great fortune in just avoiding the worst of a massive hurricane of 1780, and the American war of independence disrupting all of their food supplies for years. By 1807, when the trade but not the institution was abolished, Simon Taylor owned over 2,000 slaves – worth £128,550 – and managed many more. He described the slaves as stock; he viewed these people as his to be bought and sold and put to work as he saw fit. He expressed as much as an Assembly member in Jamaica and in political circles in Britain against the rising tide of voices in Scotland in favour of abolition of the trade.

Simon Taylor was wealthy enough to guarantee many, many planters' slave purchases. He achieved his own ambition of creating 'a clear fortune in debt to no one', but George Nugent, the Governor of Jamaica, said in 1806 that Taylor financed so many business loans to planter members of the legislative Assembly that he wielded 'a worrying degree of influence'.[18] Taylor died in 1813, leaving £750,000. To put this wealth into perspective, between 1809 and 1819, only 214 people died in the British Isles with personal estates valued at over £100,000, and just nine died with estates valued at over £500,000.

John Taylor was Simon's nephew. He was born at Marykirk, in Kincardineshire, Scotland in 1755, and worked successively under his uncle's guidance and financial support as a factor and trader in Glasgow, Virginia and New York, before moving to Jamaica in 1782. He initially handled plantation supplies and dry goods for the firm of McBean, Ballantine & Taylor. A year later, John Taylor switched operations and set up a new venture: Taylor, Ballantine & Fairlie. He reserved half of the shares in his new venture for himself and acquired two Scottish partners, Peter Ballantine and James Fairlie; together they became the second-largest human traffickers into and out of Kingston, with 54 slaving vessels under their name from which 17,295 captives were sold.

Trading slaves around the Caribbean was the most profitable and least risky end of the slave trade. John Taylor moved to London partly due to ill health, but also to manage the London offices of Taylor, Ballantine & Fairlie. The company was approached by merchants trafficking slaves across the Atlantic from the African coast and asked whether they would handle the sale of a planned slave cargo. The merchant would give details of their ship, the intended number of Africans on board and where they were from, plus an estimated time of the ship's arrival at Kingston. John Taylor would then set up a financial guarantee, based on his uncle's vast wealth and reputation, for the buyers in Kingston and any onward sales to America. A promise that Taylor, Ballantine & Fairlie would honour payments for slaves by a large list of buyers was sufficient for a British merchant in Liverpool or Bristol to proceed forward to fund a voyage. Business in these times was based on trust, clan contacts, marriages and family relationships. Good Scottish connections could make or break a new venture. In January 1794, John Taylor informed the London merchant William Collow that Taylor, Ballantine & Fairlie would guarantee slaves from the Gold Coast on his vessels the *Eagle* and the *Countess of Galway*, using William Miles of Bristol as a business partner. Miles was a vastly wealthy resident of Bristol, a retired Jamaican planter and Taylor's employer as a young man. He helped ease Taylor's entry into the community of slave traders in Liverpool. He sent letters of recommendation to friends at Hayhurst, Poole & Fletcher of Liverpool, requesting introductions 'to the principal Guinea Houses'.[19] A mutual friend, Edgar Corrie, a Scottish brewer and corn factor in the city, well-acquainted with Liverpool merchants, was also supportive. His recommendation to use Taylor, Ballantine & Fairlie was crucial to building the business. In 1798, John Taylor retired and bought back his father's old estate at Kirtonhill, near Montrose. He never returned to Jamaica. He died in 1816, leaving an estate worth nearly £100,000. Both Ballantine and Fairlie returned to Scotland as well. Ballantine died in 1810, leaving £26,025, while Fairlie died in 1819, leaving £46,294.

CHAPTER 6

Inventing apartheid

The distinction... to be kept up in this island,
between white persons and negroes, their issue
and offspring.[1]

BLACK PEOPLE LIVED IN Britain from the 1500s, if not earlier. There is evidence of black court trumpeters, black silk weavers and black divers salvaging shipwrecks, including the famous Marie Rose. In May 1668, Samuel Pepys was called from work by his wife to meet a special visitor to their home,

> A very pretty black lady, that speaks French well, and is a Catholick and merchant's daughter.[2]

Pepys recorded in his diary that, after sitting and talking a little, he took his wife and lady visitor out to meet his friends. Group prejudice and discrimination have always existed, but until the growth of the sugar industry in the West Indies, ideas about white supremacy had not been systematically promoted. The British Government initially gave diplomatic status to the kings and princes of West Africa with whom they traded in slaves. They were high-class men and were treated as such. African slave traders often trusted their Liverpool counterparts to transport their children to the city and enrol them in good, fee-paying schools. There were normally 50 or 60 such African boys and girls learning the business habits and language of the port to prepare them to take on their fathers' trade. In 18th-century Britain, people were high or low class depending on their income, with the highest class living on unearned income from land rents. Initially, black captives and indentured white men laboured alongside each other as poor, exploited workers, though indentured servants were able to leave at the end of their contracts. Men who owned slaves ensured that white waged and indentured workers arriving from Scotland passed on their skills to the more permanent slave workforce. Indentured labourers would serve their time and move on, but barrel making, carpentry and stone-cutting know-how were essential to sugar production. There was no suggestion that Africans could not take the place of contract labourers, although they were never paid skilled wages. These skilled Africans made up more than half the male workforce on plantations. They were bought, trained in Jamaica or occasionally in Scotland, then sold for two or three times their original price. Tradesmen working in Jamaica could make money by buying an unskilled slave, training him, and hiring him to families and businesses in need of a skilled man. Contracting companies were formed in this way and small fortunes made by hiring out enslaved labour for daily rates. These slaves were as skilled as those who owned and controlled them. They would be able to make a good living if free to do so. In the closing years of the 18th century, Scottish sugar estates were paying £140 for a good carpenter.[3] Much of the impressive early infrastructure in Jamaica, including country houses, har-bours, arched aqueducts, canals and dams, was built by highly skilled enslaved men.

Slave resistance was always a potential threat to the smooth running of a profitable business. Bryan Edwards wrote in 1801 that a planter's fear of his slaves 'left no choice... it superseded all questions of right'.[4] Keeping slaves under control was the task the overseer or bookkeeper was employed to carry out. Controlling the inputs of food and clothing and ensuring a maximum amount of work was the only concern of the owner of enslaved Africans. Great brutality was necessary to main-tain control over a large body of strong men and women. The planter might not consider the morality of his use of violence, but he did develop elaborate myths about the unfeeling nature of Africans to defend his behaviour.

Planters were active in ensuring their views were heard in Scotland. They would be sensitive to a Christian visitor from home viewing cruelty, which was being discussed as unac-ceptable amongst the enlightened in places like Janet Schaw's home city of Edinburgh. To avoid any difficult questions and to uphold their reputation at home, planters felt it necessary to head off possible criticism by spinning racist myths about the nature of Africans to visitors like Janet. They would hope that she would pass on such explanations to friends and family at home. Janet was clearly quite gullible. Whatever her eyes might have told her, she was prepared to accept the assertion that 'black' described a different 'species' of humanity that needed white authority, while 'white' was the name for even the lowest class of European. This distinction was a new idea which became more strident as the century progressed and criticism of slavery mounted. Janet Schaw marvelled at the fabulous wealth and ostentatious hospitality of her Edinburgh planter friends. She was charmed by one lady who,

> had standing by her a little mulatto girl whom she retains as a pet. This brown beauty was dressed out like an infant sultana and is a fine contrast to the delicate complexion of her lady.[5]

Little children like these became fashionable on both sides of the Atlantic. They were ostentatiously dressed like princes but treated like lap dogs, public symbols of white authority over lesser beings. We may remember that when Schaw set sail from Edinburgh, she was horrified at the treatment of a chained African brought on board. She pronounced him 'worthy' and his owner 'a scoundrel' despite the owner being a family friend.[6] After staying with friends in the West Indies, however, she was no longer sure about the essentially worthy nature of black people. One of the many excursions arranged for Schaw's entertainment in Jamaica was a trip to see the sugar plantations. As an outsider, she was shocked to see a whip cracked over the naked backs of both women and men.

> Every ten Negroes have a driver, who walks behind them holding in his hand a short whip and a long one. You will too easily guess the use of these weapons; a circumstance of all others most horrid. They are naked, male and female, down to the girdle, and you constantly observe

where the application has been made. But however dreadful this may appear to a humane
European, I will do the creoles justice to say,
they would be as averse to it as we are, could
it be avoided, which has often been tried to no
purpose. When one comes to be better acquainted with the nature of Negroes, the horror of it
must wear off. It is the suffering of the mind that
constitutes the greatest misery of punishment,
but with them it is merely corporeal... sufferings
are not attended with shame or pain beyond the
present moment... each has a little basket, which
he carries up the hill filled with manure and
returns with a load of canes to the Mill. They
go up at a trot, and return at a gallop, and did
you not know the cruel necessity of this alert-
ness, you would think them the merriest people
in the world.[7]

In her letter home, she repeated what she had been told by
her hosts. She assured her reader not to be concerned, because
these people, in her new understanding, 'do not feel things
as we do'.[8] Yet many of those who wielded the whip knew
in their hearts that black men and women had hopes, fears
and feelings. Intimacy with the skills and emotions of African people was a daily occurrence. The sugar fortunes of the
landed classes in the islands were completely dependent on
the knowledge of a group of expert black sugar boilers. Black
Africans ran white homes, were their sexual partners, breast
fed their children, cooked meals for them and gossiped around
the home. Schaw speaks of Africans' feelings again when she

describes her impressions of a slave market where the Africans being sold were

> stood up to be looked at with perfect unconcern. The husband was to be divided from the wife, the infant from the mother; but the most perfect indifference ran thro' the whole. They were laughing and jumping, making faces at each other and not caring a single farthing for their fate.[9]

We may wonder whether Schaw mistook pain and trauma for 'perfect unconcern'. We can certainly contrast her impression with a slave girl's own account of the experience of being sold:

> We had been bought... by Miss Betsey's grandfather, and given to her, so that we were by right her property, and I never thought we should be separated or sold away from her.

Miss Betsey was called and told,

> to take leave of us... you will see them no more, 'Oh, my poor slaves! my own slaves!' said dear Miss Betsey, 'you belong to me: and it grieves my heart to part with you'... Miss Betsey kissed us all, and, when she left us, my mother called the rest of the slaves to bid us good bye... The slaves could say nothing to comfort us; they could only weep and

lament with us. When I left my dear little brothers and the house in which I had been brought up, I thought my heart would burst... We followed my mother to the market-place. Where she placed us in a row against a large house, with our backs to the wall and our arms folded across our breasts. I, as the eldest, stood first, Hannah next to me, then Dinah; and our mother stood beside, crying over us. My heart throbbed with grief and terror so violently, that I pressed my hands quite tightly across my breast, but I could not keep it still, and it continued to leap as though it would burst out of my body. But who cared for that? Did one of the many by-standers, who were looking at us so carelessly, think of the pain that wrung the hearts of the negro woman and her young ones? No, no! They were not all bad, I dare say, but slavery hardens white people's hearts towards the blacks; and many of them were not slow to make their remarks upon us aloud, without regard to our grief – though their light words fell like cayenne on the fresh wounds of our hearts. Oh those white people have small hearts who can only feel for themselves.

At length the vendue master, who was to offer us for sale like sheep or cattle, arrived and asked my mother which was the eldest. She said nothing, but pointed to me. He took me by the hand, and led me out into the middle of the street, and,

turning me slowly round, exposed me to the view
of those who attended the vendue. I was soon surrounded by strange men, who examined and handled me in the same manner that a butcher would
a calf or a lamb he was about to purchase, and
who talked about my shape and size in like words
– as if I could no more understand their meaning
than the dumb beasts. I was then put up to sale.[10]

Jamaica maintained a façade of strict separation and difference
between white and enslaved black society, but in reality, race
relations were much more complex. Affectionate household
and neighbourhood relationships between slave women, people of colour and white men were not at all unusual, although
such friendships co-existed with harsh cruelty between owners and their slaves. William Loch gave his son of colour his
surname; the son was Robert Loch. He left Robert in charge
of the day-to-day running of the estate when he returned to
Scotland. Robert had an education probably in Virginia, judg-
ing by the words he used. He wrote regularly to his father in
Lanarkshire. In September 1809, he reported that all of their
slaves had been sent to dig cane holes for a neighbour for two
and six a day. He gossiped that 'all the ladies' had been asking
after his father 'as they always do'. Robert says he had been
sending them little presents of honey and ackees. Since ackees were definitely not for white ladies, we must assume that
Robert and his father were friendly with some of the thousands of free black and mulatto men and women who had
gravitated towards the towns along the north coast. There
were now 6,000 such residents in the free and easy community

of Montego Bay, where dances were organised specifically to help the better off white men meet respectable mulatto girls. Robert also sent regards from all the white neighbours and gave news of a very poorly slave called Trunnion, and another, 'old Frank', he reported, was keeping a bit more sober. 'The pickaninnies are growing well' he said, and 'Belinda has had a healthy boy'. He closed by passing on greetings from his sister and Drummond who 'tells you howdye' and all the 'Negroes too'. He added that his mother was taking good care of any sick 'Negroes' and the babies.[11]

Over time, black–white sex became well-established as a part of island life. Married and single men alike had black mistresses. In Jamaica, there was no stigma attached to a man's sexual involvement with a woman of African descent. A shortage of white women and the ease and availability of black ones ensured mixed unions became so normal that it would have been impossible to outlaw them. As James Stewart, the Edinburgh observer, noted,

> Between the whites and the blacks, in the West
> Indies, a numerous race has sprung up, which goes
> by the general appellation of people of colour.[12]

Most black or partners of colour were slaves, and the children of slave mothers were the property of their mother's owner. A child and her mother could only be freed by their owners, who had to enact a costly legal process known as manumission. In order to do this, owners needed not only to own the person they wished to free, but also to pay a fee for the transaction.

The price paid to manumit was not the normal market price, but a sum that recognised the slave as property on which an owner might be paying off a loan. The price to manumit was therefore fixed to cover this possible loan repayment, calculated on what the slave might earn for the master over time, plus any interest. Funds left by white men to their children were mostly for this purpose; we might therefore suppose that £100–200 was needed to complete the transaction. Young Scottish men, such as surveyors and bookkeepers on the lower ranks of the white social ladder, would be earning £50 to £80 per year, a successful doctor nearer £1,000. It was impossible for most of these men to free their partners and children, even if they wanted to. As already mentioned in Thomas Thistlewood's case, long-term partners like Phibah and their son were more often rented. Because it was expensive and not a priority use of valuable capital, men usually chose to wait and leave instructions in their wills that part of their inheritance should be used to free their Jamaican families and help them to make their way in the world. The other way to avoid an immediate expense was to arrange to exchange a slave of equal value for the one you wanted to free. Only a free son or daughter could inherit anything at all from a white parent. As noted previously, manumission payments and arrangements for exchanges in wills or letters written in the hope of sorting out such family complications were often how families at home in Scotland found out about long-standing Jamaican relatives.

Adam Fergusson from Perthshire was the attorney for a Scotsman called Mr Cameron. Mr Fergusson wrote to Hugh Hamilton, the owner of Pemberton Valley (the sugar plantation where John Hamilton was sent to improve production in the middle of the century, since its profits were disappointing to the Hamilton family) on Mr Cameron's behalf. Hugh was now residing in the family mansion in Ayrshire. One of the slaves belonging to Hugh Hamilton's estate was now Mr Cameron's partner. She was probably Margaret, the mulatto girl, the probable daughter of Mr Stirling, from his time as the overseer at Pemberton Valley. Mr Cameron and Margaret were now in a long-term relationship and had four children together. Hugh Hamilton, his wife and sister, the owners of the estate slaves, were still intent on pushing up estate profits. They drove a hard bargain. Seizing the opportunity to expand their labour force, they demanded strong adult replacement slaves, rather than money, not only for Margaret but also for the four children she had with Mr Cameron. Adam Fergusson was not happy with this offer. He wrote back pleading a shortage of slaves on Mr Cameron's estate and passed on the disappointing news for his employer's consideration.

We know nothing much about Isaac Grant, who was no doubt Scottish, except that he was an overseer in Jamaica involved in a relationship with a slave girl called Rebecca and wanted to arrange for her freedom. Her father and owner was a returned Scot called Stothert, a doughty defender of the planter class who owned Dundee Estate in the latter half of the 1700s. On return to his turreted country home at Cargen just outside Dumfries, his child Rebecca, whom he still owned, was left, possibly rented, to a cattle farm where Isaac worked called Brae near Montego Bay. Isaac wrote to her father in Dumfries,

> I took the liberty of writing you some time ago
> respecting your daughter Rebecca, at present my

housekeeper. I have now only to observe in case
you have not already given her her freedom that
I'll give you a good & picked new negro [for her].[13]

Another Scot, Thomas Hamilton, was the overseer managing
Moore Hall estate for many years in the late 1700s. He wrote
to a Mrs Dickson, an absentee owner living in Scotland.[14] She
had inherited Moore Hall, a sugar and cattle estate. At the time
he wrote, she was in the process of selling the land and resident
slaves. He drew her attention to 'a Mulatto Child belonging to
your Estate named Peggy Young'. He informed Mrs Dickson
that the girl's father had not provided for a replacement slave
in his will, which would have been one way of eventually buying Peggy Young's freedom. Thomas wanted to put this right,

as her Father was a relation of mine I am willing to
put a new Negroe boy or girl... on your Estate as
an equivalent for her.

One cannot help wondering whether Thomas Hamilton, who
had lived on the estate for so many years, was in fact her father
and which unfortunate child he intended to exchange for Peggy's freedom.

It was claimed in the Jamaican Assembly that by the early
1800s, young Scotsmen were nine-tenths of the men running
sugar estates for absentee owners. How many of them had
black partners, paid for sex or simply abused the women they
controlled, we do not know. What we do know is that many
men indulged in all three, simply because they could. Most

children of colour were never registered, but many were. More than a third of the thousands of coloured children in Jamaica were therefore likely to be Scots, sons and daughters of a Scottish father. Long-term partners from the black community were admitted into polite society, and illegitimate children of colour who had high-class fathers were socially acceptable in certain circles. It was normal for a white man to have a black sexual partner, and since contraception was virtually unknown, it was normal to have at least one family of children of colour. Almost every Scottish planter family had one group, but sometimes several sets of mixed-race children, fathered by the young men who travelled back and forth across the Atlantic managing the Jamaican end of the family business. By the 1790s, about a quarter of white Jamaican wills left something for sons and daughters of colour. A long list of Scottish planters, the minority of whom cared about at least some of their children and could afford to leave something to them in their will, can be found amongst the surviving records. However, a child of colour, despite a degree of acceptance, could not be baptised or move around the island freely unless they were formally and expensively manumitted. If they had been unable to buy their freedom, all the rules that applied to enslaved Africans applied equally to them. However, they would be equal citizens in law in Scotland after the courts in both England and Scotland decreed that slavery was incompatible with the law.

A Reverend Donald Sage recorded in his memoirs that when he was growing up in the small seaside town of Dornoch in Scotland in the late 1700s, he had three brown skinned schoolboy friends with the surname Hay.[15] The attendance of the Hay children at a Scottish school was not unusual at the time. There were few schools on the island of Jamaica, and those which existed did not admit children of colour. This presented a difficulty for fathers who wanted to provide a secure future for their Jamaican children. Scots looked to home, the well-developed primary school system, and the range of secondary academies for the education of their Jamaican children. The medical schools in Edinburgh, Aberdeen and Glasgow had links with the professions in Jamaica, having already trained and exported hundreds of slave doctors. Universities and academies began to see not only white, but also children of colour arriving from the West Indies.

Schooling was not the only reason that Jamaican children arrived in Britain; many Scots also wanted to help their offspring escape the restrictions that curtailed black children's chances for life in the West Indies. William Davidson, born in Kingston in 1781, was the son of the island's Scottish Attorney General and his enslaved partner. At the age of 14, William, like many Scots of colour in Jamaica, was sent to Glasgow to study law. He was a radical student who joined the movement for parliamentary reform on Clydeside. He ended up in London, where he taught in a Methodist Sunday School and joined the Marylebone Union Reading Society, a radical working-class group formed after the Peterloo Massacre of August 1819 when 18 unarmed demonstrators were killed by cavalry. He was also involved with shoemaker radicals, acting as secretary of their union. He became involved in what became known as the Cato Street 'Conspiracy', though his role is not entirely clear. The Cato Street plotters had planned to assassinate Cabinet members while they were having dinner at the Earl of Harrowby's home in Grosvenor Square, but their Cato Street hideout was raided by police. Some members escaped through a window. Davidson was reported to have fought fiercely, but was taken away 'damning every person who would not die in Liberty's cause' and singing the Burns song 'Scots wha hae wi' Wallace bled', which served as the unofficial national anthem of Scotland at the time. In his court defence he told the jury,

> You may suppose that because I am a man of colour, I am without any understanding or feeling and would act the brute; I am not that sort; when not employed in my business, I have employed myself as a teacher in Sunday school.[16]

The presiding judge responded,

> you may rest most perfectly assured that with respect to the colour of your countenance, no prejudice either has or will exist in any part of this Court against you; a man of colour is entitled to British justice as much as the fairest British subject.

Five of the conspirators were transported. Davidson and four others were convicted of high treason and hanged on 1 May 1820.

James Stewart, the Edinburgh observer, was outraged to witness black–white relationships in Jamaica, but it was the openness of the illegitimate partner, the immorality of the female, which most upset him, not her colour. The family at home in Scotland would probably agree. A child's illegitimacy would trouble them far more than their colour. But a child of colour was still scandalous, because such a child advertised the unmarried status of its parents. Sometime after, the already mentioned John Taylor arrived in Jamaica to work with his uncle Simon in his shipping business (the man with a favourite girl slave on every one of his estates); John found himself a mulatto lover from amongst his uncle's slaves known as Polly. John set up his slave trading venture with his Scottish partners a little later in 1783. He was making a lot of money by the time his illegitimate slave children were born. When the first born, James, was getting towards school age, he wrote to his mother Jean to tell her about the first of his three children. She replied:

> [T]ell me what has becom of your Baby that you
> mentiont to me, is it alive or not, belive me I would
> be very happy to have it under my Car[e]... I shall
> be very glad to See James, but I would wish you to
> have no more till you have a Wife.[17]

She was naturally perturbed to have an illegitimate grandson. She would have preferred her son to leave Jamaica and make a respectable marriage before he had any children. But she accepted her grandson's illegitimacy nevertheless and reassured her son she would treat him with kindness. When he informed her James would be coming home to go to school eventually, she wrote,

> if I am alive at the time you propos Sending
> [James] you may depend on me giving him a kind
> reception.

John was reluctant to confess to Jean that there were already other illegitimate grandchildren. Jean only heard about them from her in-laws, the Foulertons, who were doctors in Jamaica, 'Mr Foulerton told me that you had two fine Boys & another on the way', she wrote. When John consulted his brother in London about his son's schooling, it was suggested that it might be for the best if his children went to a school in Yorkshire. Some Scots used English schools to hide their children of colour from prying eyes at home. When Jean Taylor heard that her grandchild would be sent to England, she was not happy. She wrote back:

> Bob told me that you was to Satel James in Ingland
> as he had wrot you that he thought it much better
> than in this Country.

She did not think little James should be sent away on his own and suggested that Taylor should

> let him Stay Some time with Ketty (Taylor's sister)
> as he is So very young & not proper to go to a
> publick Scool.

Jean felt that she could not help her grandson directly because she had now moved to Montrose, but

> had I been living in the Country I would Sertenly
> have kept him with me – but this Town (Montrose)
> is not So proper.

Maybe it was too proper. The neighbours in Montrose might gossip about her illegitimate grandson. John's brother Robert nevertheless reassured him that he was sure their mother would

> treat him with the same Kindness and attention as
> if he had been born in [wed]lock.

His Scottish grandmother had her way. We do not know what his mother Polly thought of the four-year-old James boarding a boat with strangers to make what turned out to be a stormy ocean crossing, but he received a warm welcome into the home of his aunt Catherine (Kitty) and her family when he arrived in Scotland. Though he had the support of a loving family around him, when James arrived, racial attitudes were hardening as British slave traders and planters defended their ownership of slaves against growing abolitionist sentiments. Unaware of a growing debate about the inferiority of Africans going on in the wider world, James started at the local parish school and played happily with his white Scottish cousins. The Taylor family thought him 'a very fine boy'.

When John Taylor moved to London to manage the London offices of his slaving company Taylor, Ballantine & Fairlie, he was sad to part from James's mother, Polly. She was pregnant again at the time, and John had a great affection for her. He nevertheless then made the respectable, white marriage his mother had always wished for. James, and his brothers and a sister who arrived later, never lived with their father and his wife in London. The Taylor family and its circle were slave owners and traders. They defended their livelihoods robustly throughout James's childhood, but they nevertheless took care of James's mother, Polly, left behind in Jamaica. John's uncle Simon wrote affectionately about her. They also lavished love and their family fortune on Polly's child James and his siblings. Her feelings about her little children travelling to Scotland, never to be seen again, are not recorded.

When John Shand (1759–1825), an estate manager, plantation owner and slave trader in Liverpool, returned to Scotland to buy property in Kincardineshire,* he took with him his seven illegitimate children, four boys and three girls, whose mother was Frances Brown. Frances had been plucked from Shand's slave pool and was described in his will as 'a free woman of colour, my housekeeper'. She requested that each of her children should be given a portrait of her. Seven portraits was quite an elaborate set of parting gifts for her children. It seems quite poignant that Frances wanted each one of her children to have a portrait of their black mother, knowing as she probably did that they might be required to deny their African heritage once settled in Scotland.[18]

Taylor sent James to John Bowman's secondary school, Byers Green Hall outside Durham, where he studied mathematics and grammar, Latin, advanced accounting and

---

* Shand's property in the North East of Scotland included what became known as 'The Burn' which was bequeathed to The University of Glasgow by the family.

bookkeeping to prepare him for a trading career in the family business. At 16, he was sent to a London merchant house to get some work experience, but was unhappy there. By now, many slave traders took note of growing abolitionist organising; they knew their days might be numbered. Many were shifting their interest and their merchant activities to India. James's father wondered about a post for his son in the East India Company army. Since 1791, the company had ruled that they would not admit any 'whose Parents are not Natives of Great Britain or Ireland', but the Taylor family had influential friends and family prepared to help James.[19] An interview with the East India Company was arranged for him. His father admitted that James had been born and baptised in Kingston, but claimed he had lost the baptismal certificate, which would have exposed James as illegitimate and the son of a mulatto woman. James had to deny his African parentage and swear that his mother Polly, though born in the West Indies, was white. In the days leading up to his interview, James was wined and dined in London by the family's kin, who surveyed his skin colour in trepidation. They wondered if he could pass as wholly white. They had a sleepless night worrying whether the East India Company, which was now particularly strict in not allowing any who might be supposed to have 'Black blood' in them, would find him out. They tried using makeup to lighten James's skin, but it only 'made him much worse'.[20] They cut off his tight curls and dressed him in blue, which they thought made him look lighter skinned. Less than a week later, after barely passing the company's scrutiny, James boarded a ship bound for India and a distinguished future career. John Taylor's in-law, the slave merchant from Glasgow, George McCall, went with James to see him off. His grandmother was rather poorly, and James let his father know, 'I have today wrote my Grandmother a farewell letter'.

The 1785 will of Dugald Malcolm, of the transatlantic Argyll family introduced in the previous chapter who started off with a cattle farm called Argyle, left funds and slaves to a mulatto carpenter (no doubt a son of the family) and further money to a mother and her mulatto daughter. Malcolm had obviously educated and bought a commission for a favoured illegitimate son, described, as was the practice then, as 'a natural son'. Malcolm's fortune was to be drawn upon to ensure the future of a young man called

> Captain Alexander Malcolm, late of His Majesty's 97th Regiment, now retired on an annuity of £250 until he shall obtain a commission in an old regiment on full pay of the rank of Captain at least and I do further direct that so much money that shall be sufficient to purchase for him a Captaincy in an old regiment shall be advanced and paid for that purpose and I further direct that the sums of money sufficient to purchase the commission and regimental rank of Lieutenant Colonel shall be in like manner advanced.[21]

His daughters were also left enough dowry to ensure they would be attractive partners for white men in Jamaica.

Though vast numbers of children were born to Scots, and many were acknowledged and provided for, few sons and daughters of Scottish men were as fortunate as Captain Alexander,

James Taylor and their siblings. When George Barclay returned to Scotland after 30 years in Jamaica, he married his white Scottish housekeeper shortly before he died. His brother James wrote from Jamaica to George's widow appealing for a part of the inheritance to help George's children he had left behind in Jamaica,

> You know my Brother has three Children here: Sukie & two Lads. I think 'tis hard they should have been forgot in his Will & something should be done for them. I wish you would mention them to [the executor].[22]

Jamaican women often had difficulty proving their partners' desire to use some of the inheritance to free and maintain them, especially if Scots families were prepared to hire lawyers to protect their inheritance against claims regarded as illegitimate. For those who had returned with great wealth and respectability, black relatives could also be awkward reminders of their less respectable past. James Wedderburn, one of the doctor brothers known to Thistlewood, returned to Scotland with his newfound wealth and a fashionable black servant. He made an elite marriage and re-established the family on a country estate. As I have noted, Robert Wedderburn was the child of James and one of his Jamaican lovers, Rosanna. Young Robert grew up with his black grandmother, Talkee Aimee, the resourceful woman we met in chapter 3. Robert arrived in London and became a minor celebrity amongst the abolitionist fraternity, having published his life story, *The Horrors of Slavery*. He was not at all welcome at the family home in Scotland, and his father denied all knowledge of him.

Slavery could be justified so long as African people were seen as 'brutes only suitable for field work' or 'handy servants' who could only work under strict supervision.[23] Mixed-race children, especially educated and wealthy mixed-race children, were visible proof that this was not true. The personal and familial habits of merchants and planters were undermining the myths on which their family fortunes depended. As the attacks on slavery became more vocal, the racial divide grew more pronounced. Slavery's defenders excused the way they made their fortune by insisting black people were unequal in talents, feeling and intelligence. The island's elite, despite their lifestyle and sexual habits, developed and defended the idea that blacks were inferior. They needed this ideology to justify their inhuman planter regime and the brutal trafficking of humans. Their children, like James Taylor and Alexander Malcolm, could somehow pass as white, but the growing numbers of skilled and wealthy people of colour in all of the island's towns, and the large numbers turning up in Britain, were a threat to what they needed to establish as a natural order. A visible breakdown in the strict separation between Africans and Europeans pushed the island's elite to take further action to strengthen boundaries.

The numbers of mixed-race Jamaicans receiving education and other opportunities had always troubled the island government. Beginning as early as 1711, the Jamaican Assembly barred the employment of all persons deemed 'mulattos' from public office. By 1733, mulattos had lost the right to vote in elections. A decade later, the Jamaican Assembly removed their ability to testify against whites in court. Fearing that mixed-race children had acquired too large a share of the island's wealth, Jamaica's Assembly undertook an investigation into how much property lay in their hands. It examined a selection of wills lodged with the Island Secretary over a ten-year period, and found 13 containing large bequests to mixed-race children. The total sum of personal bequests was over £246,806; bequests of land were worth a further nearly £200,000. In 1762, the Jamaican Assembly limited the amount of money that could be inherited by Jamaican children to £2,000. The planter class that had spun the myth of race to protect its fortunes now found its children were the victims of that myth and the legislation put in place to defend slavery. Planters were not the only people with an interest in preserving the system: banks, insurers and slave traders were all concerned with the system's survival. The black–white hierarchical class system was firmly enshrined in law. In Jamaica, the belief that white men of property were uniquely qualified to govern must not be upset by Africans and their descendants obtaining the status and power which flowed from property ownership. A preamble to the legislation decried that those fathers giving property to mixed-race children did so

> to the particular prejudice and detriment of their [white] heirs and relations, and to the injury and damage of the community in general.

Such property allocation

> destroy[ed] the distinction requisite, and absolutely necessary, to be kept up in this island, between white persons and negroes, their issue and offspring.[24]

A system of what we now refer to as 'apartheid' legislation came into being, a model for the control of British colonies in the future. All non-white people had to carry tickets whenever they travelled around Jamaica. They had to register with the Assembly if they wished to trade goods in its markets, and a range of punishments, including death, were reserved for any individuals suspected of being sympathetic to or possibly involved in slave rebellions, including those who had knowledge of a slave rebellion or the whereabouts of a runaway and kept it to themselves. Landowners and small businesses were given minimum numbers of white people they were required to employ. Robert Loch in Jamaica, who had hitherto managed the family estate and mixed freely with black and white neighbours, wrote to his father in Lanarkshire, Scotland to tell him that the law now forbade him to run the business and manage its slaves; they would have to employ a white man to do the job. It was not surprising in these circumstances that many fathers wrote into their wills that they wanted their children to live in Britain rather than stay in Jamaica. Many, such as John Stewart (1789–1860), son of a wealthy Scot and a black Jamaican woman, left Jamaica but chose to settle in England rather than Scotland. He was elected to Parliament for the Tory party in Lymington, and as far as we know, was Britain's first black Member of Parliament. Stewart was a staunch defender of the slave system. He inherited 433 of his father's slaves and was compensated by the British Government to the tune of over £22,000 at abolition; he invested much of this windfall into British railways.

By the end of the 18th century, there were around 15,000 black people in Britain in the community that became Toxteth in Liverpool, around the port of Tiger Bay in Cardiff and in the developing community of St Pauls in Bristol. London had several thousand Black West Indians, many of them poor, such that those concerned about slavery had set up a subscription company to take home to Africa all those people of colour who wanted to go. They planned to set up a company to build trade in African goods from Sierra Leone. The idea for the company was to prove that Africa had other things to sell apart from its people. Wealthy abolitionists bought shares in the Sierra Leone Company, launched in 1791. Zachary Macauley, son of the minister in Inveraray, Argyll, was an investor in the colony and its first Governor.

It is remarkable that as far as we can tell, no visible community of black Jamaican Scots, rich or poor, ever settled in their fathers' homeland, despite almost weekly packet sailings into ports on the Clyde and Forth, hundreds of merchant ships trading across the Atlantic from Scottish ports, and the many Jamaican Scots who attended Scotland's schools and universities.

CHAPTER 7
Commerce or morality?

*If it be a truth that modern government and
commerce cannot be preserved without enslaving a great part of mankind, it is a melancholy
truth indeed.*[1]

IT WAS NO SECRET that slave trading and plantation profits ultimately depended on cruel levels of violence against transported
Africans. By the late 1700s, middle-class Scots were better educated and more enlightened in their ideas; violence to others
was less acceptable to these enlightened minds. To the deeply
religious, of all classes, the buying and selling of humans was
sinful. The justification for slavery, which Janet Schaw heard in
the West Indies, that you should not judge the treatment of 'these
people' because Africans are different, became a much-debated
subject. The question mattered to national pride. If black skin
indicated that a person was somehow not fully human, then
the brutal slave trade upon which much of Scotland's wealth
rested would be much more acceptable. The country was building an enviable reputation abroad in banking and insurance,
textiles and iron, shipping and the funding and management of
international trading ventures. This growing commercial reputation would be damaged should condemnation of Scotland's

involvement in slavery get out of hand. Apart from wanting to protect their commercial reputation, Scotland's transatlantic families also wanted to protect their status in high society from accusations of riches won through brutality. Racial difference became their justification, but it came at a cost. In the mid-1780s, Dugald Malcolm was able to establish his favoured son of colour, Alexander, in a British army career without difficulty. Less than ten years later, the wealthy and influential Taylor family was forced to powder their son James's face to hide his 'black blood' when he was interviewed for a commission with the East India Company. James himself had to swear that he was born to a white mother, rather than the mulatto slave Polly, John Taylor's beloved Jamaican partner for many years. The idea of the black race was inferior had now become East India Company policy.

Not everyone was convinced that there could be an inferior race of humans. The enlightened in the cities were avid readers of public intellectuals. Printed pamphlets, newspapers, magazines and books all took up the issue. The country's major intellectuals considered claims about Africans; the exact nature of the difference between black and white skinned people became a public talking point. Lord Kames (1696–1782) was a leading commentator, a respected judge and founder of the Philosophical Society of Edinburgh. Janet Schaw's brother Alexander chose one of Kames's books as suitable reading for their journey to the West Indies. As they rounded the north of Scotland and the boat began to lurch horribly, Janet sorted through their reading matter to find something which might take her mind off the motion of the boat. She could find nothing light-hearted and had to content herself with the philosophical works of Lord Kames. These were read aloud by her seasick 18-year-old companion. The young woman complained that she did not have a clue what the book was about, but Janet urged her to keep reading. French philosophers had put forward the idea that climate could explain differences between peoples. Kames thought the French view of the evolution of black and white people must be nonsense. In his *Sketches on the History of Man*, published in 1774, he argued that environment, climate or society could not be sufficient causes to produce an entirely different species. He floated the view that black people must have come from entirely different roots. He speculated that humanity could be descended from several different pairs, rather than simply one, each pair being fitted by God for their particular circumstances and role in life. He wrote,

> Hottentots were so obviously different to Europeans that the mere fact of ability to breed with other races should not dissuade one from what his eyes told him, that the differences were enough to pronounce them a different species.

The assembled Kirk was the voice of Scotland's established religion, the arbitrator of public morals across the land. Free thinking might be fashionable, but to be branded a heretic would destroy a reputation and lead to exclusion from public positions. If what Kames termed the 'character' of the races arose from separate roots, this resolved the moral question of whether people should be treated equally. It allowed for the idea that diverse humans could be arranged in a hierarchical way. If God had conferred rights to spiritual, moral and intellectual superiority to one group over lesser mortals, slavery could easily be justified as part of God's plan for the Scottish Nation. As Kames put it, 'sacred and profane history' could be reconciled. But this solution of multiple pairs was not allowed according to scripture; he drew back because he knew it was a heresy. Anxious to lead enlightened ideas, but not to court too much controversy, he added,

> But this opinion, however plausible, we are not permitted to adopt; being taught a different lesson by revelation, viz that God created but a single pair of the human species.[2]

David Hume (1711–76), perhaps Edinburgh's foremost enlightened thinker, supported the idea that peoples could be arranged hierarchically. Some years before, in *Of National Characters*, published in 1740, he considered the question and wrote:

> I am apt to suspect the negroes to be naturally inferior to the whites... there was never a civilised nation of any complexion but white.[3]

Such ideas would have pleased Thomas Thistlewood in Westmorland. He certainly sent for copies of Hume's writing and passed them around his slave-owning Scottish friends. They also read Hume's contemporary, Adam Smith (1723–90). Smith did not openly refute his friend Hume's argument, but he clearly thought that one man owning another was not good for morals or industry. In 1759, in his *Theory of Moral Sentiments*, Smith wrote that

> there is not a Negro from the coast of Africa, who does not, in this respect, possess a degree of magnanimity which the soul of his sordid master is too often scarce capable of conceiving.[4]

He was a little more restrained later, perhaps held back by his friendly relations with Glasgow merchants and cognisant of their power over his university. He confined himself to his area of absolute expertise and the issue of maximising profit, to which he knew his planter audience would give more attention. In his 1776 *Wealth of Nations*, Smith argued that paying for labour was always a more efficient system, since the investor paid only for work received and was not responsible for feeding and housing old or sick workers.[5]

The young academic, James Beattie (1735–1803), was rewarded with a professorship at Marischal College, Aberdeen, and established his public reputation by roundly refuting Hume's argument. That his writing was a much talked about bestselling success reflected the public's engagement in a young man of lesser reputation confronting the controversial but well-established Hume. It also showed widespread public sympathy with the explicit nature of his reply. According to James Beattie, slavery was not a technical question, and Scots could not evade the fact that slavery was a live and everyday moral question. He summed up the nation's dilemma by questioning whether slavery could be justified just because of its importance to prosperity. In his 'An Essay on the Nature and Immutability of Truth in Opposition to Sophistry and Scepticism', published in 1770, Beattie argued forcefully that

> [t]he necessities of government and commerce are urged as an excuse for enslaving the Negroes. If it be a truth that modern government and commerce cannot be preserved without enslaving a great part of mankind, it is a melancholy truth indeed. But it is incumbent on those who urge this argument to prove that commerce is of more consequence than Christianity, and that the produce of America and the West Indies, such as Peruvian Bark, Rum and Sugar are of more importance than justice and mercy.[6]

A great number of Scottish people bought his book because they agreed with him that commerce could not ignore the moral questions that the buying and selling of human beings raised. Profit did not make slavery right.

Most Scots made their living on other people's land. As the century progressed, landlords were more likely to be West Indian returnees buying into Scotland's landed class or old clan leaders made grander and more commercially minded by West Indian wealth. There may have been more English people in Jamaica than Scots, but given the size of the Scottish planter and slave merchant population, they represented a much greater concentration of power and influence in Scottish life. They gave to charity, donated to grand public building projects, funded academies and churches – the scale of their activity was immense. They controlled almost every Scottish parliamentary seat, forming the backbone of the pro-slavery lobby within the Westminster parliament. They kept up a barrage of propaganda in newspapers, public meetings and parliament, and they reorganised rural lives irrevocably.

Rural farming had been organised under an age-old system by which middle managers or 'tacksmen' allocated clan land to small communities of farmers. Family plots or rigs had been rotated annually and rent collected in farm produce. An Act of 1695 ensured clan chiefs had the right to abolish this system. By the mid-18th century, farmers were already distanced socially and economically from their clan chiefs by the growth of these commercial middle men who set rents and increasingly demanded at least part of the rent in cash. Jamaican returnees accelerated this process. Families like the Malcolms of both Kilmartin in Western Argyll and Westmorland in Jamaica, and the Hamiltons in Ayrshire, were enthusiastic land improvers. Their sugar money was invested in commercial woodlands, fishing, water mills, slate quarries and better housing for tenants. They improved the infrastructure of roads, bridges and harbours, and they brought market forces into land management by auctioning their tenancies to the highest bidder. Jamaica taught them that estates could be managed from afar. They lived in fashionable London and looked to their land managers and hired wage labourers to extract the maximum income from their much-expanded Scottish estates. The Hamiltons amalgamated tenant farms to make larger holdings, with rents paid in cash. They experimented with different kinds of fertilisers and put their money into turnpike roads, improved harbours, tile works and eventually new rail networks. By this process, they developed counties and improved communications and small-town facilities, but rural families lost the last vestiges of their old relationships to land and clan in the process. They became farm labourers, cleared from the remaining fermetouns, sometimes amidst angry clashes over evictions. Though Jamaica was far away and many white Scots of the era might never meet a black person, small farmers learned some of the lessons brought back from managing black labourers in Jamaica. Scotland's landed class were now driven by a ruthless pursuit of scientific development and investment for profit. The days of paternalistic clan relations were finally over.

Jamaican merchants and estate owners left behind their Jamaican families of colour, consolidating their position at home with marriages to young women from the British landed class. Returnees built themselves substantial country homes; old elite families built and furnished in a fashionable Jamaican planter style. In 1767, John Campbell of Orange Bay was supervising improvements at home near Inveraray. He wrote,

> I am glad to find improvements are going on so fast... I must beg you to turn your attention to a proper piece of ground for an orchard.

He suggested a particular plot,

> close to where the mansion house is intended to
> be... in my opinion the country life without the
> amusements of a garden must loose halff it's relish.[7]

The 'nouveau riche' chose more baronial styles that conveyed a
sense of old, landed money and helped to establish them within
the landed gentry. Anyone riding around rural Scotland down
the east coast, across the Central Belt, in Argyll and Ayrshire
or around Kirkudbright would pass many estates, each in the
hands of ex-planters and their families, slave traders and sugar
merchants, their bankers and close friends.

Though most children of colour born to Scots were left
behind in Jamaica, many wealthy families brought home at
least some of their children and established them with commissions in the armed forces, the navy or the colonial administration in India. John Shand, the estate manager, plantation owner
and slave trader, whose children accompanied him to Scotland
carrying a portrait of their black mother, graduated from St
Andrews in 1775. Shand transferred the vast sum of £127,348
from Jamaica to purchase an estate in Kincardineshire. One
of his Jamaican sons eventually managed South Wales coal
mines for the Bute family, and a daughter joined him there
and used some of the family's vast fortune to establish the first
Welsh school for blind students. Alexander Erskine graduated
from Glasgow University in 1791. His many children inherited
£180,000, much of which came from an estate called Lima
in Jamaica. He had a home in Middlesex along with land in

Scotland, on which his Scottish home, Dun House, stood in Montrose. Thomas Renny Strachan, husband of Harriet Strachan née Moyes, was owner of two estates in St David, Jamaica, and extensive landholdings in Forfar, Scotland. The Montgomery family were merchants in Port Glasgow and Glasgow, with property in the West Indies and the Estate of Clune Park overlooking the Clyde. Sir John Gordon had properties, slaves and livestock in Jamaica. He was born in Kirkudbright and retired to Earlston House and estate in his home county. The Grants of Moneymusk had land in both Jamaica and Aberdeenshire. The Stirling family of Hampden and Frontier in Jamaica held the estates of Kier, near Bridge of Allan, and Cadder in the north of Glasgow. The Grahams entered into a slave trading partnership with the Taylor family (who had powdered young James's face to get him accepted by the East India Company). They greatly developed their estates in central Scotland with proceeds from the slave trade, building a 26-bedroom planter-style mansion, Gartmore House, from which they enjoyed views across the Forth to Stirling. They brought a favourite slave, whose name was not recorded, to Scotland; he acted as the family butler. He eventually died in Scotland and was buried in their grounds. On the east coast, the Gordons, Taylors and Wedderburns were also building, buying land and expanding their influence. Jamaica is a small island, and members of these prominent families knew each other as neighbours and as the island's magistrates. They sat in the Jamaican Assembly together. They had business partners in England in the slaving centres of Liverpool and Bristol and the merchant centres in

London. Together, they had formidable patronage and power in their hands. They did not need to worry about Scotland's intellectuals debating the nature of Africans, so long as it was just talk. No one in Scotland seriously challenged men of independent means like these.

Owning land was not just about gracious living. In a society where independent landowners were believed to be uniquely qualified to make dispassionate political decisions, land ownership translated wealth into political power: power in the Jamaican Assembly and power also in both houses of the British Parliament, where the all-important slave laws were made. Families with large enough fortunes were thought to rise above the day-to-day pressures, see the bigger picture and make a balanced judgement. An independent gentleman with a considerable fortune was believed to be the only one qualified to know what was best for the nation in Scotland, just as much as in England.

Only two or three thousand people elected the 45 Scottish parliamentary seats in the late 1700s. Individual peers controlled many county seats; towns were mostly grouped together and sent delegates to a meeting to choose the Member of Parliament. The rest were elected by a small group of the more wealthy in the district, a group which would include such people as the Montgomerys, Weymss, Houstons, Taylors, Wedderburns, McDowals, Campbells, Oswalds, Shaw Stewarts, Laings, Grants, Hamiltons, Grahams, Cunninghams, Ewings and many more. They were tied together in business, and they influenced the Kirk and small-town decisions. Men from these families married each others' sisters and jockeyed and manoeuvred with one another to control public positions as magistrates, town councillors, Lord Provosts and parliamentarians. On the other side of the Atlantic, members of these same families managed each other's estates, lent each other capital, invested in shared merchant houses and slaving voyages, and supported each other in the Jamaican Assembly. These elite families were also deeply loyal to the British Government in its fight against the 'all men are created equal' ethos and independence of the American colonies. Despite their affection and ambitions for a select few of their Jamaican children, they were determined to protect the privileges enjoyed by their transatlantic trade and the slave trade that underpinned it.

As I have noted, returning planters often brought their more trusted house slaves to Scotland. Naturally, some of these men and women, on experiencing a free country for the first time, were determined to escape captivity. It was not uncommon for Scottish newspapers to publish advertisements offering rewards for the recapture of runaway slaves or seeking information regarding their whereabouts. They were usually dressed in expensive suits of clothes that were described in detail: good woollen breeches, velvet trimmed coats and shoes with silver buckles. The price of such suits of clothing would maintain a Scottish family for many months, if not years. Court cases in both England and Scotland deliberated on the recapture, shipping back to Jamaica and beating of escaped slaves. The Somerset case in England in 1772 finally agreed

Map of Scotland in 1750.

Map of Jamaica in 1749.

Kingston Harbour, from above the town. Drawing by James Hakewill from
A Picturesque Tour of the Island of Jamaica (London: Cox and Baylis, 1823).
Propaganda funded by planters to counter rising criticism in Britain.

Simon Taylor's Holland Estate, inherited by his niece, Anna Susannah Watson
Taylor (1781–1853). Simon's fabulous fortune was squandered by Anna's husband,
George. Drawing by James Hakewill from *A Picturesque Tour of the Island of Jamaica*
(London: Cox and Baylis, 1823).

List of Pemberton Valley enslaved men and women, Hamilton Family papers, AA/DC17/113 1 January 1756 (reproduced by permission, Ayrshire Council Archives). Slaves were mortgaged to buy replacements. Lists of enslaved Africans and their work duties were sent to Scotland to reassure bankers and absentee planters.

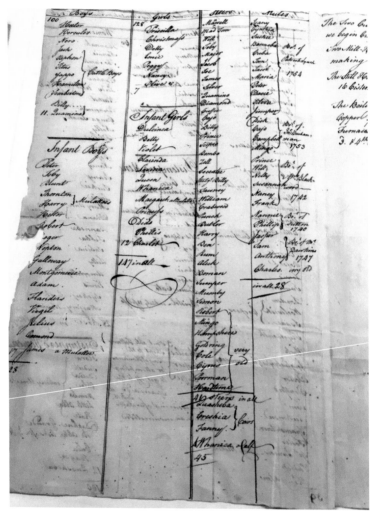

List of Pemberton Valley enslaved children. Steers and mules have similar names; unlike the children, some animals have an age recorded. Hamilton Family papers AA/DC17/113 1 January 1756 (reproduced by permission, Ayrshire Council Archives).

Trinity Estate, home to over 1,000 slaves, was among the five estates captured by Tacky – leader of enslaved people – in December 1759, causing years of uprisings across the island. Trinity estate was one of several estates managed by William Miller from Glasgow, whose fortune was made managing estates and selling enslaved people. Note the estate style which became widespread in Scotland. Drawing by James Hakewill from *A Picturesque Tour of the Island of Jamaica* (London: Cox and Baylis, 1823).

Port Maria, showing the sugar works of the Frontier Estate, also captured by Tacky in 1759. The estate was owned by the Stirling family of Kier and Cadder and managed by Alexander Stevenson. On the right of this image can be seen the homes of the 400 slaves. Drawing by James Hakewill from *A Picturesque Tour of the Island of Jamaica*(London: Cox and Baylis, 1823).

Golden Vale, home to 500 slaves. Owned by Alexander Kinloch from Stonehaven, Kincardineshire and John Steel. Alexander's riches came from renting out slave labourers. Drawing by James Hakewill from *A Picturesque Tour of the Island of Jamaica* (London: Cox and Baylis, 1823).

Montego Bay. Drawing by James Hakewill from *A Picturesque Tour of the Island of Jamaica* (London: Cox and Baylis, 1823). Samuel Sharpe preached in the Baptist church here. On 28 December 1831, looking down from this hillside, the Scottish minister Mr Blyth counted 16 blazing sugar works.

The sugar harvest, cutting canes. The harvesting months, January to April, were very dry with little food available in provision grounds. Planters were resistant to reducing profit by buying food. Long hours of heavy cane-cutting with little to eat for several months of the year destroyed the health of enslaved people. *Ten Views in the Island of Antigua* (London: Thomas Clay, 1823) via British Library, https://unsplash.com/photos/atIgjLlFryg.

Milling the cane. Cut canes had to be crushed in mills which were turned by wind, water or animals. The resulting cane juice was boiled at very high temperatures to crystallise it, a process which went on day and night during harvest. Tired workers feeding sugar cane into heavy rollers and stirring vats of boiling sugar regularly had horrible accidents. *Ten Views in the Island of Antigua* (London: Thomas Clay, 1823) via British Library, https://unsplash.com/photos/Sh3FPPouOug.

Treadmill, Jamaica 1837. Treadmills were widely used when slaves became apprentices and personal violence by planters was outlawed. James Williams' account of life as an apprenticed labourer shocked the British public. Governor of Jamaica, Lionel Smith, announced to the House of Assembly that the whipping of females was unlawful and must stop. Copyright British Library Board, Tr.148(k).

AN

ADDRESS

TO THE

PEOPLE of GREAT BRITAIN,

ON THE UTILITY OF REFRAINING FROM

THE USE OF

West India Sugar and Rum.

Why did all-creating Nature
  Make the Plant for which we toil?
Sighs must fan it, Tears must water,
  Sweat of ours must dress the Soil.
Think ye Masters, iron-hearted,
  Lolling at your jovial Boards,
Think how many Backs have smarted
  For the Sweets your Cane affords!

COWPER'S NEGRO'S COMPLAINT.

The Sixth Edition, corrected.

Printed and Sold by T. REED, Bookseller, High-Street,
Sunderland. 1791.

Price 1d. or fourteen for a shilling.

N. B. Persons wanting a larger Number to give away
may be supplied at Five Shillings per Hundred, by apply-
ing to T. REED.

Pamphlet explaining why households should boycott sugar. Printed in Sunderland in 1791.

Flogging men and women to instil obedience was routine practice. The mode of flogging slaves, engraving, (London, J Hatchard and son, c 1825), Library of Congress Prints and Photographs Division Washington, DC 20540 USA.

that although slavery was tolerated in the colonies, the courts were bound to apply the law of England. They ruled that,

> no master ever was allowed here [in England] to take a slave by force to be sold abroad because he deserted from his service... therefore the man must be discharged.[8]

The ruling in this case only applied in England. James, one of the Wedderburn doctors, returned to Inverness, bringing with him his long-standing personal slave, Joseph Knight. Knight became a Christian, met and married a Scottish servant in the Wedderburn household and requested his freedom to live with this Scottish wife. Wedderburn refused him. Knight bravely stood up to Wedderburn and appealed to local Justices of the Peace, but failed to gain their support. With the considerable courage of his Christian convictions, Knight took his case to the court in Perth, which ruled unequivocally,

> the state of slavery is not recognised by the laws of this kingdom, and is inconsistent with the principles thereof: That the regulations in Jamaica, concerning slaves, do not extend to this kingdom.[9]

Wedderburn fought this ruling. He argued that Knight still owed him service, in the same way that an indentured servant might. The case was of sufficient public interest to be dealt with in the Court of Session in Edinburgh, Scotland's supreme civil court, in 1777. Twelve judges were assembled; the great legal minds of the day were to deliberate on whether Christian morality, which did not recognise that one man could own another, should triumph over commercial and landed interests. Although the case was about two individuals, it was also a chance to resolve the national dilemma that had occupied so many of the country's educated classes. The nation's economic success in the colonies was being pitted against its moral reputation. Wedderburn was represented by leading churchman James Ferguson; the panel of judges, including Lord Kames, was chaired by no less than Henry Dundas, the Lord Advocate, who would later become a political figure of some significance. Many notable and learned people, such as James Boswell and Samuel Johnson, helped to pay Knight's legal fees and looked forward to an exposition of the subject. Dundas presented Knight's case as a moral question, that no man could be the property of another. This was an argument that would have found favour in Kirks up and down the country. Set against this was an opposition arguing for a man's right to own the work of others. This argument about commercial rights to own a man's future work would have found favour amongst large and small business, merchants and, of course, the landed with interests in the West Indies.

The moral argument won the day. The court rejected Wedderburn's appeal. Dundas summed up the view of the judges, 'The law of Jamaica, being unjust, could not be supported in this country'.[10] The court declared that slavery was not recognised under Scots law. Despite the judgement on Jamaican law, the Wedderburn case only affected African slaves in

Scotland. Although the moral arguments accepted by the court would have unsettled many Scots at home and in the West Indies, the conclusions of a Scottish court made little difference to slaves outside of Scotland, since the laws governing their captivity in the colonies were made in Westminster.

At that time, what happened in Westminster was of little interest to the average Scot. However, elite families with deep interests in sugar and slaves were well aware that their lifestyles and much of Scotland's commercial wealth was dependent on laws made in London. From 1730 onwards, at least 70 members of transatlantic families had seats in the House of Commons. Of these, 50 were absentee proprietors and the rest merchants, about half of whom were directly connected with Jamaica. Almost all of Scotland's Members of Parliament and some Scots representing English constituencies belonged to this group. Glasgow Lord Provost and MP, James Ewing, was a Jamaican slave holder, estate owner and banker. He and his family were early and successful participants in the West Indian trade. His Levenside estate consolidated his political status. William McDowal, his fellow MP for Glasgow, had property in St Kitts and Grenada. The Campbells had clan relationships across Argyll, held numerous positions in Jamaica, controlled a large merchant house in Glasgow as well as banks, manufacturing, insurance companies and land across Scotland, including many acres of land to the east of the River Kelvin, and several seats in the British Parliament. They were leading members of the Glasgow West Indian Association and founder members of the Glasgow Chamber of Commerce. The MP for

Renfrewshire was Baronet John Shaw Stewart; his mother was from the Houston merchant family. They were related to the Maxwells of Pollock. Johnstone, the MP for Cromarty and Nairn and later Shrewsbury, controlled his wife's fortune and land in the West Indies. He was subsequently known by her family name of Pulteney. Robert Cunninghame Graham, who resided in the mansion at Gartmore, Stirlingshire, became Member of Parliament for the county in 1794. The family had estates which stretched from Perthshire, through Dunbarton-shire and across the Clyde to Renfrewshire and Lanarkshire. In addition, they had Jamaican plantations, including Roaring River. John Anderson, the nephew of Richard Oswald, the Scottish merchant and slave trader who married one of the Hamiltons and jointly owned the slaves at Pemberton Valley, also sat in Parliament. He had inherited part of his uncle's empire and had been a slave ship captain. Anderson also spoke and voted with the MPs representing sugar and slaves.

The courts had outlawed slavery in Scotland while ordinary citizens were disputing the claim of a superior white race. However, Scotland's transatlantic families had established themselves as powerful voices and well-respected benefactors in towns and counties across the country. As rich and wealthy landowners, they were above criticism; moreover, they formed a formidable lobby in the Westminster Parliament where the legislation that protected slavery had been made and the only place where such protections could be reversed. For the moment, the landed gentry were safe, but as the century progressed, public faith in the unquestionable wisdom of this class in all matters of national importance became less secure.

CHAPTER 8

The fight to abolish the slave trade

*Our cause gains ground. The slave ships have
been put up in the Banks, Public offices, Coffee
house &c here, with an excellent effect.*[1]

A CALL TO ACTION by a particular Scotsman profoundly influenced the tactics of those who wanted to see the slave trade abolished. That man was James Ramsay (1733–89). He was born in Fraserburgh in North East Scotland. As a young surgeon with a medical education from King's College, Aberdeen, he served aboard the naval ship *Arundel* in the West Indies. In November 1759, the *Arundel* rescued a British slave ship, the *Swift*, with over 100 Africans imprisoned in disgusting conditions; many of the crew and Africans had already died from dysentery. Ramsay was a determined man who had been schooled in a religion where men and women not only read their Bibles but lived by them, and where the minister and Kirk elders sat in judgement on those whose standards slipped.

Ramsay set himself a mission to demonstrate that persuading masters and slaves to live by Christian values could reshape the institution of slavery. A congregation of black and white people could surely live in harmony if the congregants had a shared morality. He became ordained as an Anglican priest, the only established and salaried religion in the colonies, and found a position on the Island of St Christopher (now St Kitts). He welcomed both black and white parishioners to his church and attempted to improve the morals and behaviour of both. He was appointed surgeon to several plantations. He spoke to slave owners about Christian treatment of their slaves and to their captives about God's love for all men. Slave owners deeply resented his interference. He was not easily deterred, as he later wrote:

> those who look no further than present profit, may laugh at my far-fetched expectations... but men like me who believe in Revelations, cannot indulge in doubt.[2]

Ramsay finally left St Kitts in 1777, after 19 years, exhausted by the impossible task he had set himself and the hostility of the slave-owning community. He returned to a quiet parish in England and started to write. The first anti-slavery essay by an Anglican Christian, 'An Essay on the Treatment and Conversion of African Slaves in the British Sugar Colonies', published in 1784, was the result. 'An Inquiry into the Effects of Putting a Stop to the African Slave Trade' followed shortly afterwards.

Ramsay had learned lessons. He now knew preaching would not change the nature of slavery. The problem was not one of bad masters who could be converted to better behaviour, but a whole system that encouraged abuse and immorality. He argued that slavery was immoral; moreover, it made no economic sense. By pressing for short-term profit by working Africans 'beyond their ability', planters shortened their lives and reduced their fertility, leading to a constant traffic of kidnapped people from Africa to replace a shrinking and worn-out workforce. Absentee planters, incensed by Ramsay's accusations, responded in the only way they could: by attacking his integrity.

In the last years of his life, Ramsay was drawn into a circle of politicians, philanthropists and churchmen concerned about the situation of enslaved Africans. Some of them were involved in the Committee for the Relief of the Black Poor, distributing charity and demanding parliament do something for the thousands of ex-slaves now living on the streets of London. In 1784, at the age of 24, Thomas Clarkson (1760–1846) won a prize from the University of Cambridge for a Latin dissertation on slavery. Using an English translation of his essay as a means of introduction, he met many members of this anti-slavery community. He read and was fascinated by Ramsay's firsthand knowledge and analysis that showed that the abolition of the slave trade was a practical proposition if the lives of slaves were improved so that more children were born and these children were raised to accept the Christian value of hard work. These were the years when democratic ideas were becoming more widespread, when people were beginning to reshape their world for themselves. The French were asserting their rights before eventually storming the Bastille in 1789. English people were becoming critical of the unrepresentative nature of their parliament. As Tom Paine later wrote in his *Rights of Man*,

> The Independence of America, considered merely
> as a separation from England, would have been

> a matter but of little importance, had it not been
> accompanied by a revolution in the principles and
> practice of governments. She made a stand, not for
> herself only, but for the world.[3]

People were asserting themselves and attempting what had seemed impossible. Anglican vicars like Ramsay, along with some peaceful Quakers, were inspired by what they saw. They were learning that sermons were not enough to bring about social change, while a determined public, fired up by emotion, might. The possibilities that could be won by ordinary people, once aroused, seemed boundless. Although he did not live to see their goal achieved, Ramsay's call for moral action helped to turn a debate about the rights and wrongs of slavery into a campaign to change public hearts and minds, and ultimately put enough pressure on the parliamentary process to bring about legislation.

Clarkson spent a month with James Ramsay in Kent in 1786. The older man shared both his missionary zeal and his ultimate failure with the young man. Together they resolved that they might

> release the Africans from the scourge of this cruel
> trade... by turning public attention to their misery.[4]

Fired by enthusiasm, at dinner in the vicarage with the Ramsay family, Clarkson was moved to declare that he was ready to devote himself to the cause of enslaved Africans. The following morning, he wondered if he had been a bit hasty in giving up comfortable prospects in the church for a campaign to improve the lives of black men and women. However, he decided to make a start. To remedy his ignorance of the realities of the modern trade, he visited the port of London where he viewed slave ships and talked to their crews. He was horrified. He began making notes and promised Ramsay a weekly progress report on his researches. After a month, he had too many notes to post them all to Ramsay.

Those concerned about Africans were mostly Quakers who were independent small manufacturers, bankers and businessmen with no connections into politics. To make some parliamentary contacts, it was suggested that Clarkson give copies of a shortened version of his essay to Members of Parliament. In the course of his meetings to distribute the essay, Clarkson met William Wilberforce, Independent MP for Yorkshire (1759–1833), whom he reported as 'becoming more interested in the fate of Africa'. The anti-slavery network had talked of forming a more permanent committee. If Wilberforce could be persuaded to become involved and take up the question of slavery in Parliament, a committee would back him up. Clarkson was sent to ask Wilberforce if he would do this. At this point, he noted that Wilberforce had not 'dropped the least hint' that he would be prepared to raise the anti-slavery cause in a hostile House of Commons. Clarkson met Wilberforce several times, but he could not quite pluck up the courage to ask him the all-important question. Clarkson's naive Quaker friends seemed to underestimate the power of the West Indian lobby. Clarkson had become only too aware of the daunting nature of what was being requested. He confessed his failure to one of the abolitionist group, who suggested they invite Wilberforce to a dinner where it might be easier to put the question to him. An invitation was duly sent which Wilberforce could not refuse. Sir Joshua Reynolds, Mr Boswell and other distinguished guests were invited to join them. The after-dinner conversation was gently steered around to slavery, and finally the question of Wilberforce bringing a measure to Parliament was put to him. Wilberforce had no objection. He immediately agreed to request a Parliamentary Inquiry. In response, the Committee for Abolition of the African Slave Trade was formed in May 1787, and the first modern, public campaign to right this wrong began.[5]

Clarkson set off on horseback to tour the slave ports of Bristol, Liverpool and Lancaster, with the difficult task of finding brave and credible individuals who could be persuaded to give evidence should the requested inquiry take place. This was no easy task, since those who knew the slave trade were also dependent on it for their livelihoods. In Liverpool, he was surprised to find a shop window displaying the chains, shackles, neck collars, thumb screws and mouth gags used by slavers. He asked for an explanation of exactly how each instrument was used and bought samples to be produced in evidence.

As I have noted, the merchant and planter class had astutely ensured their place amongst the landed from which all of the legal privileges and protections that the sugar and slave trades enjoyed could be well defended. Taking on this planter and slave merchant lobby would not be an easy task. Then, as now, groups in and around Parliament worked together to defend particular business interests. With the help of most of the Scottish Members of Parliament, the 'West Indian interest' could count on support from around 70 Members in the House of Commons and a solid presence in the House of Lords. Though there was widespread public disquiet about slavery, the London Committee for Abolition of the African Slave Trade was at this stage just 12 individuals, most of them Quakers, with a scattered group of contacts and sympathisers around the country. They set themselves a limited goal: to concentrate on legislation to halt the trafficking of Africans. They calculated that by this means they could save thousands from being sold into slavery. Furthermore, when slaves could no longer be bought, owners would be forced to take better care of the captives they already possessed. The Committee members began reaching out to friends within their religious networks. Their objective was to bring together a body of respectable and well-informed people who would petition Parliament in support of Wilberforce's request for a slave trade inquiry. Politics was the preserve of the landed and educated and would remain so for some time.

Believing slavery should be abolished did not in any way imply support for inciting emotions amongst the wider public. Older and more conservative men were learning different lessons from the revolts in France and the British Colonies. Some members of the anti-slavery committee were uneasy about popular involvement. They firmly believed in the importance of an objective balancing of facts by an educated mind. Public emotion, as they saw it, was dangerous and an unreliable guide to arriving at the truth, which for them was the goal of any public debate. Wilberforce himself was not in favour of widening the franchise even to middle-class voters and definitely disapproved of women debating political questions. Wesley (1703–91), who later joined the abolition campaign, had taken Christianity out to the people and built the Methodist movement, but thought public petitioning would only raise negative feelings against planters and traders, which in his view would not be helpful. The committee was, therefore, particularly concerned that support should be confined to the well informed and respectable. In the course of his travels for the abolitionists, to spread information and request petitions to Parliament, Clarkson, who was now working full time for them, was being exposed to quite different views. He met many who thought all men, rich or poor, had a right to speak and be heard.

The landed and moneyed classes of slave owners and traders that the committee now had in its sights were not accustomed to having their integrity questioned, but they were vulnerable. Once its true nature was exposed, trafficking in humans for financial gain would not be acceptable to the more enlightened middle classes or to many religious congregations. To achieve the committee's goal, a vast amount of simply worded, explicit publicity was distributed to Christians, particularly those belonging to reformed and non-conformist congregations. They were drawn into a unity of purpose with enlightened opinions by a series of public meetings to form local committees and a campaign of letters and press releases to local newspapers. All were urged to petition Parliament to call for legislation to right a terrible moral wrong. During his months on the road, Clarkson discovered he was not alone in his thoughts about the people finding a voice; a community of sympathisers in the provinces, who supported and guided his progress around the country, was ready to take action. In October, a couple of months after he set out, Clarkson was on his way to the slave port of Lancaster when he realised that a shortened version of his essay had now been widely distributed by the abolitionist committee. In the north of England, public meetings to expose the evils of slavery were already underway. He had become a minor celebrity in these circles and was rushed to Manchester, although he protested that he was incapable of public speaking, to preach to a meeting of anti-slavery supporters. Though initially trained for the church, he had never attempted to preach to a large crowd. As he got up, with some trepidation, to face his audience, he looked down and spotted 40 or 50 friendly black faces looking up from the front rows, which instantly calmed his nerves and stiffened his resolve. The Manchester committee clearly had no reservations about who had a right to an opinion on slavery.

By the end of the year 1787, subscriptions to the anti-slavery committee were arriving in London. Hundreds of hand-written letters with what we would now call model press releases were posted out to groups. Public meetings were announced and held. Provincial newspapers advertised and reported them. Letters to news editors followed. Five thousand leaflets were printed and distributed by the London committee providing facts and arguments. A seal was developed with an illustration of an African in chains and 'Am I not a man and a brother?' inscribed. The poet Cowper wrote several emotive verses including 'The Negro's Complaint', which included the lines,

> Men from England bought and sold me,
> paid my price in paltry gold.
> But though theirs they have enrolled me,
> minds are never to be sold.[6]

Thousands of copies of Cowper's poem were distributed under the heading 'a subject for conversation at the tea table'. In Derby, the local theatre put on performances of Aphra Behn's farce *Oroonoko*, which lampooned slave owning.[7] This movement for abolition of the African slave trade, despite the initial reservations of its leaders, through the targeted distribution of pamphlets, the organised waves of letters and press releases, the repetition of slogans and wearing of badges, developed a long-lasting model for national, extra-parliamentary campaigning. All reservations about involving 'even those who have no vote' and rousing public emotion became irrelevant. The campaign had taken on a life of its own. During the year 1787, almost 100 anti-slavery groups became active. Haverfordwest and Swansea were busy in Wales. Plymouth, Bath and Gloucester were amongst those from the South West of England, and Liverpool, Yorkshire, Manchester, Leicester, Nottingham and Sheffield were some of the many groups formed in Britain's industrial midlands and north. The first circular letter from the committee hoped that 'the general sense of the nation' would be roused and 'expressed by Petitions to Parliament.' Supporters were also urged to approach their Members of Parliament 'in order to procure their assistance'. Manchester abolitionists sent the first petition to parliament in December 1787. *The Times* reported that

> An abolition of the slave trade is again a serious
> topic of conversation in most parts of the provin-
> cial towns not concerned in that inhuman traffic.[8]

Newspapers published the Manchester resolution in full. Thirty-five more petitions were received by February 1788. This rose quickly to 100, by which time the King felt obliged to agree with Prime Minister Pitt that a committee of the Privy Council should investigate what was troubling so many of his subjects. A Mr Allison was the committee's contact in Edinburgh. He established a society of the respectable and liberal-minded in 1788. A Mr Campbell Haliburton was the group's secretary. The Edinburgh committee saw itself as a national partner to London and undertook to build up support across Scotland.

When the Privy Council inquiry opened, the pro-slave trade witnesses fell back on old arguments. The first, that according to the scriptures, slavery was not un-Christian. This line of reasoning was rapidly demolished by James Ramsay in his publication 'Objections to the Abolition of the Slave Trade, with answers'. Five thousand copies of this pamphlet were printed, including one for each Member of Parliament; copies were also sent to all of the provincial and national press. The rest went out to anti-slavery groups across the country. Thomas Clarkson attended the Privy Council sessions.

He watched with some dismay as the anti-slavery witnesses were 'brow beaten' and treated as 'suspicious characters'.[9] On listening to the simple mariner, Isaac Parker, giving evidence against admirals, he was incensed that only those of 'high character' and an 'elevated life' were taken seriously. This was still a time when truth could lose out in the face of rank and riches. The second line of evidence to the Privy Council was about the nature of Africa and Africans and their treatment on slave ships. This led to heated exchanges during later discussion of the Privy Council report by the whole House of Commons. It was claimed that the public were ignorant of Africans and their ways. It was said that cannibalism was commonplace in Africa, as those who had visited knew. Africa's people, they argued, were glad to escape this mayhem and lead peaceful, useful lives in the West Indies. Mr Norris, a Liverpool merchant, authored most of these statements. He was a former slave captain who had impressed Clarkson when they previously met in Liverpool as a man willing to give damning evidence against the trade. But Norris surprised them. He was now appearing at the Privy Council inquiry for the Liverpool slave traders, in return, no doubt, for a fee. A Mr Herniker, MP for New Romney and Eton-educated military man, backed up Norris's evidence claiming,

> Africans are naturally savage people, and that we do them a great kindness by taking them from their country.

The planter lobby argued only for tighter regulation of the trade. Tory MP, Mr Fox, was so incensed by this nonsense he exclaimed that,

> the slave trade could not be regulated because there was no regulation for robbery and murder.

Disorder ensued. The speaker intervened to ask Mr Fox to retract his remarks, but he refused. In summing up, Pitt lampooned Norris's evidence to the house saying:

> he had painted the accommodations on board ship in the most glowing colours... their apartments... were fitted up advantageously... they had several meals a day... the best sauces of African cookery. After breakfast they had water to wash themselves, while their apartments were perfumed with frankincense and lime juice. Before dinner instruments of music were introduced, song and dance promoted, the men played and sang whilst the women and girls made ornaments from beads.

Pitt added sarcastically that their prejudice must be 'capable of spreading a film over the eyes thick enough to occasion total blindness'. He then drew the house's attention to the physical dimensions of slave ships, which he had taken the precaution of sending government servants to measure. He repeated the physical constraints placed on captives, the witness statements of slave conditions on board, and closed by saying that despite the objections of West Indian planters, abolition rather than tighter regulation was the only remedy.

Hard-working abolition committee members refuted statements such as those by Norris. They were determined that the many public speeches, articles and letters published in the papers by slavery's supporters would be analysed and refuted 'inch by inch and point by point'.[10] In modern campaign terms, they established a rebuttal unit. In June, the Privy Council report was accepted overwhelmingly by the Committee; 56 were in favour and five against. Between May 1787 and July 1788, the Abolitionist Committee had held 51 meetings, sent out 26,526 reports of parliamentary proceedings and 51,432 pamphlets, according to the hard-pressed Clarkson, who had sent most of them. Wedgwood had the seal of the African made into china brooches, which it became fashionable to wear. Ramsay, who had done so much to inspire the campaign, died in July. He was still being hounded by scurrilous attacks on his character, but the informed public action he had hoped for was now growing rapidly. He declared that he was

> able to bid farewell to the present scene with the
> satisfaction of not having lived in vain.[11]

The campaign for abolition took the wealthy, respectable and previously deferred to sugar lobby by surprise. The planters in Jamaica were alerted to the reception given to the Privy Council proceedings and resolved to head off further attacks by informing London that things were improving and that they were developing new slavery regulations. Simon Taylor, young

James's great uncle and a prominent member of the Jamaican Assembly, wrote to his friend, the Westminster MP and Jamaican planter, Arcedeckne:

> I sent home... a copy of the consolidated slave act... they will then see that slaves are better provided for than any of their poor at home... what would these people say if we were to attempt to rob them of their property and the means of their existence, as they are attempting to do with us.[12]

These new regulations said slaves could no longer be killed or mutilated by owners, elderly slaves could not be turned off estates to die of hunger, and slaves must be fed and clothed by their owners. Simon Taylor's colleagues in the Jamaican Assembly wrote to Westminster arguing that interference in the slave trade would ruin Britain. Government revenue would be half annihilated, naval strength undermined, merchants and manufacturers bankrupted. What was more worrying, since British law had agreed that slaves were a mortgageable asset, banks would be affected if planters could not obtain labourers to produce the sugar which paid their debts. Defaults on a vast number of loans would be inevitable if the trade in slave labour was ended, bank bailouts would cost the government millions. In addition, planters demanded hundreds of millions in compensation. When these papers from Jamaica were circulated, they had an immediate effect. They left the Members of Parliament panic-stricken. Parliamentarians retired to the country to consider the weighty report of the Privy Council. Each was also offered 'Letters on Slavery' by a Scotsman from Moffat and anti-slavery committee member, Dr Dickson (1751–1823). Dickson's 'Letters' refuted the planters' alarmist claims and put forward the abolitionists' campaign at that point, which had the limited goal of ending the transatlantic slave trade. They believed that this could be achieved by better feeding and care for young enslaved women and their babies, which would ensure greater fertility and better infant survival rates, leading to more labour born in the colonies. They were impressed by evidence from Virginia, where many more children were born to enslaved girls and survival rates of little children were much higher than they were in the islands, including Jamaica, where working conditions were more brutal but profits greater.

The 'Letters' steadied Mr Pitt's nerve, who was relieved that he was not about to destroy the colonies. On 12 May 1789, Pitt presented the Privy Council report to the House of Commons with the confidence that he was doing the right thing. The House voted to consider the slave trade early in the next session. In the new session, slavery's defenders played for time; they demanded many more witnesses and evidence. As a result, vast amounts of paperwork had to be written up and abridged. Delay after delay saw the issue drag on, and the parliamentary session ended in July 1790 without resolution. The optimism and drive of the early months was being dissipated; the pro-slavery lobby had time to regroup.

Thomas Clarkson was aware that the tide of opinion was turning. Thomas Paine had now published his *Rights of Man*. The French Revolution was pulling down the old order. Both events led to widespread unrest in England and alarm amongst the propertied classes. Demands were made to the revolutionary French Government for full rights for people of colour in the French colony of St Domingo, which eventually became the black republic of Haiti. Column inches in the national press in Scotland were devoted to shocking reports of slave violence against white men. Further reports came from the French colony of Martinique and vivid scenes of insurrection in the British colony of Dominica. Newspapers across Britain published lurid eyewitness accounts of white men being hacked to pieces by their black slaves. The predictions of ruin and mayhem in the colonies as a result of abolitionist campaigns now seemed to be coming true. Slavery's advocates demanded a military force be sent to the islands to preserve the lives of white people and their property. Whilst most of these events had nothing at all to do with the trade in slaves, when a bill to stop all further importation of slaves was put to the house by Wilberforce at the end of the following session in July 1791, it was defeated. Members were again reminded by the planter lobby that a fund of at least 60 or 70 million pounds sterling would be needed to compensate them. But it was a more general fear of radical change that ensured that Wilberforce's proposal was lost.

The campaign had not given up. Public participation was now essential to keep up the pressure on Parliament. Thomas Clarkson printed and sold, for one penny each, 70,000 copies of his 'Address to the People of Great Britain on the Utility of Refraining from the Use of West Indian Sugar and Rum', a suggestion which came from members in London and Tewksbury. As many as 300,000 responded by boycotting sugar. Giving up sugar encouraged women to connect with the movement.

Ladies' societies sprung up and sent their own petitions. The public became more directly connected to events in Jamaica. A slogan that eating a pound of sugar was like whipping a slave was repeated in letters to the Scottish press.

> Let it never be said that slavery is countenanced by
> the bravest and most generous people on earth.[13]

These words were those of James Beattie, the popular Aberdonian philosopher, referring to his fellow Scots. It has puzzled later generations why Beattie, having taken on Hume and condemned slavery so successfully in his youth, should not have stepped forward to become Scotland's foremost anti-slavery advocate. Most of the London Committee were Quaker businessmen who were perfectly free to follow their consciences. Religious certainty and moral condemnation by Scots annoyed the sugar lobby and made religious critics easy targets. Ramsay suffered persecution, as did another outspoken Scot, the son of the Presbyterian minister from Inveraray, Zachary Macauley, the young man who had arrived in Jamaica as a 16-year-old bearing a letter of recommendation from Archibald Campbell. Disgusted by the life he found there, he eventually defied his father and returned home to live with his married sister. It was in her home that he met abolitionists, including Wilberforce, and began to devote his considerable talents and energy to the anti-slavery cause. His Christian voice became well-known and he edited the anti-slavery movement's publication, the *Anti-Slavery Reporter*. Through its columns, Macauley researched and provided brief summaries of all the information activists needed to argue their case. He was consequently trashed in newspapers and pamphlets, pilloried for his 'bible dinner snuggeries' and 'godly tea drinking', denigrated for his 'care for black slaves, but not for Britain's labourers'. He was known as 'Saint Zachariah' and 'Zaccarine' for supporting the sugar boycott. Anti-slavery activists like him were regularly accused of collecting money dishonestly. Those pursuing Macauley vowed,

> We will never quit the subject until we have torn
> the veil of hypocrisy asunder and displayed the sys-
> tem of macaulyism to the broad glare of the day.[14]

Beattie's earlier interventions in the debate had led to public attacks on his integrity by fellow Scottish academics. He was accused of being too populist, a pretend philosopher appealing to herds of unthinking followers. Beattie was close to Ramsay, and would have been aware that the views he shared with his friend made Ramsay the target of lifelong, unrelenting abuse. The doctors Beattie taught would take positions in the British army and navy, on slave ships and in plantations. He did not hold back from lecturing his students about the immorality of slavery, but Beattie had a livelihood to protect. He therefore wrote regularly to Wilberforce, offered advice to the Manchester Committee and helped to arrange meetings in Aberdeen, but he no doubt felt compelled to hold back from spearheading a Scottish campaign.

From January to March 1792, Dr Dickson, author of 'Letters on Slavery', was funded to tour Scotland on behalf of the Abolitionist Committee. Thomas Clarkson was now more than

ever convinced that 'the common people' should be involved
and wrote to Dickson explaining that ordinary folk like

> those of Leadhills, &c, may certainly petition...
> after all... the manufacturers of earthenware, in
> Staffordshire, petitioned in 1788, and what is more
> in point, the Cutlers of Sheffield did themselves
> immortal honour by petitioning.[15]

He need not have worried on that score. When William Dickson arrived in Edinburgh in January 1792, he could see that
the Scottish Committee had been busy. Plymouth abolitionists had commissioned an engraving of a crammed slave ship.
The resulting prints illustrated the lower deck of the slave ship
packed with slaves. In December 1788, the local committee
printed 1,500 copies for circulation and also sent the plan to
London. Posters of an enlarged version of the slave ship had
been distributed. Dickson wrote from Edinburgh,

> Our cause gains ground. The slave ships have been
> put up in the Banks, Public offices, Coffee house
> &c. here, with an excellent effect.[16]

Not all of the committee members in London were enthusiastic. There were echoes of the Paris commune and the revolutionary campaigns in France associated with poster campaigns; this was a step too far for some of them.

Campbell Haliburton of the Scottish Committee in Edinburgh had helped the London abolitionists to abridge the vast
amount of evidence presented to the Privy Council inquiry

which they now referred to as 'the abstract'. It was a powerful document, a clear and precise exposure of the brutality of the trade. The Scottish Committee now reduced the 128-page summary further to produce a 25-page 'Short Address to the People of Scotland on the Subject of the Slave Trade'. Haliburton had a full-time job as an excise man. He regretted that he therefore could not travel the length and breadth of the country 'to explain the contents of the abstract'. His fellow Scottish Committee members were confident that they would reach the far corners of the land by sending it out to every minister of religion. What is more, they knew that Kirk sessions would need no help in digesting its contents. Scottish Christians would judge the evidence against a thorough knowledge of their Bibles. James Stothert, the returned planter and father of the slave girl Rebecca who worked on his cattle farm, wrote from his splendid turreted home in Dumfries to David Hood, his attorney in Montego Bay, reminding him not to order imported goods to feed his slaves but to ensure the slaves were encouraged to grow their own food by not giving out too many bought rations. He also complained bitterly about the actions of the Edinburgh Committee.

> Even in North Britain, where they are in general so totally ignorant in the business, the frenzy spreads amazingly, for which great pains are taken by some individuals and religious motives are of course introduced. I am now told [Mr W]* is sending

---

* I assume that this refers to Wilberforce.

copies of the evidence taken before the committee
of the House of Commons to the minister of every
parish, no doubt to obtain charitable contributions to carry on the Bill now [before Parliament].
I am sorry to add that no great spirit appears on
the planters' behalf to counteract these dangerous
machinations against the Colonies.[17]

He was right to sense danger. Although the Scottish press published opinion, letters and reports from Jamaica, rural Scotland
had hitherto been ignorant of the depths of brutality involved
in the slave trade or Scotland's widespread involvement. Petitioning Parliament, which they were now urged to do, was not
new; Scottish town councils and traders regularly petitioned
in defence of their commercial interests, but they had never
publicly challenged the behaviour of the landed class in the
way they were now encouraged to do. The 25-page 'Address
to the People of Scotland' was probably the first direct and
widespread communication of Westminster business distributed throughout the country. If the Presbyterian mission was
to build Christian communities within a righteous nation, they
would learn that a substantial portion of the Scottish merchant
and landed elite had taken a wrong turn and involved the
country in what must now be condemned as gross immorality.
Hitherto, Kirk sessions had refrained from commenting on the
morals of their betters. Activities in Africa and Jamaica might
be distant, but the merchants and planters involved in buying
and selling people had now settled themselves back home as
local lairds, Members of Parliament and leading figures in the

community. Presbyteries now felt that they had a duty to make their views of these Scots known.

Despite their association with the slave trade, the town council, magistrates and tradesmen of Kirkudbright drafted a petition to their Member of Parliament saying the trade was 'unjust, oppressive and cruel, and utterly disgraceful to the national character'.[18] There was understandably no petition from Ayr given the overriding presence and charitable activities of the Hamiltons comfortably residing in landed estates just outside the town. An anonymous letter-writer to a west of Scotland newspaper, however, asked why so few landholders were petitioning; one would suppose he knew the answer, as many of their landlords were prominent slave holders. Religious petitions sent from the small towns of rural Ayrshire such as Kilmarnock, Beith, Kilbirnie and Maybole would certainly be a rebuke to the Hamilton family. Evidently, the people of Forfar were only too aware of who was wearing all of their Osnaburgh cloth. Their Minister was reported by Dickson to be sympathetic to the cause but knew a petition condemning slavery sent from that town 'might cause a riot'.[19] The absence of an Aberdeen City committee and petitions might be explained by a reluctance to rebuke Allardyce, their Lord Provost and Member of Parliament since 1792. Allardyce, who began his working life with the Royal African Slave trading company, had children of colour and land in Jamaica. He boasted loudly and confidently that he had 'sold more black men as there are white' in Aberdeen.[20] Allardyce had enough support in Marischal College to be elected rector in 1796. Given his great power locally, a petition from Marischal College itself, no doubt urged on by Beattie, was either foolhardy or rather brave. James Stothert, Rebecca's father, need not have worried; the people of his local town of Dumfries did not petition, but that did not mean that they had not read the address. He had seen some kind of commotion outside the grocers in the high street over a barrel of sugar.

Dickson had come up from London prepared to explain the campaign tactics. Scottish petitions were needed to support a limited objective, a new bill before Parliament in the spring calling for a ban on the trade only. A disproportionately large number, more than a third of all the resulting petitions to Parliament, came from Scotland's churches. The limited tactics proposed by London were not in the Presbyterian vocabulary. Many proclaimed the necessity and the moral imperative of sweeping away the whole slave system; nothing less would do. Divine judgement featured in many of Scotland's 187 responses, from a British total of just over 550, which arrived in Westminster in early 1792. National feeling once aroused was strong in slavery's condemnation. A Kirk historian later wrote that Scotland should be proud. Petitioning voices went some way to ensuring that the Scottish nation did not go down in history for its 'eager and... unscrupulous pursuit of material wealth'.[21]

Despite well-organised local commercial interests in support of slavery, an abolition committee was formed in Glasgow in February 1792. The inaugural meeting was chaired by David Dale (1739–1806), the independent cotton manufacturer of New Lanark Mills, a founder member of the Glasgow Chamber of Commerce and well-known philanthropist. David Dale moved in elite and respectable circles, which must often have been hostile to his enlightened views, but he was a wealthy man of independent means and therefore free to make his opinions public. *The Caledonian Mercury* of 9 February 1792 reported under the banner 'Slave Trade Glasgow' that

> A General Meeting of the Society of this city, for the Abolition of the African Slave Trade was held with David Dale esq in the chair.

After 'mature deliberation', it had agreed several resolutions unanimously, which were printed in full:

> When a new application to Parliament for procuring the abolition of the African Slave Trade is made it would be highly becoming of the inhabitants of Great Britain at large, to make a public declaration of their views... that the traffic in the human species is founded on the grossest injustice, is attended with the utmost cruelty and barbarity to an innocent race and that its continuance, in this enlightened age, is disgraceful to the nation, and utterly inconsistent with the professed beliefs of Christians. A draft of a Petition to the Hon. House of Commons, in name of the Society and of all the other inhabitants of Glasgow... would be... lodged in a proper place in the city, that those inclined may have access to exhibit their subscription may do so.

The article finished by remarking that 'some degree of infamy and guilt' for the trade 'must be carried by the whole nation' and that 'commercial views' cannot excuse 'the price paid in morality... the united voice of a people must wipe this sin'.

Though it never equalled its rival, long parliamentary delays allowed a pro-slavery propaganda machine to get going. People interested in Africa would have been eager to read a book which was published in 1793 and purported to be the memoirs of the former Scottish doctor Dalzel, who had worked for the Committee of Merchants in managing their slave depots along the African coast 30 years previously.[22] Dalzel now recounted his experiences in Africa as Governor of Dahomey. His writing was circulated to parliamentarians and widely commented on in letters to most provincial newspapers. The book was actually the work of three people, Dalzel, Norris, who had made discredited claims in his evidence to the Privy Council Committee, and Dalzel's successor on Cape Coast, Lionel Abson. The book began with a serious attempt to record the geography, agriculture and lifestyles in West Africa. Descriptions of kings' palaces and stories of an African king's delight at being gifted a sedan chair with curtains would have fascinated 18th-century Britain. The book had an authentic feel and was widely quoted. 'Many essays have lately appeared in the newspapers', one writer observed in the columns of *The Scots Magazine* in June 1793, 'by writers who are not well informed about... the true state of the African'. The columnist asserted that the slave raiding voyages to West African villages saved slaves from the greater evil of becoming human sacrifices. The book's passages on cannibalism, especially the tale of a white man declared to be 'tasty english beef' by the 'savages', as the columnist described them, 'gorging' on him, must have impressed readers, since comic images of white men being boiled in pots by black men lived on for the next two hundred years. The book quotes the African King Adahoonzon's insistence that 'we only sell prisoners of war'. Since all three authors were being paid by Liverpool slave traders, their dishonesty should not surprise us.

The Abolitionist Committee spent the first months of the year 1792 building support and encouraging petitions in expectation of another attempt to get a bill through Parliament. Colonel Tarleton, MP for Liverpool, dismissed the petitioners as useless fanatics. But Parliament could not help but be impressed by the opinions of so many people and the extraordinary number of petitions claiming slavery was a stain on the nation's reputation. In April 1792, Wilberforce thought the time was right to try to ban the trade once more. Press reports and meetings encouraged the people of Edinburgh to sign the petitions available in drapers and book shops, grocers, ironmongers and hosiers. Posters of the packed slave ship were talking points in coffee houses. Henry Dundas (1742–1811) was Edinburgh's Member of Parliament. He personally received a huge petition from the city with 10,885 signatures in March 1792. He promised to give it his full attention. It was said that crossing Dundas in any way was political and social suicide. No one won a parliamentary seat in Scotland without his blessing; money, favours and business deals were all exchanged in the cause of party discipline. Dundas was rewarded for efficient management of the Scottish Tories with a seat in Pitt's cabinet. His views would therefore greatly influence the House.

Dundas began his address to Parliament by stating that he was a 'warm friend' of abolition. He only 'differed over the mode of effecting it'.[23] This was not untruthful. As Lord Advocate, he had stood up for the African Joseph Knight at his ground-breaking trial 20 years before, at which it was argued that Joseph had arrived from Africa a heathen but a Christian education had transformed him, a view which was accepted by the court. Dundas was obviously inclined towards the widespread view that a Christian mission to bring education and legal marriage to slaves might somehow transform them into a hard-working labouring class who would establish families in which they would raise another generation of hard-working children.

The big decisions in politics are never made in a vacuum. Dundas had a dilemma to resolve. As a senior cabinet member, he did not want to openly oppose his Prime Minister, Pitt, who was an enthusiastic abolitionist. He had received a petition from his city which was only rivalled in size by the one from London. Twenty years previously, the Ayr Bank had collapsed, taking down most of Scotland's banks with it. One of the very few Scottish Banks which survived was that of the Coutts family, now based in the Strand in London. They would no doubt have attended one of Dundas's 'Burgundy and Blasphemy' parties in Wimbledon to remind him that government had already been required to bail out the West Indian merchant bankers who had been rather too enthusiastic in giving loans for slave purchase and had accumulated a lot of bad debt. Another shock to the system could have serious consequences for Scottish banking. Moreover, transatlantic trade was about to become more difficult: France had declared war on her neighbours and Britain was stockpiling weapons, preparing to join a European war. The morality of the question before him was obvious, but the commercial consequences could be disastrous.

Dundas spoke for Scotland at Westminster. He was sometimes referred to as 'the uncrowned king of Scotland'. He could not therefore possibly allow Scotland's banks and commercial success to be undermined by a sudden disruption of the labour supply to the colonies. He also recognised the personal stake that many of his Tory friends in Scotland had in the West Indies. He argued to Parliament that Britain had legalised the slave trade and many had legitimately invested in it. It would be unfair to them to suddenly outlaw their legitimate business. He explained that he favoured better regulation of both slaves in Jamaica and the trade. He proposed education for slave children to ensure that in ten or more years a new, 'civilised' generation could be freed. He suggested that more children could be born and raised in the West Indies if bounties were offered to traders for transporting extra women. Mr Fox scoffed that this idea would be an incentive 'for any crew of ruffians' to seize members of the 'weak and defenceless sex'. In a devastating move, Dundas then recommended that 'gradually' be added to Wilberforce's motion in front of the phrase 'to be abolished'. Debate then followed as to how long gradually might be. With the help of Lord Frederick Campbell, third son of the Duke of Argyll, the 'West Indian interest' again played for time; the bill staggered through various stages before it was eventually lost.

Wilberforce did not give up; he made many attempts to re-introduce a bill in the next ten years, even when the slaving and banking Lascelles family was threatening to put up the vast sum of £100,000 to fund an election campaign in which a Lascelles relative would stand against him. Union with Ireland in 1802 introduced many new men to Westminster, men who had no interest in preserving slavery. This opportunity to gain the support of Irish Members of Parliament encouraged Wilberforce and the London Committee to prepare a further attempt to abolish the trade. They printed and sent out 12,000 copies of the account of the life of that son of a Scot, Robert Wedderburn, child of the slave Rosanna and raised by his proud grandmother Talkee Aimee in Kingston Jamaica. His book, entitled *The Horrors of Slavery*, was sponsored by the Society of Friends. Times had changed. The French and American revolutions had stoked public fears about violent propaganda and large gatherings of common people. The abolitionists now moved quietly and cautiously, not to arouse too much opposition. In 1805, George Stephen, a Scot and a lawyer, assisted the abolitionists to draw up another bill. Mr Pitt introduced the debate by revisiting its long history.

> For the last sixteen or seventeen years of my life, I have been in the habit of uniformly and strenuously supporting the several motions made by a respectable gentleman [Mr Wilberforce], who has so often, by his meritorious exertions on this

subject, attracted the applause of this house, and claimed the admiration of the public.[24]

Lord Tarleton replied and reminded them of the commercial value of the trade, calling their attention to the situation of Liverpool,

> a town which, from a miserable fishing hamlet of about 150 huts, had within a century risen to be the second town in point of commercial wealth and consequence, in the British dominions, entirely by the African trade.

Mr Wilberforce replied that,

> our religion... forbade all those odious means by which slaves were procured... expressly prohibited the practice of man-stealing, and called us to act on a principle of universal philanthropy, and kind goodwill to all men.

Wilberforce then read out his resolution,

> That this house, conceiving the African Slave Trade to be contrary to the principles of justice, humanity, and sound policy, will... proceed to take effectual measures for abolishing the said trade.

Parliament finally agreed that from August 1806, no slaving vessel should clear out of British ports, and by March 1807, no more slaves could be landed in the British Colonies. The importation of enslaved people into all of Britain's colonies was outlawed. The Atlantic trade was ended, and William Wilberforce received a standing ovation. In the intervening years between Wilberforce's first attempt to ban the trade and its final abolition, a further 117,021 captive men, women and children had been trafficked in British ships by British sailors, funded and directed by many wealthy Scottish merchants and carried out with the enthusiastic participation of many Scots.[25]

Reflecting on 20 years of campaigning, Thomas Clarkson felt that an important lesson had been learned by the British public, 'that commerce itself should have its moral boundaries'.[26] With hindsight, we can see how important was that lesson of putting people before profit. Understanding how easy it would be to smuggle slaves brought to the West Indies from Africa by traders from Spain, or via America, James Stephen, MP for East Grinstead, former lawyer in St Kitts and chief architect of the Abolition Bill, attempted to close loopholes. Ending importation did not end slave holding in the British colonies, as the enslaved were still property. The navy would police the oceans, but Stephen was concerned about the policing of buying and selling within the colonies. He followed up with a bill that finally passed in 1815 requiring each planter to return an annual list of all the slaves on his plantation. This strict check on any movement of slaves not only curbed smuggling, but it shone a light on slave survival rates and the low birth rate in Jamaica, which was about to become a contentious issue.

CHAPTER 9
Keeping everything under control

*[W]e were obliged to pass close by the pole, on
which was stuck the head of a black man who
was executed a few days ago.*[1]

RUMOURS OF SLAVE PLOTS and reprisals against their masters
were always circulating in the white community in Jamaica.
News of buildings set on fire and overseers attacked, grim
fantasies of planters having their heads cut off and slaves eating their hearts, were sometimes recounted in white gatherings. Men like John Hamilton, sent from the family in Ayr
to get more work from the slaves in Pemberton Valley, were
alone with over 100 adult slaves. Hamilton, like other slave
owners and managers, lived with the fear that however biddable his workforce might seem, he could have his throat cut
at any time. We may remember Thistlewood, who escaped by
the skin of his teeth and the help of his loyal slave Lincoln
from an attack by a group of black men. He also records an
instance of enslaved men sticking together to protect their
interests. A white neighbour was killed after ignoring warnings he had received from the slave community not to 'mess
with' a particular slave woman. Thistlewood's own nephew
was found drowned in a ditch after similar warnings, though

in his case, nothing was ever proven. When John Hamilton reassured his uncle that everything was under control on Pemberton Valley estate after serious disturbances among the slaves in 1754, he knew this control could never be guaranteed. Tensions between masters and slaves were always present, and slaves regularly tried to run away. Hamilton transported three of the plantation's strongest men to Honduras when he arrived in 1756 because, as he explained to his uncle, he feared they were plotting 'an insurrection'.[2] White men like Hamilton were vastly outnumbered by the strong black women and men working for them. A white man alone on an estate could be overcome quite easily by such a group.

Thomas Thistlewood left vivid descriptions of the 1760 rebellion, during which his neighbours ran in terror from groups of 'armed negroes' taking over or burning their estates while the armed militia was sent for. To ensure order on the island, a company of British soldiers was stationed in Jamaica, assisted by this militia. Every landholder had to serve, with many white men mounted on their horses and foot soldiers largely made up of loyal African slaves. Thistlewood remained a foot soldier. He looked into the possibility of joining the exclusively white, mounted class, but decided that the necessary horse, pistol and red coat were a bit too expensive for him. An unarmed group of Africans on an estate could not hold out for long against the armed and mounted militia, especially if supported by regular soldiers from the army barracks in the mountains above Kingston.

They could, however, slit quite a few white throats before the militia grabbed their guns, got on their horses and arrived. The slave holders were much more worried about slaves on several estates coordinating plans, as the militia found it hard to spread itself across numerous estates; it lacked any rapid means of communication. The fear of slaves from several estates meeting and plotting together was one reason why Africans were beaten if they left the estate on which they lived without explicit permission and a ticket.

White men responded to the threat of violence and the fear it gave them by ensuring that their slaves were also very afraid. It made no sense economically or morally for a planter to subject his most valuable asset to cruel torture, over and above already harsh routine discipline. Nor was it sensible to damage something you might be still paying for. The House of Commons Select Committee, which investigated slavery in 1788, concluded that violent abuse was the result of the planters' unlimited power. They heard from surgeons called to attend to slaves who had been almost destroyed by their mistress or master in moments of fury. A Mr Coor told the Select Committee of a house girl who had spilt a cup of tea and was nailed to a post by the ear and left overnight as punishment. She escaped by literally tearing herself away. She was soon brought back and her master, in his fury, clipped off both her ears with a large pair of scissors. A Mr Cook spoke of a slave having his upper and lower teeth knocked out as punishment for stealing a turkey. The committee heard of whole legs cut off after masters had severely damaged them, of women hung from trees and fire put to their private parts. Acts of extreme violence like these were said to be the result of a master's fury, but white violence was not simply a momentary lapse; it was much more calculated. Slave control was assisted by terror tactics. Planters, the slave courts and the island government supported public brutality as a means to terrorise slaves into submission. Only two weeks after Thomas Thistlewood arrived in Savanna la Mar in 1750, he watched his employer, William Dorrill, order the body of a dead runaway dug up and beheaded, and the head fixed on a pole. Just months later, Thistlewood

> saw a Negro fellow nam'd English belonging to Fuller Wood Tried, lost, and hang'd upon ye 1st Tree immediately (for drawing his knife upon a White Man), his head Cutt off, Body left unbury'd.[3]

As a young overseer on the Egypt sugar plantation, Thistlewood received two returning runaways, 'also Robin's head, who was hanged yesterday for running away with those two boys'. As a warning to others, he

> put it upon a pole and stuck it up just at the angle of the road in the home pasture.[4]

Slave owners justified their actions by saying that the living must be shown they could not escape, even in death. An African's body could never return whole to their homeland because it would be burnt to ashes or chopped into pieces by white men in Jamaica.

Scots arriving in Jamaica in the mid-1700s would have been familiar with brutality and public hanging used to terrorise the living. The Wedderburn brothers had watched their rebellious Jacobite father hanged, drawn and quartered on Kennington Common after being captured at Culloden in 1746. With no possible future in Britain, they found a ship's captain in Glasgow who would let them work their passage to Jamaica. On arrival, they found doctors from home who gave them work and passed on a bit of medical knowledge. They soon revived their fortunes and began supporting their mother and several brothers and sisters at home. When the loyal Campbells were appointed by the Crown to manage a confiscated Jacobite estate in northern Argyll, someone shot the Campbell manager in the back in Glenure. The culprit was never found, but James Stewart, a recently evicted tenant, was accused. The subsequent trial in Inveraray was little more than a device to allow the Campbells to take their revenge on the Stewarts. The Duke presided over a jury packed with Camp-bells. James Stewart was convicted of aiding the murder and hanged above the settlement of Ballachulish. His body was left swinging in the wind for the next 18 months, his family afraid to remove it.

Though in the minds of white men, violence remained imperative to preserve the social order in Jamaica, by the late 1700s, abolitionist sentiments were growing, and European sensibilities were changing. The Northern Irish Governor of

Jamaica was critical of the planters' worst excesses. Lady Maria Nugent, his newly arrived wife, on her way to church in 1803 protested to her diary that had she not already promised attendance to the clergyman at Kingston,

> I would not have gone, for we were obliged to pass close by the pole, on which was stuck the head of a black man who was executed a few days ago.[5]

Scots at home took a keen interest in the safety of their relatives in the West Indies. *The Caledonian Mercury* ran a regular column called 'Plantation News', which carried details of happenings in the islands, including slave revolts. On 29 June 1754, the column gave more information about the disturbances John Hamilton had found in their neighbourhood and on the Pemberton Valley property, about which he wrote reassuringly to the Hamilton family in 1756. The newspaper congratulated the Governor for his vigilance in putting down a revolt of the 'wild Negroes at Crawford Town'. These 'wild men', known as the Maroons, were the descendants of indigenous Jamaicans (Taíno), some Spaniards and their slaves, and formerly enslaved Africans who had run away from Spanish and British plantations. 'Wild' was intended to distinguish these Africans from the captured and supposedly 'tamed' men and women on the plantations. Constant attacks from the Maroons had forced the Governor into making a peace treaty with their leaders in 1740. The Maroons were skilled in guerrilla warfare and knew the mountain tracks better than any white soldier. They agreed that in return for recognition of their rights to the land they controlled, freedom of movement on the island and a sum paid annually to them from the British exchequer, they would in the future return runaways for a fee and help the regular British troops should there be a slave insurrection.

It was reported in 1754 that a group of Maroons was in revolt. They had killed Ned Crawford, one of their leaders, captured the three white government representatives stationed in Crawford town to keep an eye on their community, and seized the British soldiers' arms. As the *Caledonian Mercury* observed, this might 'have proved of very bad Consequence' without prompt action.[6] His Excellency (the Governor and one of the Campbell clan) was proudly declared to have acted promptly and sent one of the companies of African foot soldiers.[7] The soldiers' adventures in getting across the island were described in *Plantation News* in heroic detail. It had been raining hard, which slowed their march, burdened as they were with provisions and ammunition. They were reported to be 'up to their armpits' fording the rivers. The comforting news that great numbers of loyal Africans had been involved in putting down the insurrection was given prominence in the report. Government troops had been joined by 'Negroes' from Scotts-Hall and another band of loyal African soldiers from Port Antonio. Terms were offered to the Crawford Maroons, but when they refused, a battle ensued. Several soldiers were wounded on the Government side, one mortally, but they managed to kill three Maroon ringleaders and brought in their heads. The victors now reported that the

> weather was fair, the Men all in Good Health and
> Spirits, and the Negroes faithful and willing.[8]

The next day they would divide into parties to search the wooded hillsides to put a final 'End to this Affair' – until the next time.

In May 1760, a serious revolt broke out on several sugar estates in the parish of St Mary in the west of the island. One of them, Frontier Estate, was owned by the Scotsmen Robert and Archibald Stirling. Archibald was one of the early and successful planters who arrived in Jamaica as a young man and returned to Scotland in 1748, having made the small fortune of £18,000. He left the plantation in the care of an overseer and purchased the Cawder estate near Glasgow from another brother, John. The brothers' success in Jamaica catapulted all three into the ranks of the super-rich. A further generation of Stirlings would play a pivotal role in Jamaica's later history, which I will consider in chapters 10 and 12. Archibald died in 1783. At that time, his share of the family's Scottish and West Indian estates was valued at £125,000.

Tacky was an Akan African* trafficked from the Gold Coast and working at the Frontier Estate. He figured that slaves could not rely upon the support of the Maroons. Two or three Africans fleeing to freedom might survive in the mountains alone, but in order to free, a whole estate population of hundreds – nothing short of a revolutionary takeover – was needed. He knew that his white masters would

---

* From modern-day Ghana.

not survive long without their slaves, but Africans, on the other hand, could survive well without their white masters if only they could capture and hold onto enough land to make money and grow food. The white people who possessed the land, the overseers and planters, were isolated but armed. The long-term survival of Africans as free men and women would only be possible if they could capture and control the land. Tacky's plan to seize a section of the island was not entirely fanciful – the white community with all its fire power had never managed to defeat the Maroons, who controlled areas of the Blue Mountains. The British Government had been forced into a treaty with the Maroons because it could not entirely defeat them. Tacky's ambitious plan must have been discussed and agreed amongst the slaves on several plantations: Frontier, Trinity, Ballards Valley, Esher and Haywood Hall. Trinity was 1,546 acres of good sugar-producing land owned by the wealthy Bayley family. The estate had two sugar mills, one powered by wind and the other by cattle, and would later have an elegant and spectacular aqueduct with hundreds of arches to bring water from the mountains to power a third mill. Ballards Valley was owned by a Mr Cruickshank, who lived there with his slave wife and three children. Esher was owned by one of the Beckford family, who was one of John Taylor's partners in slave dealing activities in Kingston. These were large, productive estates with probably more than 1,000 resident slaves. Tacky's bold plan was to arm a group of slaves. These slaves would use their weapons to destroy their white masters, seize and then defend the captured estates. If they could gain control of a block of land, much like the Maroons had gained control of land in the mountains, it might be possible to eventually force a treaty. The Africans might then be able to live freely on their own land, use their expertise to make a little money and grow enough to eat their fill every day. All they needed was fire power and some battle training to make the initial strike against their masters, neither of which would have been at all easy to organise.

There were rumours in the white community over the Christmas holidays in December 1759. Some said they had heard that on 1 January, 3,000 Africans from Hanover and Westmorland would muster in a certain place. Though no one thought this possible, they were nevertheless on their guard. On 1 January, Tacky led a small band from Frontier and Trinity estates to Port Maria where they attacked the fort, killed the guard and seized arms and ammunition. From there they moved inland, collecting support and travelling on foot from estate to estate, killing all of the white men and taking control of their estates. Trinity, Frontier, Ballards Valley, Esher and Haywood Hall were all taken before a hundred or so whites and some trusted black men arrived to try to halt the progress of Tacky's band. Meanwhile, news of the rebellion was rushed to the Governor on the other side of the island. He responded by sending two companies of regular troops, as well as a band of Maroons. With such overwhelming numbers and fire power, the troops attacked and scattered Tacky's forces in a fierce battle in which 50 white men and over 400 slaves were killed.

Tacky was shot and killed by one of the Maroons, but many armed slaves ran into the mountains and remained at large. Terrible punishments followed: mutilations, gibbeting and slow burnings.

The enslaved African communities did not entirely give up on Tacky's mission; not all of the stolen arms were recovered. At the end of May, there was further action by slaves in Westmorland during which Thistlewood's neighbours, Mr Smith and Captain Hoar, were killed; Thistlewood fully expected to be murdered in his bed. He recorded ongoing guerrilla warfare, with bands of marauding Africans roaming the west of the island and attacking white men. Over 1,000 slaves were now reported to have freed themselves. Recounting events in his diary, Thistlewood wrote that his neighbour John Jones had his house burnt down. Critically wounded militia men returning from the fighting passed by Thistlewood's home each day. His neighbours, the Crawfords, feared that their slaves might join the revolt. His neighbour Mr Reid was afraid to sleep at home because he had been warned that he was on the Africans' hit list and might be killed at any moment. The Maroons, according to Thistlewood, remained loyal to the white planters and fought for them. Admiral Holmes sent for army and militia reinforcements, but the war of Africans against those who enslaved them continued without a clear end. The Africans of Salt Spring reportedly refused to work. The militia was still on patrol night and day when Thistlewood went to Savanna la Mar in September to see 'negroes hung up alive'.[9] High food prices, caused by the Anglo–Spanish war of 1762–3, ensured many slaves went hungry; indeed, some were starving because cheap supplies could not be imported from the American colonies. This widespread hunger did not help the situation, and peace was not entirely restored. Just as the worst seemed to be over in Savanna la Mar, trouble broke out on the other side of the island. Soldiers were dispatched in September to St Thomas in the east, then St John near Kingston, followed by St James and then Hanover in the west again. These continuing revolts were almost equal to Tacky's original uprising. Thistlewood had his most trusted slaves guard his property and approach roads every night for months on end. Patrolling continued in Westmorland at regular intervals over the next two or three years. Thistlewood recorded in his diary in 1763 that the band of Maroons led by their leader Cuddie

> [l]ately came up with eleven runaways in a hut in the mountains. Killed 3 and took the rest, who were tried today at Savannah La Mar. one is kept as evidence against others which may be taken, and the others, some of them hanged, and the others burnt alive by slow fire, in the morass behind the court house.[10]

Horrible punishments from white slave holders did not work. By August 1776, the island was again considered to be on the verge of rebellion. The Governor of Jamaica published a statement confirming that

> a great number of negroes in the parish of Hanover [in the Western corner of the country] have been and now are in a state of actual rebellion... to

> prevent any further attempts by the slaves... mar-
> tial law shall now be in force.[11]

He warned planters to be vigilant and placed an embargo on all movement of ships in and out of the ports of Jamaica until peace and tranquillity could be restored. This, of course, made the lack of food even more serious. A letter from Port Royal, Jamaica, dated August 1776, brought news of the insurrections to families and businesses at home. It arrived into Falmouth by the ship *John and Mary*. The letter was printed in several British newspapers in October 1776:

> Dear Brother, Our present situation is very deplor-
> able. We have been now under arms ever since the
> beginning of August, on account of an insurrection
> of the negroes, who have been exceedingly trouble-
> some for some time past, occasioned by the scarcity
> of provisions, our supplies from America being long
> cut off. We were in great hopes the execution of
> about thirty of their ringleaders would have quelled
> the sedition, but it has not had the desired effect, as
> they still continue very outrageous, and have laid
> waste many plantations... I will write to you again
> by the first opportunity, as you must be anxious for
> our safety. I am, your loving brother, &c.[12]

Though it was often said that troops had put an end to 'negro revolts', there never was a final end of these uprisings. White men were vastly outnumbered by black men and women.

They were few in number and therefore dependent on the help of loyal Africans – slave drivers on plantations and foot soldiers in the militia. African compliance was won by spreading terrible fear amongst slaves, executions, 'slaves hung up alive' and on occasion the display of severed heads. By the late 1700s, white slaveholders in Jamaica were angry but vulnerable. Violence against slaves appeared to be no longer working; moreover, it was receiving a much less sympathetic audience amongst radical Christians in Britain. Planters like John Hamilton attempting to maximise sugar profits for their families in Scotland might reassure them that everything was under control, but he knew this would never be the case.

CHAPTER 10

The civilising mission

Men must be polished and refined in their manners before they can be properly enlightened in religious truths.[1]

RELIGION IN THE 18th and 19th centuries was much, much more important to Scots than it is today. Christian acceptance of the immorality of slavery was therefore crucial to building a Scottish campaign against it. Access to Christianity also became important to many slaves. The reformed and more radical churches introduced captive Africans to a higher authority, a God who judged their white masters and supported Africans as thinking, feeling, fully human beings. The next part of our story, the ending of slavery and Scotland's role in it, cannot be fully understood without a brief guide to the position of Scotland's national religion in Jamaica and in Scotland. The dignity that flowed from a right to worship God and be received into the Christian faith, the knowledge that the Bible taught that all people, black and white, were God's children, gave hope to many slaves. That right was an equally important moral principle for many worshippers at home.

Slavery had many defenders in Scotland. Not only the wealthy transatlantic families, now integrated into the British political elite, but also a great range of people who had invested a bit of money in one or two slaves which were managed and rented to various businesses in the colonies. These small investors included ministers of religion, widows using slave income to survive, and the many traders and businessmen with trading interests and families in Jamaica. Such people made up the ownership and readership of a growing number of pro-slavery newspapers and magazines published in Scotland, such as *The Glasgow Courier* and *Blackwood's Magazine*. If a rural family fished herrings to be smoked, spun linen at home or toiled in a workshop making hoes or chains, they were less likely to concern themselves with where their produce was exported to. For most of the 18th century, such families were, as far as we can tell, unconcerned about slavery in Jamaica. Their own lives were hard, struggling to feed and clothe their families on a pittance. Before the Edinburgh Anti-Slavery Committee sent out the 'Address to the People of Scotland' in 1792, if these families knew anything at all about the West Indies, it was probably that a carpenter could earn two or three times their Scottish wages there. Despite growing towns, most Scots lived in rural communities where life centred around the Kirk, and the virtues of hard work and Bible reading shaped opinions. Kirk sessions presided over by the parish minister, landowners and the ruling elders elected by the congregation had far more influence on small-town and rural culture than far away Westminster. Throughout the 1700s, there was a widespread view amongst Kirk congregations that they were living with a mission. Universal education and Bible reading, hard work and faith in God, would make Scotland the first truly Christian nation. Scotland's prosperity was proof for some that God recognised their efforts.

As national feelings for and against slavery became more prominent, a group of radical Presbyterian ministers sought to ensure that the Church Assembly opposed slavery and regularly tabled the question for discussion in the conference of Scotland's established church. The Scottish Church was, however, a state-funded religious body controlled by ministers of a moderate persuasion. In keeping with ideas of the time, they gave advice to rather than made demands of the British Government. They therefore passed on the concerns about slavery expressed in the Assembly and asked Westminster simply to take 'such steps as they think proper'.[2] In 1789, amid rising public pressure, the issue was again raised in the Assembly. Alerted to the importance of what promised to be a heated debate, several black men watched from the gallery. They were members of 'Sons of Africa', a group of former slaves living and campaigning against slavery in Britain. One of their number, Olaudah Equiano (1745–97), was so moved by the emotions expressed by members of the Assembly that he wrote a letter to the *Edinburgh Evening Courant* offering 'warmest effusions... from a heart over flowing' for the success of the church's efforts to end slavery.[3] Though the

Assembly issued a statement that slavery was 'incompatible with the great principles of morality and religion' and urged Westminster to act speedily, it had no intention to involve itself further.

Rural people read their Bibles and accepted without question that we were all descended from Adam and Eve. In free-thinking but respectable Edinburgh, Janet Schaw's assertion on viewing the whip-scarred backs of field workers 'that these people do not feel things as we do' because they are a different sort of being was accepted by many.[4] Elsewhere, such ideas upset a biblical certainty. Ordinary Scots read their Bibles; they believed they knew right from wrong. Though they attended the Kirk, no one had asked them to consider the question of whether slaves, like other human beings, had a right to be introduced to God's message. That situation was about to change. In Jamaica, certain branches of Christianity had always been suppressed because of this literal reading of the Bible. The simple assertion that we all came from the same parents was not compatible with buying and selling our fellow women and men. It was also believed by many that since a Christian could never be a slave, Christianity in all its forms was a danger to the practice of slavery.[5] From the earliest days, Scottish planters kept a wary eye on the little ports around the coast of Jamaica. They were particularly concerned about the possible arrival of members of the Roman church in the form of preaching Jesuits from neighbouring French colonies. They believed, and were probably right to suppose, that attempts to convert French slaves to the Catholic religion had helped to fuel insurrection amongst the African population in the French islands. Although as late as 1839 the Catholic Church was relaxed about the buying and selling of humans and the church's official view that slavery could be just and compatible with God's will, planters maintained their fears, since democratic French intellectuals profoundly disagreed with the Church's stance, with some missionary Jesuits amongst them.

The idea of taking religion to foreign non-believers, of converting others to Christianity, had always been important to Christians. A belief in the civilising influence of religion was eventually used to justify Britain's powerful domination of large parts of the globe. Scotland's established religion was divided on this question of missions to convert others to Christianity. In the last decade of the 18th century, a heated debate regularly took place in the Church Assembly about funding missionaries. It was argued that Christ had commanded Christians to 'preach the gospel to every creature under heaven'. Dr Hunter, professor of theology in Edinburgh and a popular lecturer, led the dissenters. He argued to the Church Assembly that it was 'unchristian and unconstitutional' to oppose the propagation of the gospel abroad. The ruling hierarchy was, however, more inclined to believe that nature had ensured that some men and women were not 'refined enough... to be enlightened' by religious truths. Proposals to send missionaries to 'heathen' lands were defeated by a large margin. When put to vote, the Assembly, including many ministers considered to be enlightened, agreed,

> To spread abroad the knowledge of the gospel among barbarous and heathen nations, seems to be highly preposterous, in as far as it anticipates, nay it even reverses, the order of nature. Men must be polished and refined in their manners before they can be properly enlightened in religious truths.[6]

It was not until 1825, after much deliberation, that a compromise was reached and the first official missionary was sent by the national Scottish church. He went to a less controversial place than the West Indies: India.

Though tasked by the King to 'discourage vice and debauchery', the Jamaican Assembly never had any intention of encouraging missionary work with the thousands of Africans who arrived to the island.[7] The Assembly did not want anyone else to do this work either. The only form of religion allowed in Jamaica was the established Anglican Church. In 1723, the Jamaican Assembly limited preachers to those who were licensed ministers of the established church and who had signed an oath of loyalty to respect the planters' property rights over their slaves. No one could preach to a slave without the slave owner's permission. In return, ministers of the established religion were paid generous salaries which were two or three times that of a bookkeeper. A number of small churches were established, some with a minister's house, a little land and slaves to work it. In the latter half of the 18th century, 36

Anglican ministers took the oath and were licensed to preach in Jamaica. There were still no church buildings in the island's smaller towns, even in the 1780s, but services were held. In his last years, in 1785, Thomas Thistlewood joined the Anglican worshippers in Savanna la Mar once or twice and reported that half the congregation was black. Many masters turned a blind eye to African attendance at Anglican services. Since their presence did not imply any questioning of the vast disparities of power and wealth amongst the black and white members of their congregation in Jamaica, the authorities tolerated these black church-goers.

Curiously, Jamaican ministers were often Scots converts to the Anglican faith. According to a contemporary church survey, one minister working in the wilds of Westmorland had been banished by the Presbyterian congregation in London for lewdness and intemperance. Since his move to the Church of England and Jamaica, it was reported that he was 'not much' mended in his ways. A second, James Spence, from Aberdeen, was thought 'not so regular in his life as he ought to be'. He was reduced to preaching in his own home with seldom more than family to hear him. Another Aberdonian, Mr White, was described as

> a poor, unhappy man, who lives, Salamander like,
> in the fire of contention with all man kind.[8]

His preaching, it was recorded, consisted of railing against Papists. His parishioners regularly petitioned the Governor to turn him out. The Codringtons were an English planter family of vast wealth, more renowned for their sexual exploits and high living than piety. They were responsible for a prolific number of mixed-race descendants in both Jamaica and Barbados over more than a century. In the early 1700s, the family left a small chunk of its considerable fortune to the Society for the Propagation of the Gospel in Foreign Parts. The family's bequest consisted of land and the far more valuable gift of over 200 slaves. Though it was said that the Codringtons had treated their slaves well, the Anglican Society used a branding iron to mark each of the hundreds of slaves with the word 'society'. The organisation appears to have lacked missionary zeal in propagating the gospel and made no conversions to Christianity in the West Indies beyond some of the people they enslaved. Admittedly, the Society were hampered by island legislation: what you did with your own slaves was up to you, but no one had a right to interfere in any way with other people's property. Education, Bible reading and church-going needed the permission of a slave's master.

Presbyterian Scots in Jamaica made no attempts to proselytise. They knew that their favoured religion was not, and never could be, compatible with slavery. There was no easy route into the Presbyterian faith. To be received into the Kirk, a person must study the Bible and establish a relationship with God for him or herself. Scots knew that slaves learning to read the book in English would be moved to question their situation. It is not surprising, therefore, that Scottish planters were wary of encouraging slaves to join them in their branch of Christian worship. It was left to the Wesleyans, Baptists and

Methodists to expound the Christian doctrine of the equality of all men. George Lisle (ca 1750–1828), a gifted African preacher, arrived in Jamaica from North America in 1782 and attracted large audiences to a chapel that had been built for him in Kingston. The Jamaican authorities turned a blind eye for a while, though planters complained that Lisle was a dangerous agitator.

The 'Address to the People of Scotland', sent out to ministers of religion in every corner of the country by the Edinburgh Committee in early 1792, ensured that many of the voices raised against slavery now came from ordinary members of Kirk congregations across Scotland.[9] The idea that captive Africans had a right to know God's word was gaining ground, and the idea that marriage and Bible reading would 'civilise' Africans had much more widespread acceptance. The debate about missionaries being sent to Jamaica now extended far beyond the church hierarchy in the Assembly of the Church of Scotland.

Planters saw no danger from the established church, but wanted the more radical branches of religion suppressed. As a result of the completely uncompromising attitude of members of the Jamaica Assembly, Lisle was chained, charged with seditious practices and thrown into prison. The Jamaican Assembly passed an Act in 1802 hardening its opposition to all but the Anglican religion. The Act made it illegal for all unestablished Christians to preach to slaves. Religious services by unauthorised persons, at unauthorised times, were prohibited. To offer religion to a slave without the consent of the slave's owner was not just unlawful, but seditious. Several ministers were imprisoned for continuing to conduct religious services. The town authorities closed the Wesleyan chapel, built on the Parade at Kingston, and Wesleyan worship was prohibited altogether from 1807 to 1815. These actions were received with anger and dismay by Christians at home in Britain. Thomas Coke, a Wesleyan, wrote angrily to the Secretary of State for the Colonies. He could not believe that the Christian country of Britain had allowed 400,000 slaves to be excluded from all public worship and from Christian instruction of any kind. A law excluding

> such a large body of the human race from all the means of salvation, was, I think, never passed before by any Legislature.[10]

To deny slaves access to religion fuelled more strident opposition to slavery, especially from the excluded churches. This further alerted slaves in Jamaica to the idea that Christians in Britain were on their side.

Scots in Jamaica argued that the Presbyterian religion was an established church in Britain and as such should, like the Anglican faith, be approved and properly funded by the state in Jamaica, just as it was at home. Assembly members disagreed, arguing that as Jamaica was a British island, not a Scottish one, it could not have two established churches. Finally, in 1819, the Jamaican Assembly, whilst it did not agree to establish the Presbyterian religion, did grant some funds which, together with money given by

wealthy merchant families in Scotland, allowed the Presby-
terians to complete and open the massive Scottish Kirk in
Kingston, with places for 1,000 people. By taking funds to
build the Kirk from an Assembly still implacably opposed
to encouraging Black Christianity, the Scottish Presbyteri-
ans were aligning themselves with the views of the Angli-
cans, that a slave could only access Christian services and
teaching with the permission of her master. Commercial
concerns overruled religious rights. There would therefore
be no mission to encourage slave attendance at the Kingston Kirk, no Bible education or preaching of ideas that
would disturb the planter class. It seemed unlikely therefore that any of the 1,000 places in the Kirk in Kingston
were ever filled by Black worshippers. Much later, in August
1830, the *Anti-Slavery Reporter* was still informing its
readers that,

> though members of the Scotch Kirk say they are
> not unfriendly to the religious instruction of slaves,
> in Kingston no slaves attend the ministry of the
> Rev Mr Wordie [the Kingston minister].[11]

Rev Peter Duncans, under oath to a Parliamentary Committee
investigating the suppression of religion on the island, repeated
this claim, saying of the Church of Scotland,

> there is only one in the island, and I have attended
> that frequently, but I never saw a slave there.[12]

The Scottish Church, however, gave considerable autonomy to its congregations, and not all of them were happy with the official view of the National Assembly of the Church of Scotland. Glasgow and Edinburgh Presbyteries decided to take matters into their own hands and set up their own missions to spread God's word. New generations of Scots planter families were inheriting Jamaican estates. Many of these families were less keen to settle in Jamaica. They preferred to enjoy their sugar wealth at home and leave their estates in the safe keeping of managers. They found themselves owners and beneficiaries of a system which denied a Christian education to their hundreds of captive workers, and they were exposed to a rising tide of criticism against this system at home. The more enlightened were supporters of improving slave lives through education, Christian marriage and family life. Whilst these planters did not want to risk their incomes, they were keen to make moves to improve the conditions of those they enslaved and to banish what they saw as ignorance and immorality from their estates. Circumventing the entrenched position of the National Assembly of the Church of Scotland, they approached sympathetic individuals and independent congregations to join them in funding missions to the slaves on their own estates. This move was unpopular with many of their planter neighbours, but it was well within their rights. By this means, the new generations avoided collision with the law on the island and the rulings of the Church Assembly in Scotland.

The Stirlings of Kier pioneered the process with funding help from James Stothert of Cargen, the outspoken defender of slavery, father and owner of the previously mentioned slave, Rebecca, left behind in Jamaica. In 1823, with absentee planter families bearing half the expense, a Mr Blyth became the first Presbyterian missionary to Jamaica from Scotland. He landed in February 1824 to begin to educate and convert a limited group of Africans owned by the Stirling family at Hampden plantation in Trelawny. As we shall see in the next chapter, this was a most difficult moment to begin his mission. 1823 was the year when anti-slavery activists had reorganised and shortly afterwards won a programme of reforms to the slave code at Westminster, which had been sent to the Jamaican Assembly with orders that it must be implemented. By 1824, a wave of determined resistance was sweeping the island's planters. Slaves, knowing that Britain had proposed reforms, were becoming openly rebellious, and planters were intent on rooting out any signs of trouble amongst them. Planters believed that missionaries were the cause of this growing unrest. Mr Blyth reported to his slave-owning benefactors that he was

> materially restricted in his labours, in common
> with other missionaries, in consequence of the per-
> secuting acts of the legislature of Jamaica.[13]

He was able to defend himself by telling them that he 'was sent by honourable characters to teach the slaves Christianity not rebellion'. In his reports to Scotland, Mr Blyth assured them that the Hampden slaves were not mixing with any 'troublemakers':

> the Managers of some estates forbade the negroes
> to assemble at night... knowing how danger-
> ous such meetings might be to the peace of the
> community.[14]

Mr Blyth 'readily advised the negroes' to obey the orders of their superiors in this matter.

CHAPTER 11
Anti-slavery campaign revived

*A property can only be made valuable in the West
Indies at the expense of injustice. It is labour
alone that gives value to land.*[1]

IN 1823, THE SCOTTISH newspapers printed claims that families were being overcharged for sugar. East Indian sugar growers had complained to Parliament that their sugar was being unfairly taxed to artificially raise its price and prevent it being cheaper than sugar from Jamaica. It was estimated that the public might be paying an extra £2 million altogether for the sugar in their tea. Adam Smith's view that market prices were fixed to subsidise slavery was now much quoted. Many years back, he had written in his *Wealth of Nations* that

> [n]othing but high prices can ever support the
> Slave Trade... their system of cultivation cannot
> exist unless the country is taxed to support it.[2]

It was argued that making slave sugar meet fair competition would force planters to adopt the more efficient system of paid labour. A comparison was made between a waged family who could live on a few shillings each week and a family in a parish workhouse whose keep cost a good deal more. Wages were more efficient. A level playing field for east and west would lead to savings for consumers, more children in better fed families in the colonies and improvements in the lives of Africans. The institution of slavery was now being attacked from a different perspective. The morals of slaves, white British people argued, could only be improved by the discipline of hard work. It was therefore supposed that strictly enforced paid work could be used to 'civilise' slaves and prepare them for an orderly freedom. This idea that Africans could keep up sugar production as paid workers greatly influenced thinking about slavery and breathed new life into the abolition campaign from a new point of view. A transition to wages and waged work seemed like a perfect solution.

There was one problem with this line of logic. Just as John Hamilton and his kinsmen dreamed of lives as landed gentlemen of leisure, surveying their parks and walled gardens at home in Scotland, Jamaican slaves had dreams as well. These dreams did not include long hours of forced hard work for their current masters. They could not return, like their Scottish owners, to their homeland. But memories of that homeland filled the stories told by their mothers and the music of their menfolk in their villages at night. The faraway Africa informed their dreams. Just like those who enslaved them, many Africans in Jamaica dreamed of the independence which came from a home and land of their own. Black Jamaicans had the skills to build their own houses. They were adept at growing their own food, and most had other marketable skills. The women were experts in raising pigs and fowls, producing eggs and growing vegetables. Land, a bit of skilled work to raise cash, some growing and selling, and the leisure to watch your children and garden grow were among the dreams of former slaves. Planters and overseers were determined to resist this possibility.

In the autumn and winter of 1822, a core group of abolitionists met in the Kings Head Tavern in London, and on 31 January 1823, the Society for the Mitigation and Gradual Abolition of Slavery throughout the British Dominions was formed. Thomas Clarkson and Zachary Macauley were both on the committee. The Society's agreed aim was to improve slave lives gradually and to prepare them for eventual freedom as waged labourers. Thomas Fowell Buxton, who had replaced the ageing Wilberforce in Parliament, planned to revive the campaign and introduce his first motion on slavery on 15 May 1823. He asked for petitions, but was aware that he faced a Parliament in which fear of public agitation and resistance to any attempt at social reform in the colonies was stronger than it had been for perhaps 15 years. In September, Zachary Macaulay wrote to 'old warriors of the slave trade campaign' to try to rebuild activities.[3] They needed funds and subscribing members in order to write and publish information. Macaulay was now editor of *The Christian Observer*. Through its columns, he sent out a rather stronger message than 'mitigation' and 'gradual' abolition. His robust views would receive a sympathetic response from Kirk members in Scotland. His message in the *Observer* was clear:

> Woe unto him that buildeth his house by unrighteousness, and his chambers by wrong; that useth his neighbour's service without wages, and giveth him not for his work... The time, we trust, is at length arrived... when they will no longer be

permitted to impede the progress of civilisation...
to stain the character of our country, and to outrage the Holy Religion by which we profess to be
guided.[4]

In the little time available, only 225 petitions were received in Westminster, and most of these came from Christian churches in Scotland. Some spoke of gradual change, but just as many contradicted the committee's strategy and demanded 'immediate' freedom. The Society for the Mitigation and Gradual Abolition of Slavery's campaign was satisfied; shortly afterwards, the Government formally accepted the need for 'ameliorating' the conditions of slavery. Their plan included slaves having time off to attend services on a Sunday, restrictions on punishments, and the encouragement of marriage and family life. The Government's rather sudden agreement sapped the efforts of abolition supporters, but Clarkson stressed that supporters must keep up the pressure to prevent the Government giving in to 'the Clamours and misrepresentations of the West India opposition'.[5]

The Glasgow and Edinburgh Committees divided the country between them. Dr Macgill, Professor of Theology at the University of Glasgow, chaired the Glasgow Committee. With fellow academics, he divided the west coast between different Committee members. Edinburgh organised sub-committees for correspondence, publication and finance and prepared to tackle the rest of the country. Soon afterwards, societies began meeting in Aberdeen, Dunfermline, Kirkcaldy and many more of Scotland's smaller towns. Together, they kept up the pressure. The Edinburgh Committee continued to collect signatures. *The Scotsman* of Wednesday 15 February 1826 carried a notice informing the public of all the local traders around the city who had petitions for signing.

> Negro Slavery, Petitions to Parliament for the Mitigation and Ultimate Abolition of Negro Slavery. Which must be forwarded this week to London. In order to give an opportunity to those who have not yet signed, it is still possible to do so. Copies of the Petition will lie at The Depository, South Street, Tile Tract Depository in Register Street, Messrs J. & J. M'Donald's Ironmongers 5, High Street, Mr David Brown Bookseller, South St and Andrew's Street, Messrs John Lindsay & Co Booksellers, South St and Andrew's Street. Mr A.W. M Jean, West Register Street, Cruickshank and Dollis Hosiers, 51 Jeburgh Street, Mr Samuel Hoppoton, Grocer, lawn Market, Messrs M.S. & \' Mountcastle Udt Manufacturers 1 Catherine street, Mr John Atkin's, Bookseller, 1 Anthony Place, near Union Canal.

Blackwood's Magazine, a monthly antidote to the more enlightened *Edinburgh Review*, was incensed that even though the Government had made a commitment to improvements, abolitionists were still pressing the issue. In an editorial on 'The West Indian Controversy', the editor argued that abolitionist societies were making unwarranted claims about slave conditions.

Is such conduct worthy of British statesmen? Are these restless, inconsistent, unreasonable mortals, the proper guides for the English mind?[6]

Zachary Macaulay was attacked as a man interfering in matters he was not qualified to understand fully:

nature and education have qualified him for vestry meetings and tavern dinners... rather than influencing the course of politics.

Their campaign, in the editor's opinion, threatened to

convert these [slaves] at once into a set of lawless banditti, revelling in blood... On every account, therefore, we are most anxious that Mr Wilberforce and his associations would be persuaded to pause.

The Scottish Association was not prepared to pause and was becoming frustrated with the lack of progress by the London Committee. The Duke of Manchester, now Governor of Jamaica*, had agreed in August 1823 that he would 'employ any influence' he had with 'leading gentlemen in the island' to persuade them to revise 'the slave code' to improve 'the conditions of the slave population'.[7] By the end of the year, the Governor informed the British Government that he was disappointed that the slave owners were more reluctant 'to part with power over the slave than might have been expected'. The Governor felt that he had done everything he could. He sent private correspondence to Britain

* Governor from 1808 to 1827.

complaining that he had 'never witnessed a more tedious and unpleasant session' or one more disposed 'to violence and trick' in the face of attempts to get the Assembly to turn the eight British proposals sent out to Jamaica into a new slave code.[8] There were many sticking points. Freedom for slaves to attend church services in particular proved to be absolutely unacceptable to Assembly members.

When Parliament met in February 1824, abolitionists had been dismayed that the King's speech did not include any mention of the promised action to reform slave conditions. Several newspapers, including the *Inverness Courier* of 1 April 1824, printed the full text of an address by the Earl of Bathurst, Secretary of State for the Colonies, to the House of Lords in which he had explained what had happened to the agreed reforms. The noble Earl read out the resolutions passed:

> for the due observation of the Sabbath among the slaves... for the abolition of the use the whip... to abolish flogging of female slaves... the infliction of punishment contrary to judicial order... means for the encouragement of marriage... regulation with respect to the sale of slaves... security for slave property... facilitating the manumission of slaves... admitting slave evidence under certain restrictions.

He reported that the Jamaican Assembly had been utterly opposed to and voted against all of these proposed regulations. The Assembly opted to bring back and tinker with their own amended bill on slavery, which had been passed two years before. Bathurst was of the opinion that this Jamaican bill 'by no means agreed' with the resolutions of the British Government.[9]

Blackwood's Magazine was not wrong in linking the campaign in Britain to restless slaves in Jamaica, where 15,000 whites were now vastly outnumbered by the 335,000 Africans. In Jamaica, news was gathered by those transporting goods to and from ports and jetties. House slaves picked up on newspaper reports discussed in planter homes. Intelligence was relayed from plantation to plantation via markets, late night meetings and community dances. Songs, news and rumours passed quickly around the island. Out of sight of their overseers, gossip travelled amongst the enslaved population. British talk of improving conditions and Jamaican Assembly discussion about the impossibility of shorter hours and extra days off were all known in the African community. Slaves were also well aware of the entrenched resistance to any kind of reform amongst their white masters. Away from overseers and the prying eyes of white owners, slaves were talking. Their owners knew that slaves were aware of the planters' resistance to granting them greater rights and freedoms. Slave owners feared that slaves were sharing oaths to work together to resist their masters. The name of Wilberforce and his campaign for abolition were famed among the enslaved Africans. Slave songs of freedom were now openly sung on the island. On his tour of Jamaica in 1823, Cynric Williams wrote that he had heard a group of slave women in Jamaica singing,

> Hi! De Buckra*, hi! Mass Wilberforce da come
> ober de sea, Wid him roguish beard and him ten-
> der look, And while he palaver and preach him

---

* Patois for 'master' or 'boss man'.

book, At the negro girl he'll winkie him eye, Hi!
De Buckra, hi![10]

Another popular song with a more aggressive tone was also
doing the rounds:

> Oh me good friend Mr Wilberforce mek we free,
> God Almighty thank ye! God Almighty thank ye!
> Buckra in dis country no mek we free! Wa negro fe
> do? Wa negro te do? Tek force wid force. Tek force
> wid force![11]

Slave overseers were faced with the appearance of calm among
the enslaved, but they knew this peace would not last. Overseers began a concerted campaign to root out all possible 'troublemakers' with the hope of preventing the spread of a slave
revolt. They searched for disaffection amongst their slaves by
using violence and intimidation to extract witness statements
and prosecuted reports of slave conspiracy, real or imagined.
Local courts heard a continuous stream of so-called evidence,
of oaths to kill made in secret places out of sight behind sheds,
near cattle pens and in the slave villages at night, of supposed
plans to burn down white homes and fields, discussed and
resolved upon at dances and markets. Evidence given to court
in Savanna la Mar on 9 October 1823 by the bookkeeper at
Caledonia estate in Westmoreland claimed he had

> heard a negro complain of they're having Satur-
> day stopped... when another said, never mind, they
> would soon have Friday also.[12]

Such stories unsettled a community of overseers already unnerved by the series of uprisings discussed in chapter 9. All the presumed ring leaders of these real and imagined revolts were hanged or deported to neighbouring slave islands.

In the summer of 1823, planter fears were heightened when, in mid-July, a revolt broke out on the Argyle estate of resident Scottish slave owner John Malcolm. He was undoubtedly a relative of the original Malcolms, now more grandly styled 'of Poltalloch' in Argyll. John Malcolm lived on the estate with his slave wife, five children and 244 slaves. The 249 enslaved people on neighbouring Golden Grove, which was managed by another Scotsman, William Miller, for a Mr Hudson, joined them. These two slave groups had shared their plans with a third estate, Alexandria, which had been jointly owned by John Alexander and Donald McIntosh, but had recently been sold following McIntosh's death. The resistance began on a Sunday night with the burning of the trash houses on Alexandria and Golden Grove estates.* Mary Wyllie, of Golden Grove, testified at the subsequent trial that

> [o]n Sunday night William Downer brought news
> to John Clarke that everybody did fight; that Argyle
> negroes did fight, and that Alexandria negroes had
> set fire to the Golden Grove trash-house.[13]

Testimonies revealed that the slaves had plotted together. William Roach of Argyle estate claimed that a man from Golden Grove came one day to check when the Argyle people were

---

*The remains of the crushed sugar canes were dried and kept as fuel for the boilers; the residues of sugar made a very hot fire.

going to fight. According to Rachel Crooks, another enslaved witness, she passed by Argyle after dinner on the Tuesday and saw one of the Argyle men shake hands with a man called George Reid from Golden Grove. When the militia arrived to put down the rebellion, all the Africans ran into the hillside forests, from which they held out for some time by making sporadic attacks on the well-armed troops. The revolutionary spirit was only finally suppressed by the appearance of a Major General commanding a large and well-armed detachment of the 92nd regiment. This show of strength promptly ensured most of the insurgents on Argyle Estate returned to order, but the revolt continued on Golden Grove and Alexandria, other properties in Hanover and in some parts of St Elizabeth. Three of the freedom fighters from Argyle refused to return to the estate. Governor Manchester reported that these three, John Clarke, John Miller, and Ben Reynolds, killed themselves, stating that they preferred to die as free men rather than be captured and killed as slaves. The court in the town of Lucea tried 11 men from Argyle estate and seven from Golden Grove. They executed 13. At the request of John Malcolm, the court decreed that the 11 men from Argyle should be hanged publicly in John Malcolm's Mill Yard. There were horrible scenes as the brave Argyle slaves attempted to rescue their fellow captives. Two men from Golden Grove were hanged in the market place in the town of Lucea, an action intended to terrify remaining slaves and force them into submission.

Governor Manchester was utterly frustrated that he could not persuade the Jamaican Assembly to implement the new slave code. He recognised that the slaves were not entirely ignorant of his struggle with their masters. Slaves knew they now had rights that were being denied. The new code had been agreed by the British Parliament and sent to Jamaica in the King's name. The Governor wrote to his superior in London expressing his frustration. Bathurst, Secretary of State for the Colonies, was no radical, but he was a lawyer and ultra-loyal to the king. He had personally sent out the circular demanding the colonies improved slave conditions and expected the King's clear instructions to be obeyed. Governor Manchester relayed to Bathurst a graphic account of what had happened on Argyle, Golden Grove and the neighbouring estates, quoting the words of the black men who had died for their rights in full:

> the Negroes belonging to the property Golden Grove were with difficulty restrained from interfering with the execution of the convicts. All those executed were fully impressed with the belief that they were entitled to their freedom and that the cause they had embraced was just and in vindication of their own rights.[14]

The question of rights for slaves was not about to go away any time soon. As he said in his letter,

> one of the Golden Grove ringleaders declared at the place of execution that the revolt was not subdued... the war had only begun.

He added that one of the Argyle men who killed himself had said on his death bed that

though it was in vain to contend against the power
of the whites, he was satisfied that he was at that
moment a free man.

He also, according to the Governor, forgave his master.
Although John Clarke, John Miller, Ben Reynolds and the
unnamed 11 gained nothing from the revolt against their masters, they did gain a lot of respect from their community. They
chose to die as free men, they spoke bravely of the continued
fight for rights and justice and they called on their fellow slaves
to continue the war, even as they went to their deaths. They
were remembered by the surviving slaves: 'Argyle' became a
byword for resistance.

When news reached Britain that planters were using hearsay and rumour in the courts to convict slaves and execute them
on scant evidence, questions were raised in the House of Commons. A substantial article publicising the debate was printed
in the columns of the *Perthshire Courier* on 9 March 1826. Mr
Denman, Irish MP, had called the

attention of the House to the subject of the administration of justice to negro slaves in the island Jamaica.
It was known to the House, that there were
four sets of trials in Jamaica, during the years
1823 and 1824. The first case was in the parish
St Mary, and its date was December 16, 1823. In
that instance, the hearsay evidence of one Roberts,
a butcher, who merely stated words spoken to him
by a negro slave, not more than sixteen years of

age, produced the conviction and death of eight persons, who all protested their innocence up to the moment of their execution. They had been seized together, tried together, and together were executed. Was this consistent with justice? Would it not have been proper to have separated them, to have examined each individual, to have collated his answers, in order to elicit the truth? Yet no such thing had been done.

The honourable and learned member, after alluding to one or two similar cases, moved the following resolution:

That this House, having taken into their consideration the accounts laid before them of the judicial proceedings in Jamaica, the trials of slaves for rebellious conspiracy, and other offences, in the years 1823 and 1824 deem it their duty to express, in the strongest terms, the sorrow and indignation with which they contemplate the perversion of law, and violation of justice displayed in those trials; they deeply lament precipitation with which sentence death, wholly unwarranted proof, was in several instances carried into execution; and they cannot refrain from declaring their conviction of the necessity of an immediate and effectual reform in the administration of criminal justice affecting slaves in that Island.

The Fife Herald reported on the same day, 9 March 1826, that,

> the great question of Negro Slavery occupied the
> House of Commons on Wednesday night... F Bux-
> ton called upon his Majesty's Ministers to explain
> what they meant by a gradual extinction of Slav-
> ery. Three years had already elapsed since that
> expression had been used, and with the exception
> of a few trivial improvements in some of our colo-
> nies, the main evil still remained untouched.

Mr Secretary Canning replied that 'Parliament was working
towards abolition by slow, gradual, cautious, and, if possible,
safe means.' He was desirous of seeing how 'that pledge could
be redeemed without direct interference on our part.' Secretary
Canning continued,

> We observe that Mr Hume, speaking of free labour
> in the West Indies [he was referring here to the free
> labour introduced in Trinidad] says, that the exper-
> iment has not been successful. It is not likely that
> it should in countries... where, by very little labour,
> an individual may subsist himself... recourse must
> be had to compulsory labour... A property can only
> be made valuable in the West Indies at the expense
> of injustice. It is labour alone that gives value to
> land... there is such abundance of fertile land in
> the Island, that millions of people could live with

ease... and therefore no human beings would be
such fools as to work for us unless compelled.

The Anti-Slavery Society and the Government continued to
hope that gradual negotiation with the West Indies would produce results. Behind the scenes, the issue was being passed backwards and forwards across the Atlantic in a prolific exchange
of letters. But times had now changed; a vocal and organised
section of the British public, angry at Westminster's utter lack
of accountability, expected answers about what had happened
to the legislation which had been passed by the house and
why had it not been implemented across the British Colonies,
particularly in the island of Jamaica. Parliament could not or
would not provide these answers. By December 1830, Governor Belmore in Jamaica (who had replaced Manchester) finally
wrote to London

with deep regret... to acquaint you that the Slave
Bill which had been introduced into the House was
thrown out on the second reading by a majority of
24 to 16,

and by March 1831 that 'the measures proposed for the consideration of the Assembly', despite being 'sanctioned under
the authority of the King's name', raised such 'intemperate discussions' that there was 'no hope of they're obtaining consideration at least during, the present session'.[15]

CHAPTER 12

A general uprising of slaves

*I would rather die upon yonder gallows than live my
life in slavery.*[1]

IN 1823, CYNRIC WILLIAMS, defender of the white community
in Jamaica, wrote:

> It becomes a serious matter for the whites to
> think of emancipating their slaves when they con-
> sider that a few hours work daily, for only a few
> weeks in the year, would enable a negro to bring
> up a family, though blacky would rather his wife,
> or wives, should work for him, while he smokes
> his pipe.[2]

There was some truth in what he said insofar as slaves had
mostly fed themselves by working their provision grounds on
their one day off. With a little more time of their own, they could
feed themselves well and still have time to spend with their friends
and family. The wealth of the white man in Jamaica was his slaves
and only his slaves. They were worth hundreds of thousands of
pounds. An approximate combined value for slaves in Jamaica
was estimated in the reports presented to Parliament during
debate on the issue. At that time, this came to the colossal sum

of £6,996,915.25* based on an average price of £21.88** per enslaved person, which was a rather low estimate. Without these valuable enslaved men and women forced to work it, the land in the hands of Jamaican planters was absolutely worthless. The fearful vision of the white man with no enslaved workers was matched by a joyous expectation amongst his captives. Free life could be simple, leisurely and secure. They had the practical skills to make an independent living. They were the experts in hoeing and planting tropical soils. Control over what they did would allow for time to swing in their hammocks, smoke their pipes, play their banjos, breast feed their babies whenever they cried and watch their children grow. Freedom meant leisure they had never known.

Cynric continued,

> Those Christians who have signed petitions for emancipating slaves should reflect on the fact that the wealth of the rich, in the colonies, is slaves secured to them in the first place by the laws of England; and that to tamper with... these slaves must produce alarm, consternation and hatred in the minds of their owners, mingled with no small portion of indignation at what they consider ignorance and presumption on the part of the Reformers... If slaves could be induced to work for wages for eight or nine hours,

---

* An approximate combined value for the slaves in Jamaica, estimated from reports presented to Parliament during debate on the 'Amelioration of the condition of the slave population in the West Indies'.

** Extrapolated from figures for the number of slaves in Jamaica and average prices given at that time. Available at www.statista.com.

for six days out of seven, emancipation could be contemplated... But how would they feel in Britain... if
landowners were forced, by the influence of religious
zealots to pass an agrarian law to give such privileges
to the very lowest class.[3]

The Caledonian Mercury relayed similar sentiments to the people of Glasgow in a letter received from a gentleman from Aberdeen, currently living in Jamaica, published in October 1823:

At the time I am now writing, we are on the eve
of absolute ruin, it is unavoidable. How will it end,
God alone knows. You will have heard how the
Government at home has interfered with our internal legislation, and how those in power here have
complied with their regulations about the negroes;
but their compliance has done us no good, for we
have had evil upon evil, and vexation upon vexation, heaped upon our heads, and the grossest and
most unfounded calumny repeated against us, under
which we have tamely sat down; and now, to crown
the whole, orders have come out, that the whole
negro population are to be emancipated, which is
only taking our whole property from us, and turning loose a set of half savages, who will soon deso-
late the island, and leave the marks of blood and fire
wherever they go; what is our lands if we have no
hands to cultivate them?[4]

Archibald Alison, the popular historian and a lead writer for
Blackwood's Magazine, joined the chorus of Scottish voices

defending white Jamaica. Britain was destroying her Empire and with it her prosperity, he thundered. He was particularly angered by interfering missionaries. In time, he said, slavery could civilise Africans, who were fortunate to have been rescued from barbarism. They 'needed European authority to discipline and improve them'. He reminded his readers that in the Caribbean, 'passions are more violent' than 'under a cloudy northern sky'. He insisted,

> We have the interests of negroes at heart... we do not love slavery... but without developing the habits of industry the appeal to religion was deranged.[5]

The loss of the American Colonies was a very expensive humiliation for the British Government. They were now particularly sensitive to any action which might provoke the same result among the planter and merchant class in Jamaica. Alison was an effective and popular writer for the pro-slavery propaganda war in Scotland. When he repeated myths about Africans, proclaimed that slaves were 'incapable of understanding what freedom is' and complained of '[i]gnorant and fanatical missionaries in the West Indies' in danger of provoking uprisings and a repeat of the American war of independence, he knew that his words would strike a chord both in Scotland and in Westminster.

Undeterred, Scotland's religious networks were reaching out beyond the cities to small town, island and rural communities. The Church of Scotland kept up its pressure on the Westminster government, with Merse and Teviotdale, Lothian and Tweeddale Synods, and the Presbyteries of Edinburgh, Paisley and Selkirk petitioning Parliament in 1830. But the largest number of religious petitions now came from the United Secessional Church, a group which had left the established church because it was particularly opposed to the role played by wealthy landowners in local decision-making. Buxton, the abolitionist's parliamentary spokesperson, noted that 2,200 of the 2,600 petitions now presented to Parliament in November and December 1830 were signed by non-conformist congregations. Many insisted that slaves had an absolute right to Christian teaching, that withholding religion was 'unworthy of a nation that bears the Christian name'. They expressed concern that the bonds of marriage and family were not respected, nor was 'the Sabbath day' with 'its hallowed sanctity' and 'peaceful repose'.[6] The accountability of the British government was now at issue. Under great pressure from the public, new rights for the enslaved populations in the colonies had been agreed upon by Parliament seven years previously; they must now be enforced in Jamaica without delay. Parliament continued to be deluged by thousands of petitions signed by one and a half million Britons, yet the Jamaican Assembly was still denying the right of the British Parliament to interfere in the internal affairs of the island. It was pretending to amend the slave code, but was in fact putting together a bill to make it illegal for anyone, apart from those of the established Anglican religion, to be paid for giving any kind of religious instruction to slaves. The bill would have been passed had the Governor not vetoed the possibility. When he pointed out that he simply could not allow this, the assemblymen became openly defiant.

Scotland continued to collect funds to send Presbyterian ministers across the Atlantic. The estates of Hampden and

Dundee and the little settlement of Falmouth in the parish of Trelawney, which looked down over Montego Bay, became their centre. In 1828, a handsome stone church was opened on the Hampden estate, owned by the Stirling family of Kier. It was built by the family with the help of a great number of small subscriptions from Christians in Scotland. A Rev James Watson arrived and began work at nearby Lucea. He extended his Bible groups to Green Island, a small harbour town further west, and began to contact sympathetic partners amongst the planters who might allow Bible classes and a church on their land. Zachary Macauley reported on their progress in the columns of the *Anti-Slavery Reporter* and publicised the growing number of attacks on black Christians to congregations at home. His readers were incensed to learn that thousands of the faithful were being persecuted for learning about God from the Bibles and preachers Scottish Christians had sent to Jamaica. One notorious story involved a Reverend Bridges, appointed in 1817 to the Anglican Church in Mandeville, Jamaica, at a salary of £500. His activities led to questions in Parliament. He was the author of a pamphlet making a vicious attack on Wilberforce and was virulently opposed to non-conformist missionaries. Vicars of the established religion had always been paid a fixed fee by the Government for each baptism they conducted. They were now under pressure from their paymasters to show that they were encouraging black access to their churches. Bridges would fulfil his obligation to encourage black Christians by requesting that planters assemble their slaves in front of the master's great house, allowing him to stand on the veranda and earn handsome fees by baptising a whole crowd altogether. He processed thousands in this way. When a local Bible class led by a Baptist teacher called Henry Williams refused to attend Bridge's Anglican service, the Reverend, who was also a magistrate, had him severely flogged and sent to the workhouse.

Despite massive petitioning in Britain, there was no visible progress towards the implementation of the resolutions passed by Westminster in 1823 to give access to religion, outlaw inhuman punishments and reform slave family life. In answer to parliamentary questions about what had happened to these resolutions to improve slave rights, the Government simply announced that it was doing what it could. Elizabeth Heyrick (1789–1831), a member of the Society of Friends and a leader of women abolitionists, had visited all of Leicester City's grocers, urging them not to stock slave-grown sugar. In her opinion, which she expressed forcefully, West Indian planters were people thieves; buying their sugar was tantamount to receiving stolen goods. Freedom could and should be granted right now, she wrote in her pamphlet 'Immediate, not Gradual Abolition' in 1824.[7] The abolitionist society was persuaded to distribute 1,500 copies of Elizabeth's views for discussion. Women were important donors and fund raisers. When abolitionist women, delegates to the conference in Birmingham criticised the society, saying that they had 'shown a great deal too much politeness and accommodation towards these gentlemen [the planters]' and threatened to withdraw their funding, the conference took note.[8] In May 1830, the Anti-Slavery Society finally agreed to drop the words 'gradual abolition' from its title and support the women's plan to campaign for an immediate end to slavery. The Rev Andrew Thomson (1779–1831) was well-known in Edinburgh as an outspoken voice from the more radical, evangelical wing of the Church of Scotland.[9] His call for Scotland to support freedom for colonial slaves immediately, took place at a public meeting in Edinburgh on 8 October 1830. 'There should be no more waiting', he insisted; enemies of emancipation would always claim that 'the earliest practicable period' was sometime 'in the future'.[10] There was pandemonium in the hall following his intervention, with many arguing just as vehemently that immediate emancipation would be 'highly injurious to the mother country'. The meeting broke up in disarray. However, a packed recall meeting a few days later voted overwhelmingly in his favour. The people of Edinburgh did not doubt Thomson was right; 22,000 signed a public petition demanding an immediate end to slavery, and a Ladies Society was formed from the many interested women.

Enslaved people knew that non-conformist Christians in Britain thought slavery was immoral and must be ended. The knowledge that radical Christians recognised them as thinking, feeling, fully human beings drew slaves towards such preachers and their message. Jamaican slave owners thought they could see a 'visible alteration' in slave behaviour and were afraid of what it might mean. An editorial in the Jamaican *St Jago Gazette* of July 1830 talked of

> mischievous misrepresentations on the part of the Missionary preachers... every sectarian must now be considered as a spy in the land... every man who has the least regard for the peace and welfare of the Colony will now watch them as enemies, and be slow to encourage them.

The Jamaican newspaper *The Watchman* agreed that

> twenty-three years experience and the visible alteration in the manners and habits of the slaves within the last ten years, teach me that these dissenting preachers will, inevitably, bring the country to ruin, especially if their most improbable calumnies are countenanced by the highest authorities in the state.[11]

The white population held a series of heated anti-abolitionist protest meetings organised by the Colonial Church Union, formed to oppose the spread of non-conformist faiths and led by the notorious defender of mass baptisms, Reverend Bridges. Slaves watched and waited. They knew that only one thing would make white men so angry. Freedom must be coming.

December was harvest time, when slaves worked all day and half the night to cut and process the sugar cane. Christmas

Day 1831 was a Sunday and a holiday. On Monday, slaves were sent back to work. But on Tuesday, they downed tools and refused to go to the fields. Instead, they set out to hold their own protest meetings to non-violently declare their claim to a better life; to demand some of the rights that Westminster had granted to them and the Jamaican Assembly had successfully resisted. All over the island, slaves stopped work to protest their inhuman conditions. Bible class secretaries and deacons supported the protests. Samuel Sharpe was a slave preacher at the Baptist church in Montego Bay, which had been welcoming black members for some years. Sharpe was widely known and respected around the island because he travelled about giving Bible lessons. He was said to have led the striking slaves and encouraged a peaceful demonstration to protest inhumane working conditions and claim the right to freely choose where and how to worship. Black protesters were quickly confronted by armed white militias determined to force them back to work, but the patience of the enslaved population had reached its limits. The protest quickly spread, with slaves setting fire to sugar works to alert their neighbours that the moment had come to get out and fight for their rights. Bands of slaves left work and protested all over the island. The planter militias were soon fighting a general uprising. An estimated 60,000 slaves joined what had become a battle. White men called in regular British Government troops stationed on the island, along with extra help from the navy and the Maroons.

On the night of 28 December, the Scottish minister at Hampden, Mr Blyth, looked down towards the coast from the handsome church at Hampden. Though peace prevailed on the Dundee and Hampden estates, he counted 16 sugar works 'lighting up the sky with the fires which laid them in ruins.' He went on to report that '[t]hroughout half the island' there was 'a general rising of the slaves'.[12] The protesters held out for several days before most slaves realised they could not win against vast numbers of well-armed troops. Some fled to the mountains, but many eventually went back to their estates and surrendered. They successfully killed 14 whites in the fighting, but more than 500 slaves were slaughtered by planter militias and troops. The Jamaican government hanged many of the slave leaders, including Sam Sharpe, in 1832. When faced with death, he was reputed to have said, 'I would rather die upon yonder gallows than live my life in slavery'. He was one of over 300 who were executed, many for minor offences such as theft. Thousands were flogged. The planters, always keeping a keen eye on their profit and loss, estimated that the property destroyed was worth £667,000. The Governor was well aware of the role that white-led militias were playing in unlawful reprisals and the danger of the British State losing control to these bands of white vigilantes in the island. He ordered the militias to be disbanded, but many planters refused to obey. They were intent on venting their anger at the destruction of their property by roaming the island, demolishing dozens of Baptist and Wesleyan chapels and terrorising their pastors. They menaced and threatened the Scottish Presbyterian missionaries and offered bribes. If the missionaries would join the Colonial Union and abide by the rules of the established church, allow no Bible reading by slaves and engage in no talk of all being equal in God's eyes, the white vigilante groups would promise Scots Kirks in every parish. When this ultimatum failed, Hampden church was only saved from destruction by the bravery of members of the congregation. Mr Watson, minister for Lucea, was imprisoned in his house by a mob of angry white men throwing stones, then forced to do military duty by the local magistrate. Rev Simpson, Presbyterian minister at Green Island, was dragged before magistrates, falsely accused, assaulted and threatened.

Rev Bridges now began to use the Colonial Church Union to form vigilante groups amongst the planters. The inaugural meeting of Trelawney Colonial Union in July 1832 was called by Alexander Campbell, and another Campbell, John, took the chair. A Mr Johnson, their Campbell son-in-law, joined the committee. Leading members of the Grant family had retired to estates in Banff with their proceeds from Bunce Island slave fort, but family members Alex and Peter Grant, managing their eight local plantations, also volunteered for the committee along with a McDowell family member and John Napier, a mulatto son of Glasgow merchants, the Oswalds, who was no doubt managing their estate. A Mr Dickinson, who joined them, was also likely to be one of their countrymen. All were now in outright revolt against the British Government represented by the Governor and the rights granted to slaves by the British Parliament. The Trelawney Colonial Union resolved 'not to permit any sectarian Missionary to disseminate their Doctrines in this parish' and to 'pledge ourselves to support the same to the utmost of our ability'.[13]

The uprising of enslaved people claiming their entitlement to basic rights and their inevitable confrontation with slave owners who refused to grant those rights became known as 'The Baptist War'; a misnomer intended to place responsibility for the destruction of property on the non-conformist religious authorities and to obscure the question of the rights planters and slave owners had denied. It was a turning point. The planters were obviously not prepared to compromise. As *The Scotsman* later reported, these actions of the white population proved, if such proof was still needed, the 'impossibility of continuing the slave system'.[14] The British Government would have to act to impose the legal rights granted almost ten years previously which had been so brutally denied.

The abolition of slavery was not the only public agitation for reform happening in Britain in the early years of the 19th century. After a long campaign, Parliament passed legislation to change the British electoral system in June 1832. The Great Reform Act widened the franchise to allow a limited number of middle classes voters. This was enough to break up the old Tory political machine in Scotland. The vast majority of those returned to Westminster from Scotland in the election of 1832 were Liberals. Only the Oswalds, Hope Johnstones,

Hays and Erskine Wemyss from the old familiar families with Jamaican connections now sat in the House of Commons. However, many still held power as landed gentlemen in the House of Lords, from which a rearguard action would now be fought. Lord St Vincent reminded his noble friends in June 1833 that

> it was of great importance that this country should
> have the co-operation of the colonial authorities

in any actions it now took.[15] He warned that any government plan to abolish slavery would need the agreement and cooperation of the Jamaican Assembly. He also reminded the Lords of a fundamental difficulty. Encouraging slaves to work long hours for money was highly unlikely in a fertile country, where

> one day's work was sufficient to supply the negro
> with the means of subsistence for a week.

The Earl of Rippon emphasised that Parliament could not withdraw 'that species of property [slaves]... without giving full compensation'. The Duke of Wellington reminded the Lords of the cost of lost revenues,

> £5,000,000 in sugar taxes which the British public
> would now have to find if production dropped.

The Bill that finally emerged from these discussions at Westminster was not what the British public had fought for or expected. The freed slaves would continue to receive some rations from their employer and keep their provision grounds but,

> All Persons who on the 1st August 1834 shall have been registered as Slaves, and shall appear on the Registry to be Six Years old or upwards, shall from that Day become apprenticed Labourers.

Slaves would not be wholly free until 1 August 1838. In return, the Jamaican slave owners would be compensated for their loss of 311,071 slaves with payments eventually totalling £5,853,975. According to the missionaries at Hampden, on the last night in July 1834,

> where there were churches, they were filled with grateful worshippers, who kneeled before God as at the stroke of midnight they entered into liberty. On the mountain tops they welcomed, with shouts of praise, the rising of the sun that shone on a free people. Again in the forenoon they crowded the church services of thanksgiving. Thereafter many of them, with a fine courtesy, paid their respects to their former masters and overseers.[16]

In Scotland, *The Scotsman* newspaper congratulated the abolitionists by advertising

An elegant well executed cheap medal with the figure of a Negro, with rays of light descending upon him his head being lifted up towards heaven in expressive gratitude. In his uplifted hands are pieces of the broken chain and the words: A record of the Extinction of Colonial Slavery in the Reign of William IV August 1834.[17]

CHAPTER 13

Learning to become wage labourers?

Had the planters and slave-owners done that for
which twenty-million was bestowed on them?[1]

WHEN SLAVERY WAS FINALLY outlawed across the British colonies, the law required freed slaves to remain as paid employees on their master's estate. The 'apprenticeship', as the Government termed this period of learning to be waged labourers, was supposed to last for five years and was understandably deeply resented by black Jamaicans. Planters remained determined to force the supposedly free black Jamaicans to work all the hours the plantation required. They were also determined to hold down wages. Meagre payments were clawed back by imposing rents for housing and provision grounds on many estates. Long hours were now necessary to earn enough to survive, leaving less time available to grow vital provisions. The apprenticeship legislation transferred the power to punish from masters to local magistrates. A system of workhouses replaced the master's whip. Since magistrates were mostly planters, the new justice regime looked in many ways much like the old one. The public in Scotland was disturbed by vivid descriptions of a newly introduced and widely used punishment, the poorly constructed treadmill which was accompanied by floggings. The anti-slavery public felt that it had been duped into paying compensation to planters with little benefit to former slaves. The *Inverness Courier* of November 1838 reported,

> attorneys, are so long accustomed to tyranny and oppression, we believe that an early attempt will be made to deprive the peasantry of their provision grounds... that they will not be permitted even to rent them; so that, by producing starvation... a lower rate of wages may be enforced.[2]

No other colony was quite as hostile to its freed slaves as Jamaica. The Assembly brought in harsh vagrancy laws. Planters took the introduction of paid work as an opportunity to stop buying food and clothing, though British legislation specifically forbade this. News of severe punishments for apprentices' minor offences, such as 'taking too long to feed a baby', were relayed to the British public.

When Mr Fowell Buxton (1786–1845) stood up in the House of Commons on 19 June 1835, he expected and received considerable opposition. He was anxious that no part of the massive 20 million pounds set aside to compensate slave owners should be handed over until it was established that planters in the West Indies had kept their side of the abolition bargain. 'Had the planters and slave-owners done that for which 20 million was bestowed on them?' he asked. He went on to answer his own question, armed with truths that were becoming much better known. The lived reality of apprentice lives, by the 18-year-old William James, a Jamaican apprentice, had now been published and circulated in Britain. In Jamaica, Buxton contended, a former slave,

> walking along the high road, in his own time... was an offender liable to punishment... he was undoubtedly a criminal if he should visit his own wife on a neighbouring estate... his wife, his daughter, his sister, may at the pleasure of the overseer of a plantation... be subject to corporal punishment upon their bare persons.

He gave an example from many he had collected:

> Ann Mahon, a girl of fifteen years of age, had given offence to her master, who had taken improper liberties with her, which she resented. Her master in consequence accused her of not watering the garden properly... took her round the waist, and carried her to the mango tree, where, assisted by two men, each holding a hand of the girl, he, after unbuttoning her frock, and taking off her handkerchief, proceeded to flog her.[3]

Fowell Buxton wanted a Select Committee to inquire into whether the law which freed slaves was working as intended. The abolition legislation protected planters, sugar estates and the merchant houses that had lent them thousands by attempting to preserve the workforce and delaying African freedom for five years. But it did not necessarily protect the African labourers who would be paid wages for which no rates were set and tied them to working for their former masters. In return, during this time referred to as an 'apprenticeship', black men and women were supposed to have customary access to the grounds provided for growing their food. In addition, they were to receive medical attention and clothing as before. Most contentiously for those used to total control over those they enslaved, there was to be no whipping or flogging, and outside of set working hours, the former system of tickets – without which a slave could not leave a plantation – was abolished. A former slave must continue to work for her master but, in theory at least, she was free to live and move around as she wished.

Fowell Buxton did not get the Select Committee he wanted. But in 1837, Joseph Sturge and other Christian friends went to Jamaica to enquire for themselves. They toured the island talking to Christians, former slaves, planters, magistrates and overseers. From Westmorland, it was reported

> that the apprentices have conducted themselves in the most tranquil and peaceable manner, and have shown every disposition to be industrious where encouragement has been afforded to them by fair and equitable remuneration.[4]

They met a Thomas McNeed who had many estates under his care. Altogether, he was responsible for 4,000 'apprentices'. McNeed told them that planter fears had been unfounded; the free black Jamaicans were not giving him any trouble, and people were willing to remain on the plantations and work for wages. He also informed them that he had bought seven slaves for £9 each in 1833 and received £20 in compensation for each one upon their emancipation.

In a detailed report, Sturge and his group despaired that a fair society could be brought about by the participation of 'the present race of white residents'. He declared that the apprenticeship system was a 'mockery of freedom'.[5] Sturge found many instances of brutal and arbitrary punishment. From his discussions with groups of former slaves, he concluded that there was no realistic way to ensure that 'apprentice' workers were treated fairly on isolated plantations. The pressures for excessive overwork to keep up sugar incomes remained. This was especially true when more and more planters had deserted the island, leaving overseers in charge who were paid a percentage of crop results and thus had every reason to pressure their workers to keep production up to former levels. These levels had always been achieved through coercion. Sturge noted work continuing late into the evening despite heavy rain and supposed regulation of the working day:

> We passed midway on our journey by Glasgow estate, belonging to R. Wallace MP for Greenock, and observed the gangs of negroes still at work in the fields.

Sturge visited the workhouse in Savanna la Mar where he saw,

76 prisoners, sent out to daily labour, both sexes
in chains, all had heavy iron collars, among them
three females with infants at the breast committed
to hard labour.[6]

Each prisoner was being punished for mundane transgres-
sions, 'one for having 3 pints of sugar, another for quarrelling
with a sister.' He noted, 'past sufferings inscribed on their
backs [they were almost nude]... severe scars from floggings.'
Many of the women he saw were too weak to execute the
tasks imposed by the 'special magistrate'. Sturge's report
described in painful detail the sufferings of a heavily pregnant woman he had watched as she struggled to work the
punishment treadmill.

The overseer at Pemberton Valley, William Millar, wrote
to the Hamilton family in Ayr in May 1834 explaining that
since the workers now worked for a daily wage, the long
hours worked far into the night at harvest time, hours which
had always been necessary for cutting and processing the
sugar crop, would require additional payment. He informed
Archibald Hamilton that he would need to send 'about £200 in
shillings and sixpences' to cover this night work.[7] The family
sent John Hamilton out to Jamaica to check that their promised compensation was 'a fair and equitable valuation of the
negroes'. Archibald and Lady Jane were setting off for a tour
of Italy when nephew John's letter arrived saying that 'the
negroes had left' the estate. They appeared to have 'purchased
small properties around us', John reported. The decision of
their slaves to walk away meant the plantation would now

have to search for paid labour. This John had tried to do, but found that negotiating with the so-called apprentices was not quite as easy as he supposed it would be. He had not had much success. He was incensed that 'a gang of men' came to take a look at some clearing and hoeing work, discussed a price, then declined his offer, swung their hoes over their shoulders and sauntered off home. He concluded that

> Our only chance to reduce the wages of Negroes
> will be an immense importation of workers.[8]

Since this was unlikely to happen soon, he recommended abandoning the plantation because it could not be run at a profit. John suggested that perhaps they could sell off land in small job lots. He thought they could probably get nine pounds per acre plot from some of the black Jamaicans who were his former slaves. Since the family had bought some of the original land for just over five pounds an acre, the sale would not be such a bad bargain, he suggested. In the process, the family would create 'a small township of labourers nearby' if they should ever want to use the remainder of their land for something else, like stock-raising.

The apprenticeship system was abandoned as unworkable before the five-year term was up. On 1 August 1838, immediate abolition was finally passed in the House of Commons by 96 votes to 93. Fowell Buxton was observing the moment from the gallery with a group of Quakers who gave such a loud shout 'that we strangers were all turned out for rioting!'[9]

The British Parliament thought it necessary to restate the law on punishment and freedom to roam:

> And be it enacted, That from and after the Proclamation of this Act it shall not be lawful to Place any Female Apprentice on a Treadmill or in the Chain or Penal Gang of any Parish, or to punish any Female Apprentice by whipping or beating her Person, or by cutting off her Hair, for any Offence by her committed... after the Fifteenth Day of August in the Year One thousand eight hundred and thirty-eight in any of the said Colonies. That it shall not be necessary for any apprenticed Labourer to be furnished with a Pass or Permission of any Kind during any Time of the Day or Night.

Some Jamaicans did continue to work for wages and made full use of their provision grounds, growing fresh vegetables and supplementing what was often an inadequate, seasonal income with cash brought in by these small-scale market gardening ventures. But many free Jamaicans avoided any further contact with white employers. A substantial number, like those who had been enslaved by the Hamiltons at Pemberton Valley, simply walked away and settled as subsistence farmers on their provision grounds, small corners of abandoned estates or unoccupied crown lands deep in the mountains. They built themselves little huts on land they had possibly bought but probably had simply settled on; 'capture land' and abandoned fields, where they were now leading the peasant life or small artisan lifestyles of which they had dreamed. Here, they built shacks out of whatever material they could find. Rows of little homes appeared on former provision grounds or parts of abandoned estates. Many such squatter communities can be seen today, as I found on my visit to Jamaica. Generations of these families have continued to cultivate and survive on plots they have never owned. The bits of land on which they live continue to belong to the compensated slave owners and their heirs or those who acquired them from parting planters at bargain prices when they would no longer make the inflated profits their owners had come to expect.

Of the 653 sugar estates in Jamaica, more than 150 were abandoned in the first year or two; many more followed. Thousands of acres were left uncultivated. Exports of sugar, rum and coffee were halved. The estates where Tacky had led his rebellion were abandoned or sold for very little in the 1840s. The Hamiltons eventually abandoned Pemberton Valley. The plantation had 305 slaves at the time of compensation, for which they received £4,580, and a further £865 for slaves they owned on a nearby estate. The money was collected and shared between John Hamilton, his wife, and her sister and husband, who owned the slaves between them.

Of the Scottish families represented at the inaugural meeting of Trelawney Colonial Union in July 1832, John Campbell senior received the largest payout to any Scot of £73,000; the Grant family received almost as much altogether from slaves held all over the West Indies, but the sum was £34,543 for their Jamaican captives. The Dickinsons pocketed £19,202 for the people they enslaved in Jamaica, and the Johnstone family walked away with £6,377.

Dugald Malcolm came from a family of cattle farmers and traders. As my story relates, in 1752 he arrived in Jamaica from Kilmartin on the west coast of Scotland with a few skilled labourers and a lot of ambition. He named his cattle farm and later sugar estate after his Scottish home, Argyle. The family set up a store in the port of Lucea where they hired out slaves, took orders for sales and arranged credit for their slave-buying neighbours. They went on to buy shares in several slave ships. The massive capital the family accumulated ultimately depended on these early beginnings, buying and selling the lives and production of several generations of Africans on plantations in Jamaica. These were long hours of back-breaking work, for which the women and men received nothing more than a few rations of preserved herrings, an issue of rough linen clothes and a roof over their heads, which they usually built for themselves. By the time the Malcolm family received their compensation, they had been Jamaican planters for several generations. Under the protection of colonial law, for over 80 years, the family had been buying and selling Africans. Hundreds of Scots did exactly the same, it was considered a respectable way to make lots of money. Though they invested their funds in all kinds of other ventures at home and abroad, their accounts show that Jamaica was always the prime source of their capital.

In 1823, slaves in Jamaica were finally granted limited but increased rights under a new Slave Code – which the Jamaican Assembly refused to implement. The Governor recognised that justice was being denied. In the summer of that year, a slave revolt was brutally put down on the Malcolm family's Argyle estate. John Malcolm, who was managing the estate on their behalf, requested that 11 freedom fighters from Argyle be hanged publicly in his Mill Yard. Terrorised but unbowed, the enslaved community attempted to free these men. Three Argyle freedom fighters, John Clarke, John Miller and Ben Reynolds, chose to kill themselves and die as free men.

Terror tactics ultimately protected a very substantial fortune. The Malcolms were entitled to file 11 separate compensation claims and receive just under £40,000, the estimated value of the people they had enslaved, at the time of abolition. Their compensation payment for 2,181 slaves would be worth around £5.3m in today's pound sterling. John Malcolm (1805–93), first Baron of Poltalloch, was described as 'an art collector and landowner' on the papers which detailed his personal compensation of £2,509. Neil Malcolm (1769–1837) left his family £500,000 when he died. They invested in other parts of the world, but Jamaica during the years of plantation slavery was always their most lucrative source of money. Buying and selling the lives and work of human beings gave them capital that would transform the lives of their family members for generations.

Making such a fortune was the dream that took many young Scots to Jamaica and kept several generations of their families there. It is a chapter in Scottish history which many prefer to forget.

Endnotes

Preface: Freeing our minds

1   Robert Wedderburn, 'The Horrors of Slavery', in *The Horrors of Slavery and Other Writings by Robert Wedderburn*, Iain McCalman (ed), New York and Princeton, Markus Wiener Publishing, 1991, p 47.

2   This was the main role of the many Scottish doctors working in Jamaica throughout most of the 18th century. They shipped vials of live vaccine across the Atlantic.

3   An agreement was signed on 31 July 2019 in Kingston, Jamaica, that the University of Glasgow would fund a £20 million programme of restorative justice; see University of Glasgow, University News Archive, 1 Aug 2019. The development of a museum highlighting Glasgow's links to slavery has been proposed; see www.museumsassociation.org/museums-journal/news/2020/09/glasgow-life-appoints-curator-focusing-on-slavery-and-empire/.

4   When writing this book, I searched our distinguished academic historians' works in vain for an analysis of the part played by the slave economies of North America and the Caribbean in our national development. Bruce Lenman's *Economic History of Modern Scotland*, Harper Collins, 1977 and Gordon Donaldson's *Scotland, the Shaping of a Nation*, London, David and Charles, 1974, are typical examples of our collective historical 'amnesia', though by 2000 Christopher Whatley, in *Scottish Society 1707–1803, Manchester, Manchester University Press*, acknowledges the importance of linen exports to the plantations and the Oswalds as a family of slave traders. Tom Devine, who has studied these matters closely, mentions slavery twice in *The Scottish Nation*, London, Penguin, 1999, (p 367) as the 'abomination' which motivated Scottish missionaries to travel to Africa to convert black slave owners to Christianity. Our new-found

wealth in the eighteenth century, according to his analysis, was the result of agricultural improvement, 'efficient business practices' in the American trade and enterprising men of 'modest means'. Efficient business practice, he explains, led to Scotland's success in the sea trading war with London, Bristol, Whitehaven and Liverpool. In addition, he admits that by the mid 1700s, Scots were 40 per cent of wealthy sugar producers in Jamaica. He describes Scottish agitation against slavery as reducing the 'complex problem' of slavery to a far too simplistic moral question (page 365). We have to wait until 2015 for an admission in TM Devine (ed), *Recovering Scotland's Slavery Past*, Edinburgh, Edinburgh University Press, 2015 that Scottish slave profits were proportionately greater than England's. It is hard not to agree with G Palmer in *The Enlightenment Abolished, Citizens of Britishness,* Aldie, USA, Henry Publishing, 2007, that the collective and willful obscuring of the part played by Black lives in building our prosperity and our failure to acknowledge the capture and working to death of African men and women is an omission which has sustained modern racism.

5   Stephen Mullen, 'Glasgow, Slavery and Atlantic Commerce: An Audit of Historic Connections and Modern Legacies', March 2022, www.glasgow.gov.uk/index.aspx?articleid=29117.

Chapter 1

1   M Campbell, 'Kilberry papers, letters by the packet', Argyll and Bute Library Service publication, 2004.

2   Quoted from Campbell, 'Kilberry papers, letters by the packet'.

3   EF Bradford, *Mactavish of Dunardry, Whitby*, Self-published, 1991, p 149.

4   Campbell, 'Kilberry papers, letters by the packet', p 97.

5   Col John Campbell of Black River 1673–1740', www.ucl. ac.uk/lbs/person/view/2146637757.

6   Janet Schaw, *Journal of a Lady of Quality; Being the Narrative of a Journey from Scotland to the West Indies, North Carolina, and Portugal, in the Years 1774 to 1776,* EW Andrews (ed), Yale University Press, New Haven, Connecticut, 1921, p 55.

7   Ibid, location 413.

8   Ibid, location 637.

9   Ibid, location 815.

10   Ibid, location 1053.

11   *Caledonian Mercury*, Midlothian, Scotland, 22 June 1749, www.britishnewspaperarchive.co.uk.

12   William Daniel, *Jamaican Courant*, Kingston, Jamaica, William Daniel, 1749, vol v, no 295.

13   D Hamilton, *Scotland, the Caribbean and the Atlantic World 1750–1820*, Manchester, Manchester University Press, 2005, location 1391.

14   The UCL https://www.ucl.ac.uk/lbs/ (slavery database) has an interactive map of all known estates in the Caribbean where all the plantations mentioned in this book can be found.

15   Thomas Salmon's set of 22 maps published in London in 1758. Schaw, Journal of a Lady of Quality, location 1031.

16   The voice of John Campbell is quoted from Bradford, *Mactavish of Dunardry*, p 146.

Chapter 2

1   Robert Hamilton to a friend, Oct 1747, Hamilton Family papers, bundle AA/DC17/113.

2   Hamilton Family papers, bundles AA/DC17/113: DC17/v3, AA/DC17/82, AA/DC17/v8. Letters and accounts are used for this chapter with additional material which can be found at 'Browse the legacies / Legacies of British Slavery', www.ucl.ac.uk>lbs>legacies. Search by name of plantation or owner.

3   *An Abstract of the Laws of Jamaica Relating to Slaves with the slave law at length,* Spanish Town, Jamaica, 1819.

4   AA/DC17/113 1740s–50s, Letters referring to the need for more enslaved workers, their purchase and prices, and also the extension of Pemberton Valley lands, details of hurricane damage and miscellaneous business.

5   These examples can be found in Campbell, 'Kilberry papers, letters by the packet', pp 19, 24.

6   Schaw, *Journal of a Lady of Quality*, location 1432.

7   Campbell, 'Kilberry papers, letters by the packet', p 105.

8   Estates in Scotland were beginning to use lime to improve crop production.

9   Quoted from Campbell, 'Kilberry papers, letters by the packet'.

10   He was educated at Glasgow around the time that Watt was working there. A mixed-race son of a Scottish Jamaican family.

11   *Acts of Assembly pased in the Island of Jamaica 1681–1759,* printed by Aikeman Alexander, London, 1802. For further discussion, see B Edwards and D M'Kinnen, *The History, Civil and Commercial, of the British Colonies in the West Indies,* 2 volumes, John Stockdale, London, 1802 and also Aaron Graham, *Jamaican legislation and the Transatlantic constitution 1664–1839,* e-text, Cambridge University Press, 2017.

12   Anonymous, *Great news from Barbadoes, or, A True and faithful account of the grand conspiracy of the Negroes against the English and the happy discovery of the same with the number of those burned alive, beheaded, and otherwise executed for their horrid crimes: with a short description of that plantation,* London, L Curtis, 1676.

13   Olaudah Equiano, *The interesting narrative of the life of Olaudah Equiano: or Gustavus Vassa, the African. Written by himself,* London, self-published, 1789.

14   Governor John Dalling's views are taken from M Wyman-McCarthy, 'Perceptions of French and Spanish Slave Law in Late Eighteenth-Century Britain', *Journal of British Studies,* 57.1, 2018, p 179.

15   Church elders took the trouble to enquire into the circumstances of anyone requesting help from the 'charity box'. Were they hard working and of good character? Church records have the details of each family member's earnings including the mother and children. I examined Maybole, Craigie, Cumnock and Dundonald in Ayrshire in 1790s to arrive at my estimate of seven shillings.

16   Letter from Simon Taylor to Acedeckne, April 1765 quoted in BW Higman, *Plantation Jamaica 1750–1850, Capital and Control in the Colonial Economy*, Kingston, Jamaica, University of the West Indies Press, 2008, p 198.

17   The International Museum of Slavery, Liverpool, displays this quote https://www.liverpoolmuseums.org.uk/international-slavery-museum/virtual-tour. Source unknown.

Chapter 3

1   H Drax, 'Instructions for the management of Drax Hall', in *A treatise upon husbandry or planting*, by William Belgrove, Boston, New England, D Fowle, 1755, p 56.

2   Schaw, *Journal of a Lady of Quality*, location 2327.

3   J Stewart, *A View of the Past and Present State of the Island of Jamaica*, Edinburgh, Oliver and Boyd, 1823, p 267.

4   Ibid, p 272.

5   Ibid, p 263.

6   Hamilton Papers AA/DC17/113 1719–186, 1760.

7   My descriptions of the slaves on these pages come from the Hamilton family papers: Local authority archive service for South Ayrshire Council, East Ayrshire Council and North Ayrshire Council, www.ayrshirearchives.org.uk. Hamilton papers AA/DC17/113: List of Negroes and Stock upon the Pemberton Valley plantation (1 January 1756).

8   The International Museum of Slavery, Liverpool display this often-cited quote attributed to former American slave William Prescott: www.liverpoolmuseums.org.uk/international-slavery-museum/virtual-tour.

9   Hamilton Papers AA/DC17/113 1719–186. Letters which contain references to the slave insurrection and rebellion on a neighbouring plantation, giving details of events, including the slaughter of whites, destruction, mood of the people and also the general consequences and effect on work on their own plantations (February 1760–24 August 1760).

10   The full list of slaves present and their allowed work tasks in 1756 can be found at AA/DC17/113 with John's comments, some of which I have included in text. List of Negroes and Stock upon the Pemberton Valley plantation (1 January 1756) found in local authority archive service for South Ayrshire Council, East Ayrshire Council and North Ayrshire Council, www.ayrshirearchives.org.uk.

11   Stewart, *A View of the Past and Present State of the Island of Jamaica*, p 263.

12   D Hall, *In Miserable Slavery: Thomas Thistlewood in Jamaica, 1750–86*, New York, Macmillan Press, 1999, location 1030.

13   Belgrove, *A treatise upon husbandry or planting*, p. 66.

14   Stewart, *A View of the Past and Present State of the Island of Jamaica*, p 256.
15   Schaw, *Journal of a Lady of Quality*, location 1863. See also pp 2–7 in Colonel Martin's 'proper care of plantation negroes' as discussed in N Zacek, 'Guide to the microfilm edition of *The papers of Samuel Martin* from the collections of the British Library Introduction to the Papers of Samuel Martin', 2010, www.research.manchester.ac.uk/portal/files/51121211/MartinPapers.pdf.
16   Edward Long, *The History of Jamaica or, General Survey of the Antient and Modern State of that Island: with Reflections on its Situation, Settlements, Inhabitants, Climate, Products, Commerce, Laws, and Government,* quoted in Sidney W Mintz, *Caribbean Transformations*, New York, Colombia University Press, 1989, p 198.
17   Edwards and M'Kinnen, *The History, Civil and Commercial, of the British Colonies in the West Indies*, pp 162 (for attachment and use of provision grounds in Jamaica), 192 (for the law).
18   Hall, *In Miserable Slavery*, location 1521.
19   Ibid, location 1386.
20   Ibid, location 1520.
21   Wedderburn, 'The Horrors of Slavery', pp 44–61.

Chapter 4

1   RB Graham, *Doughty deeds of the Laird of Gartmore: an account of the life of Robert Graham of Gartmore, poet & politician, 1735–1797, drawn from his letter-books & correspondence by RB Cunninghame Graham*, London, William Heinemann Ltd, 1925, p 45. For a short online introduction to Cunninghame Graham, see www.answersonapostcard.weebly.com/answers-on-a-postcard/the-laird-of-gartmore-his-creole-wife-and-their-jamaican-slave-tom.
2   This paragraph is taken from a few of the hundreds of cases in the church records for Maybole old parish church between 1777 and 1813. CH2/809/8. For comparison, I consulted CH2/8252/2, CH2/73/1, CH2/261/1/1, CH12/572/6/1/1, CH2/81/7, CH2/104/2, CH2/751/14, CH2/772/3, CH2/531/7, all available from Ayrshire Archives.

3   Schaw, *Journal of a Lady of Quality*, location 1782.
4   Zachary Macaulay, 'Short autobiographical memorandum written by Macaulay in Sierra Leone in 1797', quoted in Viscountess Knutsford's *Life and letters of Zachary Macaulay by his grand daughter*, London, Edward Arnold, 1906, pp 5–9. Available online from Radcliffe College Library.
5   Ibid, pp 5–9.
6   Quoted from Campbell, 'Kilberry papers, letters by the packet', letters 1797, p 36.
7   DA Livesay, 'Children of an uncertain fortune, from the West Indies to Britain, 1750–1820', unpublished PhD thesis, University of Michigan, 2010, p 41.
8   Cunninghame Graham, *Doughty deeds of the Laird of Gartmore*, p 45.
9   Hall, *In Miserable Slavery*, location 2568.
10   Wedderburn, 'The Horrors of Slavery', p 47.
11   Schaw, *Journal of a Lady of Quality*, location 2035.
12   M Nugent, *Lady Nugent's journal: Jamaica one hundred years ago*, Cambridge, Cambridge University Press, 2010, p 273.
13   Stewart, *A View of the Past and Present State of the Island of Jamaica*, p 324.
14   The wills cited here are taken from the Jamaican geneology research library at www.jamaicafamilysearch.com (listing of wills 1756–1930).
15   Multiply by about 100 to get an estimate of the fortunes these men lavished on their children.

Chapter 5

1   This Harvie brother's quote comes from his letters in SD Smith, *Slavery, Family, and Gentry Capitalism in the British Atlantic, The World of the Lascelles, 1648–1834*, Cambridge, Cambridge University Press, 2006.
2   Skipper Duncan, 'Letter to James Campbell, 9 August 1748', in Bradford, *Mactavish of Dunardry*, p 139.
3   Scottish ships, most of them based on the Clyde, were about 12 per cent of the British total; some calculations would suggest a higher figure of 14 per cent. My figure of exports by value is 12 per cent of the British total of £5,746,353.

4   For more information, search 'Forfar' in 'The statistical
     accounts of Scotland', www.statista.com.

5   The opinions of the Laird are taken from John Maclean, *His-
     torical and traditional sketches of Highland families and the
     Highlands,* Inverness, Dingwall Advertiser Office, 1848, p 9.

6   Francis Hutcheson, *System of Moral Philosophy in 3 books,*
     London, Longman, 2009, p 227 (ebook).

7   Information found in Dumfries and Galloway Archive, Dum-
     fries and Galloway Council, Communities Directorate, Ewart
     Library, Catherine Street, Dumfries, DG1 1JB. Box GD192
     – Dumfriesshire Trade, Especially in Slaves. Letters. James
     Irving Surgeon to the African Trade Voyages 1790–1792 and
     his adventures reported in Dumfries weekly magazine. Further
     information which suggests he was probably a young relative
     of the surgeon of the same name (Irving) who was in the Afri-
     can trade can be found in F Wilkins, *Dumfries and Galloway
     and the Transatlantic Slave Trade,* Kidderminster, Worcs, Wyre
     Forest Press, 2007, p 35.

8   Schwarz, 'Scottish Surgeons in the the Liverpool slave trade',
     p 150.

9   T Clarkson, *The History of the Rise, Progress and Accomplish-
     ment of the Abolition of the African Slave-Trade, the British
     Parliament, 1839,* republished by Cambridge University Press,
     2010. Clarkson devotes Chapter XXII to a detailed summary
     of all the evidence given to the committee enquiry which is
     discussed here.

10   Clarkson presenting evidence to the Privy Council enquiry
     into slavery. He bought the wooden instrument from a shop
     in Liverpool and noted the graphic explanation of how it
     was used. Clarkson, *The History of the Rise, Progress and
     Accomplishment of the Abolition of the African Slave-Trade,*
     p 271.

11   Extracts from the evidence delivered before a Select Commit-
     tee of the House of Commons, in the years 1790 and 1791
     on the part of the petitioners for the abolition of the slave-
     trade. This can be found at www.archives.parliament.uk and
     the Journals of the House of Commons, www.commonsli-
     brary.parliament.uk/research-briefings/cbp-7460/ – Privvy
     Council Reports.

12 Detailed requirements relayed from prospective buyers can be found in Hamilton, *Scotland, the Caribbean and the Atlantic World 1750–1820*.

13 International Museum of Slavery, Liverpool. These figures are taken from a display showing the books/ accounts of slave ships and their crew working out of Liverpool.

14 This and other examples are taken from Schwarz, 'Scottish Surgeons in the the Liverpool slave trade', pp 145–65.

15 Hamilton, *Scotland, the Caribbean and the Atlantic World 1750–1820*, p 195.

16 The Jamaican geneology research library, www.jamaicafamilysearch, lists early arrivals by year and surname.

17 Smith, *Slavery, Family, and Gentry Capitalism in the British Atlantic, The World of the Lascelles, 1648–1834*, p 139.

18 Nugent Papers Box 3 quoted in C Petley, *White Fury: A Jamaican Slaveholder and the Age of Revolution*, Oxford, Oxford University Press, 2018, p 273.

19 Smith, *Slavery, Family, and Gentry Capitalism in the British Atlantic*, p 180.

Chapter 6

1 'An Act to Prevent the inconvenience arising from the exorbitant Grants and Devises made by White Persons to Negroes and to restrain and limit such Grants and Devises', in *Acts of Assembly passed in the Island of Jamaica 1681–1759*, London, Aikeman Alexander, 1802, part 11. (Originally published St Jago de la Vega, 1769).

2 Samuel Pepys, *The Diary of Samuel Pepys from 1659–1669 with Memoir*, Richard Lord Braybrooke (ed), London, Frederick Warne and Co, 1825, 12 May 1668.

3 Owners could double the value of young male slaves by sending them home to Scotland for an apprenticeship. Ovid, the black man bundled onto the packet boat in chains under the authority of Janet Schaw's brother, was possibly one such man.

4 Edwards and M'Kinnen, *The History, Civil and Commercial, of the British Colonies in the West Indies*, p 401.

5 Schaw, *Journal of a Lady of Quality*, location 2250.

6   Ibid, location 416–20.
7   Ibid, location 2310.
8   Ibid, location 2318–23.
9   Ibid, location 2314.
10 Mary Prince, *The History of Mary Prince, A West Indian Slave*, Sara Salih (ed), London, Penguin, 2000, locations 50196–235.
11 Bradford, *Mactavish of Dunardry*, pp 154–6.
12 Stewart, *A View of the Past and Present State of the Island of Jamaica*, p 324.
13 Dumfries and Galloway Council, Communities Directorate, Ewart Library, Catherine Street, Dumfries, DG1 1JB. GGD192, Dumfriesshire Trade, Especially in Slaves.
14 Livesay, 'Children of an uncertain fortune', p 151.
15 The Hays' association with the West Indies began in Barbados. They moved into Jamaica where they became a long-term planter family. One of them was a high court judge and Member of the Jamaican Assembly.
16 'The Cato Street Conspiracy', *The National Archives*, www.nationalarchives.gov.uk/pathways/blackhistory/rights/cato.htm.
17 Livesay, 'Children of an uncertain fortune', p 215.
18 See Wills, Church of England, at www.jamaicafamilysearch.com.
19 MH Fisher, *Counterflows to Colonialism: Indian Travellers and Settlers in Britain, 1600–1857*, Delhi, Permanent Black, 2006, p 201.
20 Livesay, 'Children of an uncertain fortune', p 225.
21 See Wills, Church of England, at www.jamaicafamilysearch.com.
22 Livesay, 'Children of an uncertain fortune', p 219.
23 Schaw, *Journal of a Lady of Quality*, location 2323.
24 T Burnard, *Mastery, Tyranny, and Desire: Thomas Thistlewood and His Slaves in the Anglo-Jamaican World*, Chapel Hill, University of North Carolina Press, 2004, pp 155–6.

Chapter 7

1   James Beattie, *An essay on the nature and immutability of truth, in opposition to sophistry and scepticism*, Edinburgh, A Kincaid & J Bell etc, 1771, pp 228–30.
2   Henry Home Kames, *Sketches of the History of Man*, Cambridge, Cambridge University Press, 2012, pp 17–20.

3   David Hume, 'Of National Character', Knud Haakenssen (ed), Cambridge, Cambridge University Press, 1994. Originally published in 1777, these lines were contained in note 'M' at the end of the essay.

4   Adam Smith, *The Theory of Moral Sentiments*, London, A Millar; Edinburgh, A Kincaid and J Bell, 1759, pp 206–7.

5   Adam Smith, *An Inquiry into the Nature and Causes of the Wealth of Nations*, 2 volumes, RH Campbell and AS Skinner (eds), Indianapolis, Liberty Fund, 1984, p 387.

6   James Beattie, *An Essay on the Nature and Immutability of Truth in Opposition to Sophistry and Scepticism*, Edinburgh, A Kincaid & J Bell etc, 1771, pp 228–30.

7   Campbell, 'Kilberry papers, letters by the packet', Argyll and Bute Library Service, 2004, sending instructions across the Atlantic to Archibald Campbell in Minard in 1766, p 32.

8   'The Somerset Case', *The National Archives*, www.national archives.gov.uk/pathways/blackhistory/rights/docs/state_trials.htm.

9   'Joseph Knight against Sir John Wedderburn of Ballendean Bar[onet]', 1774 in 'Slavery, freedom or perpetual servitude? – the Joseph Knight case', *National Records of Scotland*, www. nrscotland.gov.uk/research/learning/slavery/slavery-freedom-or-perpetual-servitude-the-joseph-knight-case.

10 *Caledonian Mercury*, 17 January 1778.

Chapter 8

1   William Dickson writing to Thomas Clarkson on arriving in Edinburgh on 18th March 1789, quoted in Clarkson, *The History of the Rise, Progress and Accomplishment of the Abolition of the African Slave-Trade by the British Parliament*, chapter XXIV.

2   J Ramsay, *An Essay on the Treatment and Conversion of African Slaves in the British Sugar Colonies*, Cambridge, Cambridge University Press, 2010, p ix.

3   T Paine, *The Rights of Man*, London, J Jordan, 1791, part II, p 2.

4   Clarkson, *The History of the Rise, Progress and Accomplishment of the Abolition of the African Slave-Trade by the British Parliament*, chapter VIII covers Clarkson's month in Kent with Ramsay.

5   Clarkson's account of the dinner with Wilberforce can be found in Clarkson, *The History of the Rise, Progress and Accomplishment of the Abolition of the African Slave-Trade by the British Parliament*, chapter x.

6   Reproduced in full in Clarkson, *The History of the Rise, Progress and Accomplishment of the Abolition of the African Slave-Trade by the British Parliament*, location 6314.

7   The acclaimed anti-slavery novel, written by the female novelist in 1688, was adapted for the stage by Thomas Southerne and performed many times in the 18th century.

8   M Jones, 'The mobilisation of public opinion against the slave trade and slavery, 1787–1838', DPhil thesis, University of York, 1998, p 32.

9   Clarkson, *The History of the Rise, Progress and Accomplishment of the Abolition of the African Slave-Trade by the British Parliament*, location 6386.

10   Ibid, location 6288.

11   Ibid, location 4844.

12   Taylor Family Papers, Institute of Commonwealth Studies Library in London, original papers quoted in Petley, *White Fury*, p 154.

13   Beattie, *An essay on the nature and immutability of truth, in opposition to sophistry and scepticism*, pp 228–30.

14   These quotations from the *John Bull* magazine are quoted in Ian Whyte, *Scotland and the Abolition of Black Slavery*, Edinburgh, Edinburgh University Press, 2006, p 129.

15   T Clarkson, *Essay on the impolicy of the African Slave Trade*, London, Phillips, 1788, p 55. www.digitalcollections.nypl.org.

16   These quotations are taken from Jones, 'The mobilisation of public opinion against the slave trade and slavery, 1787–1838', p 155.

17   Dumfries and Galloway Archive, Dumfries and Galloway Council, Communities Directorate, Ewart Library, Catherine Street, Dumfries, DG1 1JB. Box numbers – GGD192 Southern American States: Dumfriesshire Trade.

18   W Dickson, *Diary of a Visit to Scotland for the Abolition Committee, January–March 1792*, in Friends House Library, London, pp 106–7.

19   Ibid.

20   Allerdyce was reputed to have had a slave trading career with the Royal African Company. He owned property in Jamaica and had several children there. A background to Allerdyce can be found at www.ucl.ac.uk>lbs>legacies.

21   Introduction by George Robson, 'Story of the Jamaica Mission' in *Missions of the United Presbyterian Church*, series 1, Edinburgh, Morrison and Gibb, 1896, p 25.

22   Archibald Dalzel, esq, *History of Dahomey: an Inland Kingdom of Africa; Compiled from Authentic Memoirs with introduction and Notes by Governor at Cape-Coast Castle*, Hardpress, Sligo, Ireland, 2017.

23   The opinions of Dundas and debate in parliament are covered very fully in Clarkson, *The History of the Rise, Progress and Accomplishment of the Abolition of the African Slave-Trade by the British Parliament*, chapter IV, p 305.

24   A full account of the legislation and the debate can be found at 'An Act to prevent the importation of slaves by any of his majesties subjects', Hansard Parliament, vol 7, debates 23rd July 1806.

25   The Transatlantic Slave Trade Database www.slavevoyages.org lists all vessels and voyages, the numbers of captives, captains and investors as well as the total numbers of people transported.

26   Clarkson, *The History of the Rise, Progress and Accomplishment of the Abolition of the African Slave-Trade by the British Parliament*, p 359.

Chapter 9

1   Lady Maria Nugent to her diary in 1803. M Nugent, *Lady Nugent's journal of her residence in Jamaica from 1801 to 1805*, P Wright (ed), Kingston, Institute of Jamaica, 1966 p 239.

2   Hamilton AA/DC17/113: Letters which contain references to the slave insurrection and rebellion on a neighbouring plantation, giving details of events, including the slaughter of whites, destruction, mood of the people and also the general consequences and effect on work on their own plantations (February 1760–24 August 1760).

3   Hall, *In Miserable Slavery*, location 826.
4   Ibid.
5   Jones, 'The mobilisation of public opinion against the slave trade and slavery, 1787–1838', p 34.
6   Ibid, p 32.
7   There were never enough white men in the islands at times like this. They were dependent on employing black foot soldiers.
8   Colonial Office Papers, www.jamaicafamilysearch.com.
9   Hall, *In Miserable Slavery*, location 2150.
10   Burnard, *Mastery, Tyranny, and Desire: Thomas Thistlewood and His Slaves in the Anglo-Jamaican World*, p 128.
11   Colonial Office Papers, www.jamaicafamilysearch.com.
12   The author of this letter was a Captain Jenkins. It can be found along with similar examples in '1776 Hanover slave uprising', www.jamaicanfamilysearch.com/Samples2/ 1776slaverevolt.htm.

Chapter 10

1   Assembly of the Church of Scotland, 1797, in WM Heatherington, *History of the Church of Scotland: From the Introduction of Christianity to 1841*, Edinburgh, John Stone and Fairley, 1842.
2   Principle Acts of Church of Scotland, convened 2nd May 1789, printed by James Dickson.
3   Olaudah Equiano's letter can be found in the *Edinburgh Evening Courant* of 30 May 1789.
4   Schaw, *Journal of a Lady of Quality*, location 1863.
5   It was established English Common Law since the earliest times that a Christian could not be bought and sold as a slave. See M Kaufmann, *Black Tudors, The Untold Story*, London, Oneworld Publications, 2017, p 46. In Scotland, with its separate legal system, this was not the case.
6   The words of Dr George Hamilton reported in Heatherington, *History of the Church of Scotland*, p 694.
7   In British Government Instructions to the first Governor, 1660.
8   All details taken from 'Anglican servants in the Caribbean, c 1610–c 1740' with remarks from www.jamaicafamilysearch.com.

9   *Short Address to the People of Scotland*, Edinburgh, J Robertson, 1792, can now be accessed via Cornell University Library
Digital Collection.

10   Colonial Office Papers, www.jamaicafamilysearch.com.

11   'A history of the Scottish Church in Jamaica' and 'Early 19th
Century Jamaica Church of Scotland and Presbyterian Missionaries' at www.jamaicafamilysearch.com.

12   Ibid.

13   Mr Blyth's views are reported in Robson (ed), 'Story of the
Jamaica Mission', p 25.

14   'Early 19th Century Jamaica Church of Scotland and Presbyterian Missionaries' in *A history of the Scottish Church in
Jamaica*, www.jamaicafamilysearch.com.

Chapter 11

1   Taken from a 'Petition of the West Indian Merchants for
protection of their property' presented to House of Lords April
1826, vol 15 cc385–96.

     After the petition had been read to the house, Lord
Redesdale stressed that should there be any loss of colonial
labour, this would completely undermine 'the confidence of
capitalists' with disastrous results for the nation's banks. A
previous petition from merchants of London in 1823 claimed
'West Indian securities are become nearly valueless [...] as
transferable property' – Debate in Lords, 29 March 1823.

2   Adam Smith, *An Inquiry into Nature and Causes of the
Wealth of Nations*, p 159.

3   Clarkson, *The History of the Rise, Progress and Accomplishment of the Abolition of the African Slave-Trade*, chapter XXII.

4   Macaulay in *The Christian Observer*, vol 23, March 1823,
p 185.

5   Clarkson, *The History of the Rise, Progress and Accomplishment of the Abolition of the African Slave-Trade*, p 157.

6   Anonymous, 'The West Indian Controversy', *Blackwood's
Edinburgh Magazine*, December 1823, p 438.

7   The Duke of Manchester, later Governor of Jamaica, is quoted
in 'Governor's Correspondence 1808–1827' to be found on
www.jamaicafamilysearch.com.

8   These quotes can be found in Colonial Office Papers at www.
     jamaicafamilysearch.com.
9   Bathurst's views can be found in the Colonial Office Papers
     available at www.jamaicafamilysearch.com.
10   C Williams, *A Tour Through the Island of Jamaica 1823*,
     London, Hunt and Clark, 1826, p 68.
11   For further examination of slave songs, see Hilary D Beckles,
     'The Wilberforce Song: How Enslaved Caribbean Blacks
     Heard British Abolitionists', *Parliamentary History*, 26.4,
     2007, pp 113–26 and Karina Williamson, ed, *Contrary
     Voices; Representations of West India Slavery*, 1657–1834,
     Kingston, Jamaica, University of the West Indies Press, 2008.
          For the words of the song, see Paul Brown, 'Representati-
     ons of Rebellion: Slavery in Jamaica, 1823–1831', MA Thesis,
     Clemson University, 2014, p 10.
12   Anonymous, *Report of The Trial of Fourteen Negroes, at The
     Court-House, Montego-Bay, January 28, 1824, and The Two
     Following Days, on A Charge of Rebellions Conspiracy; With
     The Arguments of The Advocates, and The Speeches of The
     Judges, Montego-Bay*, Jamaica, 1824. Reprinted for Harvard
     Law School Library's The Making of Modern Law series by
     Gale in 2012.
13   Brown, 'Representations of rebellion: Slavery in Jamaica,
     1823–1831', p 12.
14   Anonymous, Colonial Office Papers 1816–1831 *Amelioration
     'improve conditions of the lower orders of society'*, www.
     jamaicanfamilysearch.com/Samples2/Mslavea4.htm.
15   Jamaica CO137172, Earl Belmore (Governor 1829–1832), Colo-
     nial Office Papers, available at www.jamaicafamilysearch.com.

Chapter 12

1   Sam Sharpe was reputed to have said this to reverend Henry
     Bleby, an English Methodist minister, just before his execut-
     ion in 1832. The spirit of his words evokes the actions and
     sentiments of three Argyle freedom fighters, John Clarke, John
     Miller and Ben Reynolds, who killed themselves ten years pre-
     viously, preferring to die as free men rather than be captured
     and killed as slaves.

2   This quotation comes from the short preface to C Williams,
     A Tour Through the Island of Jamaica 1823, Miami, Hard
     Press, 2019, p 224.

3   Ibid. p 75.

4   Extract of a letter from Jamaica written to a gentleman in
     Aberdeen, 9 August 1823, published in the *Caledonian Mer-
     cury* on 27 October, p 3. For further discussion, see TR Day,
     'Jamaican revolts in British press and politics, 1760–1865',
     Virginia Commonwealth University, 2016,
     www.scholarscompass.vcu.edu/etd.

5   Archibald Allison, 'West Indian Controversy', *Blackwood's
     Edinburgh Magazine*, October 1828, p 438.

6   Petitions signed by large numbers of local people were usu-
     ally published in full in the local newspaper. These quotations
     come from the *Inverness Courier* of Wednesday 17 March
     1830, pp 2–3. As we have seen, they also printed parliamen-
     tary speeches on the subject of slavery from time to time.

7   Elizabeth Heyrick, *Immediate, Not Gradual Abolition: Or, An
     Inquiry Into the Shortest, Safest and Most Effectual Means of
     Getting Rid of West Indian Slavery*, London and Boston, Isaac
     Knapp, 1824.

8   Jones, 'The mobilisation of public opinion against the slave
     trade and slavery, 1787–1838', p 186.

9   The Church of Scotland accepted a role in advising and gui-
     ding the Government. Evangelicals believed that religion pro-
     vided the moral leadership of the nation and should therefore
     not be overruled by Government.

10   Whyte, *Scotland and the Abolition of Black Slavery, 1756–
     1838*, p 255.

11   Edward Jordan, *The Watchman*, August 1828, p 68.

12   Robson (ed), 'Story of the Jamaica Mission', pp 38–9.

13   The *Royal Gazette* recorded the formation of the Colonial
     Union, listing members of committee and the resolutions of the
     meeting. See *Royal Gazette* at www.jamaicafamily search.com.

14   *The Scotsman*, 28 March 1832, p 4.

15   Lord St Vincent and Earl of Rippon, 'Debate on the Ministerial
     Plan for the Abolition of Slavery', *Hansard*, vol 18, 4 June 1833.

16   Robson (ed), 'Story of the Jamaica Mission', p 37.

17   *The Scotsman*, 30 July 1834, p 1.

Chapter 13

1   Hansard, 'Abolition of Slavery', *House of Commons Debate 19 June 1835*, vol 28, cc 918–60.
2   *Inverness Courier*, 8 November 1838.
3   Examples originally from William James. Fowell Buxton's contributions to the debate are reproduced in Clarkson, *The History of the Rise, Progress and Accomplishment of the Abolition of the African Slave-Trade*, p 290.
4   Sturge arrived in Jamaica in January and by late February/mid March he was in the west of the island. At the end of February he met Thomas McNeed in Westmorland. J Sturge and T Harvey, *The West Indies in 1837*, Cambridge, Cambridge University Press, 2010, location 2010.
5   Sturge and Harvey, *The West Indies in 1837*, location 4599.
6   On 10 March, Sturge visited the Savannah la Mar workhouse and recorded his findings. Sturge and Harvey, *The West Indies in 1837*, location 2044–3752.
7   AA/DC17/2, 1832–1845, Correspondence and accounts of Archibald Hamilton of material on the Pemberton Valley estate, Jamaica, May 1834.
8   John Hamilton's comments come from his letters to the Hamilton family about the problems of getting labourers, the ending of slavery and the introduction of a transitional apprenticeship labour system. AA/DC17/9, 1838, John Hamilton to Archibald Hamilton concerning the Pemberton Valley estate.
9   Fowell Buxton had lost his seat in the house at this point. His comments about being 'turned out for rioting' are recorded in *The African Slave Trade and Its Remedy*, London, J Murray, 1839, p 20.

Bibliography:
Principal materials used in this account

Articles and Theses:

Anti-Slavery Reporter, volume 4, London, London Society for the Abolition of Slavery, 1831.

Anti-Slavery Reporter, volume 5, London, J Hatchard, January 1832–February 1833.

Beckles, Hilary D, 'The Wilberforce Song: How Enslaved Caribbean Blacks Heard British Abolitionists', *Parliamentary History*, 26.4, 2007, pp 113–26.

Bigelow, J, 'Jamaica in 1850, estates abandoned or depreciated', *History*, 91.302, 2006.

Brown, Paul, 'Representations of Rebellion: Slavery In Jamaica, 1823–1831', Master's Thesis, Clemson University, 2014, www.tigerprints.clemson.edu/all_theses/1984.

Brown, Vincent, 'Spiritual Terror and Sacred Authority in Jamaican Slave Society', *Slavery & Abolition*, 24.1, 2003, pp 24–53.

Bryden, DJ, 'The Jamaican Observatories of Colin Campbell, FRS and Alexander Macfarlane, FRS', *Notes and Records of the Royal Society of London*, 24.2, 1970, pp 261–72.

Carlos, AM, and JB Kruse, 'The decline of the Royal African Company: Fringe firms and the role of the charter', in *The Economic History Review*, 49.2, 1996.

Day, TR, 'Jamaican revolts in British press and politics, 1760–1865', Master's Thesis, Virginia Commonwealth University, 2016, www.scholarscompass.vcu.edu/etd.

Devine, TM, 'The colonial trades and industrial investment in Scotland, c 1700–1815', *The Economic History Review*, 29.1, 1976.

Dorris, Glen, 'The Scottish Enlightenment and the Politics of Abolition', Doctoral Thesis, University of Aberdeen, 2011.

Duffill, M, 'The African trade from the ports of Scotland, 1706–1766', *Journal of Slave and Post Slave Studies*, 25.3, 2004.

Forster, Martin, and Simon D Smith, 'Surviving Slavery. Mortality at Mesopotamia, a Jamaican sugar estate, 1762–1832', *Discussion Papers 09/03*, Department of Economics, University of York, 2009.

Houston, George, 'Labour Relations in Scottish Agriculture before 1870', *The Agricultural History Review*, 6.1, 1958, pp 27–41.

Inikori, JE, 'The volume of the British slave trade, 1655–1807', *Cahiers d'Études Africaines Année*, 128, 1992, pp 643–88.

James, HF, 'Medieval rural settlement: a study of mid-Argyll, Scotland', PhD thesis, University of Glasgow, 2009.

Jones, M, 'The mobilisation of public opinion against the slave trade and slavery, 1787–1838', DPhil Thesis, University of York, 1998.

Livesay, DA, 'Children of an uncertain fortune, from the West Indies to Britain, 1750–1820', PhD thesis, University of Michigan, 2010. www.hdl.handle.net/2027.42/77875.

Livesay, DA, *Children of Uncertain Fortune: Mixed-Race Migration from the West Indies to Britain*, Chapel Hill, North Carolina, the Omohundro Institute of Early American History and Culture and University of North Carolina Press, 2018. www.hdl.handle.net/2027.42/77875.

Livesay, DA, 'Extended families: Mixed-race children and Scottish experience, 1770–1820', *International Journal of Scottish Literature*, 4, 2008.

Livingston, A, 'The Galloway Levellers, a study of the origins, events and consequences of their actions', MPhil dissertation, University of Glasgow, 2009. www.eleanor.lib.gla.ac.uk/record=b2671101.

Lovejoy, PE, and D Richardson, 'Competing markets for male and female slaves: Prices in the interior of West Africa, 1780–1850', *The International Journal of African Historical Studies*, 28.2, 1995, pp 261–93.

Mc Innes, Allan, 'Commercial Landlordism and Clearance in the Scottish Highlands: The case of Arichonan', *Communities in European history: representations, jurisdictions, conflicts*, Juan Pan-Montojo and Frederik Pedersen (eds), States, legislation and institutions: thematic work group 1.2, 2007.

Millar, AH (ed), 'Selection of Scottish forfeited estates papers. 1715 and 1745. Showing incomes in cash and kind', *Publications of Scottish History Society*, LVII, 1909.

Mitchell, MD, 'Joint-stock capitalism & the Atlantic commercial network: The Royal African Company, 1672–1752', DPhil dissertation, University of Pennsylvania, 2012. upenn.edu/dissertations/AAI3509288.

Morgan, K, 'Merchant networks, the guarantee system, and the British Slave Trade to Jamaica in the 1790s', *Slavery & Abolition*, 37.2, 2016, pp 334–52.

Morgan, K, 'Slave women and reproduction in Jamaica, c 1776–1834', *History*, 91.302, 2006, pp 231–53.

Morris, M, 'Atlantic archipelagos: A cultural history of Scotland, the Caribbean and the Atlantic world, c 1740–1833', PhD thesis, University of Glasgow, 2013.

Muir, J, 'Farm rents and improvement: East Lothian and Lanarkshire, 1670–1830', *The Agricultural History Review*, 57.1, 2009, pp 37–57.

Mullen, Stephen, 'Glasgow, Slavery and Atlantic Commerce: An Audit of Historic Connections and Modern Legacies', March 2022, www.glasgow.gov.uk/index.aspx?articleid=29117.

Mullen, Stephen, 'The Glasgow 'West India interest': Integration, collaboration and exploitation in the British Atlantic World, 1776–1846', PhD thesis, University of Glasgow, 2015.

Mullen, Stephen, 'Scots Kirk of Colonial Kingston, Jamaica', *Scottish Church History*, 45.1, 2016, pp 99–116.

Newman, BN, 'Gender, sexuality and the formation of racial identities in the eighteenth-century Anglo-Caribbean world', *Gender & History*, 22.3, 2010, pp 585–602.

Nichols, Patrick John, '"Free Negroes" – The Development of Early English Jamaica and the Birth of Jamaican Maroon Consciousness, 1655–1670', MA Thesis, Georgia State University, 2015. www.scholarworks.gsu.edu/history_theses/100.

Oldfield, JR, 'The London Committee and Mobilization of Public Opinion against the Slave Trade', *The Historical Journal*, 35.2, 1992, pp 331–43.

Paul, HJ, 'The South Sea Company and the Royal African Company's combined slaving activities', *conference paper reading*, University of St Andrews, Economic History Society, 2006.

Rugemer, Edward S, 'The Development of Mastery and Race in the Comprehensive Slave Codes of the Greater Carribean during the Seventeenth Century', *William and Mary Quarterly*, 70.3, 2013, pp 429–58.

Ryden, D, 'Manumission in late eighteenth-century Jamaica', *New West Indian Guide*, 92.3–4, 2018, pp 211–44.

Schwarz, Suzanne, 'Scottish Surgeons in the Liverpool slave trade in the late Eighteenth and early Nineteenth Centuries', in TM Devine (ed), *Recovering Scotland's Slavery Past*, Edinburgh, Edinburgh University Press, 2015, pp 145–65.

Sheridan, Richard B, 'The Role of the Scots in the Economy and Society of the West Indies' in *Comparative Perspectives on Slavery in New World Plantation Societies*, Vera Rubin and Arthur Tuden (eds), New York, The New York Academy of Sciences, 1977, pp 94–106.

Smith, Robert Worthington, 'The Legal Status of Jamaican Slaves Before the Anti-Slavery Movement', *The Journal of Negro History*, 30.3, 1945.

Smith, Robert Worthington, 'Slavery and Christianity in the British West Indies', *Church History*, 19.3, 1950, pp 171–86.

'The Jamaican observatories of Colin Campbell, FRS and Alexander Macfarlane, FRS', *Notes and Records of the Royal Society of London*, 24.2, 1970.

Thompson, Peter, 'Henry Drax's Instructions on the Management of a Seventeenth-Century Barbadian Sugar Plantation', *The William and Mary Quarterly*, 66.3, 2009, pp 565–604.

Wyman-McCarthy, M, 'Perceptions of French and Spanish Slave Law in Late Eighteenth-Century Britain', *Journal of British Studies*, 57.1, 2018, pp 29–52.

Books:

Anonymous, *Great news from Barbadoes, or, A True and faithful account of the grand conspiracy of the Negroes against the English and the happy discovery of the same with the number of those burned alive, beheaded, and otherwise executed for their horrid crimes: with a short description of that plantation*, London, L Curtis, 1676.

Anonymous, *Report of The Trial of Fourteen Negroes, at The Court-House, Montego-Bay, January 28, 1824, and The Two Following Days, on A Charge of Rebellions Conspiracy; With The Arguments of The Advocates, and The Speeches of The Judges*, Montego-Bay, Jamaica, 1824. Reprinted for Harvard Law School Library's 'The Making of Modern Law' series by Gale in 2012.

Aikeman, Alexander, *Acts of Assembly passed in the Island of Jamaica 1681–1759*, London, Aikeman Alexander, 1802.

Bradford, EF, *Mactavish of Dunardry*, Whitby, Self-published, 1991.

Beattie, James, *An essay on the nature and immutability of truth, in opposition to sophistry and scepticism,* Edinburgh, A Kincaid & J Bell, 1771.

Drax, H, 'Instructions for the management of Drax Hall', in *A treatise upon husbandry or planting,* by William Belgrove, Boston, New England, D Fowle, 1755.

Blythe, G, *Reminiscences of Missionary Life, with Suggestions to Churches and Missionaries,* Edinburgh, William Oliphant & Sons, 1851.

Box, Brown Henry, *Narrative of the Life of Henry Box Brown, Written by Himself,* Manchester, Lee and Glynn, 1851.

Burnet, GB, *The Story of Quakerism in Scotland: 1650–1850,* Cambridge, Lutterworth Press, 1952.

Burnard, T, *Mastery, Tyranny, and Desire: Thomas Thistlewood and His Slaves in the Anglo-Jamaican World,* Chapel Hill, University of North Carolina Press, 2004.

Cage, RA, *The Scottish Poor Law 1745–1845*, Edinburgh, Scottish Academic Press, 1981.

Cage, RA, *The Working Class in Glasgow 1750–1914,* London, Croom Helm, 1987.

Campbell, M, 'Kilberry papers, letters by the packet', Argyll and Bute Library Service, 2004.

Christian Observer, Editors: 1802, J Pratt; 1802–16, Z Macaulay; 1816–?, SC Wilks; 1858, JW Cunningham, London, Hatchard & Co 1802–1874, University of Chicago.

Clarkson, T, *Essay on the impolicy of the African Slave Trade,* London, Phillips, 1788. www.digitalcollections.nypl.org.

Clarkson, T, *The History of the Rise, Progress and Accomplishment of the Abolition of the African Slave-Trade,* Cambridge, Cambridge University Press, 2010. (Originally published by the British Parliament, 1839).

Craton, M, *A Jamaican Plantation: The History of Worthy Park 1670–1970,* Toronto, University of Toronto Press, 1970.

Cregeen, ER (ed), *Argyll estate instructions, Mull, Morvern and Tiree, 1771–1805,* Edinburgh, Scottish History Society, 1964. www.digital.nls.uk/127707909.

Cunningham Graham, Robert, *Doughty deeds of the Laird of Gartmore: an account of the life of Robert Graham of Gartmore, poet & politician, 1735–1797, drawn from his letter-books & correspondence*, London, W Heinemann, 1925.

Dalzel, A (ed), *History of Dahomey an Inland Kingdom of Africa; Compiled from Authentic Memoirs with introduction and Notes by Archibald Dalzel, esq Governor at Cape-Coast Castle,* Spilsbury and Son, USA, Hardpress and Sligo, Ireland, 2017.

Delaney, Lucy Ann, *From the Darkness Cometh the Light or Struggles for Freedom*, St Louis, JT Smith, 189?.

Devine, TM, *The Transformation of Rural Scotland, Social Change and the Agrarian Economy, 1660–1815*, Edinburgh, John Donald, 1999.

Devine, TM, *Scotland's Empire 1600–1815*, London, Penguin, 2004.

Devine, TM, *The Scottish Nation*, London, Penguin, 1999.

Devine, TM, *Scotland and the Union 1707–2007*, Edinburgh, Edinburgh University Press, 2008.

Devine, TM (ed), *Recovering Scotland's Slavery Past*, Edinburgh, Edinburgh University Press, 2015.

Devine, TM, *The Scottish Clearances*, London, Penguin, 2019.

Dickson, W, *Diary of a Visit to Scotland for the Abolition Committee, January–March 1792*, held at Friends House Library, London.

Donaldson, Gordon, *Scotland the Shaping of a Nation*, London, David and Charles, 1974.

Door, Alistair J, *The Scottish Linen industry in the eighteenth century*, Edinburgh, John Donald Ltd, 1979.

Douglass, Frederick, *Slavery: Not Forgiven, Never Forgotten – The Most Powerful Slave Narratives, Historical Documents & Influential Novels*, e-book, e-artnow, 2017.

Draper, N, *The Price of Emancipation: Slave Ownership, Compensation and British Society at the End of Slavery*, Cambridge, Cambridge University Press, 2010.

Dunn, RS, *A Tale of Two Plantations, Slave Life and Labour in Jamaica and Virginia*, Cambridge USA, Harvard University Press, 2014.

Edwards, B, and D M'Kinnen, *The History, Civil and Commercial, of the British Colonies in the West Indies*, 2 volumes, London, John Stockdale, 1801.

Equiano, O, *The Interesting Narrative of the Life of Olaudah Equiano, or Gustavus Vassa, the African*, London, Self-published, 1789.

Ferguson, J, *Lowland Lairds*, London, Faber and Faber 1949.

Fisher, Michael Herbert, *Counterflows to Colonialism, Indian Travellers and Settlers in Britain, 1600–1857*, Delhi, Permanent Black, 2006.

Fowell Buxton, Thomas, *The African Slave Trade and Its Remedy*, London, J Murray, 1839.

Gaines, Thomas S (ed), *Buried Alive (Behind Prison Walls) for a Quarter of a Century: Life of William Walker*, Saginaw, MI, Friedman & Hynan, 1892.

Gaskell, P, *Morvern Transformed*, Cambridge, Cambridge University Press, 1968.

Graham, Aaron, *Jamaican legislation and the Transatlantic constitution 1664–1839*, ebook, Cambridge University Press, 2017.

Graham, HG, *The Social Life of Scotland in the Eighteenth Century*, London, Adam and Charles Black, 1901.

Grandy, Moses, *Narrative of the Life of Moses Grandy, Late a Slave in the United States of America*, London, Gilpin, 1843.

Grant, A, *Report on Colonial Trade to Privy Council*, London, Richard Phillips, 1807.

Greene, JP, *Settler Jamaica in 1750s, A Social Portrait*, Charlottesville, Virginia, University of Virginia Press, 2016.

Hakewill, James, *A Picturesque Tour of the Island of Jamaica*, London, Robinson and Lloyd, 1823.

Hall, D, *In Miserable Slavery: Thomas Thistlewood in Jamaica, 1750–86*, New York, Macmillan Press, 1999.

Hamilton, D, *Scotland, the Caribbean and the Atlantic World 1750–1820*, Manchester, Manchester University Press, 2005.

Heatherington, WM, *History of the Church of Scotland: From the Introduction of Christianity to 1841*, Edinburgh, Johnstone and Fairley, 1842.

Heyrick, Elizabeth, *Immediate, Not Gradual Abolition: Or, An Inquiry Into the Shortest, Safest and Most Effectual Means of Getting Rid of West Indian Slavery*, London and Boston, Isaac Knapp, 1824.

Higman, BW, *Plantation Jamaica 1750–1850, Capital and Control in the Colonial Economy*, Mona, Jamaica, University of West Indies, 2008.

Howard, JH, *The laws of the British colonies, in the West Indies and other parts of America, concerning real and personal property, and manumission of slaves; with a view of the constitution of each colony*, London, WH Bond, 1827.

Hutcheson, Francis, *System of Moral Philosophy*, London, Longman, 2009, digitised.

Jackson, MJ, *The Story of Mattie J Jackson Incidents During the War--Her Escape from Slavery. A True Story*, in Academic Affairs Library, UNC-CH, University of North Carolina at Chapel Hill, 1866. Electronic edition, 1999.

Karras, A, *Sojourners in the Sun, Scottish Migrants in Jamaica and Chesapeake, 1740–1800*, New York, Cornel University Press, 1992.

Kaufmann, M, *Black Tudors, The Untold Story*, London, Oneworld Publications, 2017.

Knutsford, Viscountess, *Life and letters of Zachary Macaulay by his grand daughter*, London, Edward Arnold, 1906. Originally published by India Office, 1900.

Law, R (ed), *The English in West Africa: The local correspondence of the Royal African Company of England, 1681–1699, Part 3 (1691–1699)*, Oxford, Oxford University Press, 2007.

Lenman, Bruce, *Economic History of Modern Scotland*, New York, Harper Collins, 1977.

Levitt, I, and C Smout, *The State of the Scottish Working Class in 1843*, Edinburgh, Scottish Academic Press, 1979.

Lindsay, J, *The Scottish Poor Law in the North East 1745–1845*, Ilfracombe, North Devon, Stockwell Ltd, 1975.

Long, Edward, *The History of Jamaica or, General Survey of the Antient and Modern State of that Island: with Reflections on its Situation, Settlements, Inhabitants, Climate, Products, Commerce, Laws, and Government*, London, T Lowndes, 1774.

Luan, John, *An Abstract of the Laws of Jamaica Relating to Slaves with the slave law at length*, Spanish Town, Jamaica, Printed at the Office of the Saint Jago de la Vega Gazette, 1819.

Lynch, Michael, *Scotland a New History,* London, Pimlico, 1991.

Maclean, John, *Historical and traditional sketches of Highland families and the Highlands*, Inverness, Dingwall Advertiser Office, 1848.

Mann, A, *James VII: Duke and King of Scots*, Edinburgh, Birlinn, 2014.

Mintz, Sidney W, *Caribbean Transformations*, New York, Colombia University Press, 1989.

Morgan, K, 'Liverpool Ascendant: British Merchants and the Slave Trade on the Upper Guinea Coast, 1701–1808', in PE Lovejoy and S Schwarz (eds), *Slavery, Abolition and the Transition to Colonialism in Sierra Leone*, Trenton, New Jersey, Africa World Press, 2015, pp 29–50.

Mountain, Joseph, and David Daggett, *Sketches of the Life of Joseph Mountain, a Negro, Who Was Executed at New-Haven, on the 20th Day of October, 1790, for a Rape, Committed on the 26th Day of May Last*, New-Haven, T and S Green, 1790.

Nugent, M, *Lady Nugent's journal: Jamaica one hundred years ago*, Cambridge, Cambridge University Press, 2010.

Anonymous, *News from Barbados, or a True and Faithful Account of the Grand Conspiracy of Negroes Against the English*, London, L Curtis, 1676.

Paine, T, *The Rights of Man,* London, J Jordan, 1791.

Palmer, G, *The Enlightenment Abolished, Citizens of British-ness,* Aldie, USA, Henry Publishing, 2007.

Parker, M, *The Sugar Barons, Family, Corruption, Empire and War,* London, Hutchinson, 2011.

Petley, C, *White Fury: A Jamaican Slaveholder and the Age of Revolution,* Oxford, Oxford University Press, 2018.

Pettigrew, WA, *Freedom's Debt: The Royal African Company and the Politics of the Atlantic Slave Trade, 1672–1752,* Chapel Hill, University of North Carolina Press, 2013.

Pepys, Samuel, *Memoirs of Samuel Pepys, comprising his diary 1659–1669,* Richard Lord Braybook (ed), London, Frederick Warne and Co, 1825.

Prince, Mary, *The History of Mary Prince, A West Indian Slave,* Sara Salih (ed), London, Penguin, 2000.

Powers, A, *A Parcel of Ribbons, Letters of an 18th century family in London and Jamaica,* Self-published, Lulu.com.

Ramsay, J, *An Essay on the Treatment and Conversion of African Slaves in the British Sugar Colonies,* Cambridge, Cambridge University Press, 2013.

Rasmussen, DC, *The Infidel and the Professor,* Oxford, UK, Princeton University Press, 2017.

Richardson, D, 'Profits in the Liverpool Slave Trade: The Accounts of William Davenport, 1757–1784', in R Anstey and P Hair (eds), *Liverpool, the African Slave Trade, and Abolition*, Chippenham, England, Antony Rowe Ltd, 1979, pp 60–90.

Robson, G (ed), 'Story of the Jamaica Mission' in *Missions of the United Presbyterian Church*, series 1, Edinburgh, Morrison and Gibb, 1896.

Schaw, Janet, *Journal of a Lady of Quality; Being the Narrative of a Journey from Scotland to the West Indies, North Carolina, and Portugal, in the Years 1774 to 1776*, EW Andrews (ed), in collaboration with CM Andrews, New Haven, Connecticut, Yale University Press, 1921.

Schofield, MA, *The Slave Trade from Lancashire and Cheshire ports outside Liverpool 1750–1790*, Historic Society of Lancashire and Cheshire, 1976.

Slaven, Anthony, *The Development of the West of Scotland, 1750–1960*, London, Routledge & K Paul, 1975.

Slave Laws of Jamaica, printed for the Duke of Manchester, Spanish Town, Jamaica, Office of Saint Jago La Vega, Gazette 1819.

Smith, Adam, *The Theory of Moral Sentiments*, London, A Millar; Edinburgh, A Kincaid and J Bell, 1759.

Smith, Adam, *An Inquiry into the Nature and Causes of the Wealth of Nations*, London, W Strathan and T Cadell, 1776.

Smith, SD, *Slavery, Family, and Gentry Capitalism in the British Atlantic: The World of the Lascelles, 1648–1834*, Cambridge, Cambridge University Press, 2006.

Smout, T, and AJS Gibson, *Prices, food and wages in Scotland, 1550–1780*, Cambridge, Cambridge University Press, 1995.

Stedman, Joanna, 'Narrative of Joanna; An Emancipated Slave, of Surinam' in *Narrative of a Five Year's Expedition Against the Revolted Negroes of Surinam,* Boston, Isaac Knapp, 1838.

Stewart, J, *A View of the Past and Present State of the Island of Jamaica,* Edinburgh, Oliver and Boyd, 1823.

Sturge, J, and T Harvey, *The West Indies in 1837*, Cambridge, Cambridge University Press, 2010.

Southey, Captain Thomas, *Chronological History of West Indies*, 3 volumes, London, Longman, 1827.

Thomas, H, *History of the Atlantic Slave Trade 1440–1870*, London, Simon & Schuster, 1997.

Vasconcellos, CA, *Slavery, Childhood, and Abolition in Jamaica, 1788–1838*, Athens, USA, University of Georgia Press, 2015.

Warner-Lewis, M, *Archibald Monteath: Igbo, Jamaican, Moravian*, Mona, St Andrew, University Press of the West Indies, 2007.

Wedderburn, Robert, *The Horrors of Slavery, from The Horrors of Slavery and Other Writings by Robert Wedderburn*, Iain McCalman (ed), New York and Princeton, Markus Wiener Publishing, 1991.

Wilkins, F, *Bittersweet, a story of four Jamaican sugar plantations*, Kidderminster Worcs, Wyre Forest Press, 2007.

Wilkins, F, *Dumfries and Galloway and the Transatlantic Slave Trade*, Kidderminster Worcs, Wyre Forest Press, 2007.

Williams, C, *A Tour Through the Island of Jamaica 1823*, London, Hunt and Clark, 1826.

Williams, E, *Capitalism and Slavery*, London, Billing and Sons, 1981.

Williams, J, and D Paton (eds), *A Narrative of Events, since the First of August, 1834, by James Williams, an Apprenticed Labourer in Jamaica*, John Hope Franklin Center, Oklahoma State University, Oklahoma, 2001.

Williamson, Karina, ed, *Contrary Voices; Representations of West India Slavery*, 1657–1834, Kingston, Jamaica, University of the West Indies Press, 2008.

Whyte, I, *Scotland and the Abolition of Black Slavery, 1756–1838*, Edinburgh, Edinburgh University Press, 2006.

Wright, P (ed), *Lady Maria Nugent's journal of her residence in Jamaica from 1801 to 1805*, Kingston, Institute of Jamaica, 1966.

Young, W, *The West-India Common-place Book: Compiled from Parliamentary and Official Documents; Shewing the Interest of Great Britain in its Sugar Colonies*, London, Richard Phillips, 1807.

Other Useful Sources:

Anti-slavery reporter: www.wellcomecollection.org.

Blackwood's Magazine: www.google.co.uk/books/edition Blackwood_s_Edinburgh_Magazine.

Caribbean Newspapers: www.readex.com/products/caribbean-newspapers-series.

Glasgow University theses online: www.ucl.ac.uk/lbs.

Church of Scotland historical records: www.churchofscotland.org.uk.

The Emancipation Proclamation (1863): www.archives.gov/exhibits/featured-documents.

Hansard, www.hansard.parliament.uk, proceedings of parliament, Members of parliament, constituencies, www.parliament.uk/business/publications/hansard/commons hansard.parliament.uk.

HathiTrust Digital Library: www.hathitrust.org. HathiTrust Digital Library is a large-scale collaborative repository of digital content, US University consortium, research libraries including content digitized via Google Books and the Internet Archive digitisation initiatives, as well as content digitised locally by libraries.

House of Commons Library, Journals of the House of Commons, www.commonslibrary.parliament.uk/research-briefings/cbp-7460/ – Privvy Council Report on shipping March 1805.

Jamaican genealogy research library, www.jamaicafamilysearch.com: Source for wills, records of residents in Jamaica and some governor's correspondence. Also contains Colonial Office Papers 1816–1831 Amelioration, 'improve the condition of the lower orders of society' The Governor's correspondence: Colonial Office Papers 1816–1831 Jamaica CO137/172. Note from public records office transcribed by University of Lancaster Bishops survey of Anglican servants in the Caribbean, c 1610–c 1740.

'Legacies of British Slave-ownership', www.ucl.ac.uk/lbs/legacies/.

National Library of Jamaica: nljdigital.nlj.gov.jm.

Slave trade books and pamphlets printed by abolitionist publisher James Phillips in London 1791, 1792, including evidence delivered before the select committee of house of commons in 1790.

National Library of Scotland resources: www.nls.uk/digital-resources.

Newspapers: www.britishnewspaperarchive.co.uk. Search by date, place of publication, subject matter.

Slavery archive: www.columbiaandslavery.columbia.edu.

Slave trade records: www.nationalarchives.gov.uk/help-with-your-research/research-guides/british-transatlantic-slave-trade-records.

Transatlantic Slave Trade Database: www.slavevoyages.org. Lists all vessels and voyages, the numbers of captives, captains and investors as well as the total numbers of people transported.

The statistical accounts of Scotland, www.statista.com.

Microform Academic Publishers.

The Christian Observer: www.catalog.hathitrust.org New York Public Library www.digitalcollections.nypl.org.

Papers relevant to The London Committee and mobilisation of public opinion against the slave trade have been published online by Cambridge University Press: www.cambridge.org/core/journals/historical-journal/.

Trading, historic papers relevant to Glasgow: tradeshouseli-brary.org.

The American Civil Rights Act of 1866: www.african-american-civil-rights.

University of North Carolina, Chapel Hill online resources and slave accounts: www.docsouth.unc.

UCL Slavery Database: https://www.ucl.ac.uk/lbs/.

Many of my resources can now be found at www.brycchan-carey.com/slavery/index.htm.

Scottish Archives:

Sources used from Dumfries and Galloway Archive, Dumfries and Galloway Council, Communities Directorate, Ewart Library, Catherine Street, Dumfries, DG1 1JB. Box numbers:

GGD192 Southern American States: Dumfriesshire Trade, Especially in Slaves: Article by AE Truckell.

GGD620 Account book, Granton Estate, Grenada.

GGD675/1 William Kennedy Laurie of Woodhall: Accounts and correspondence relating to the Jamaican estate of Woodhall and the succession of Walter Kennedy Laurie.

Sources used from Argyll Archives, Archives, Manse Brae
Area Office Lochgilphead, Argyll PA31 8QU, archives@livear-
gyll.co.uk. Box numbers:

R/15 T MacTavish of Dunardry, Papers DR/15. GD/14
Letter from John Campbell of Saltspring, J.

DR/2 Malcolm of Poltalloch Papers.

Sources used from Local authority archive service for South
Ayrshire Council, East Ayrshire Council and North Ayrshire
Council, www.ayrshirearchives.org.uk. Box numbers:

Letter, James Stirling at Pemberton Valley Plantation. Gives
details of crops, the need for more slaves and the possibility of introducing cattle to the estate, against the wishes
of Dr Aikenhead.

AA/DC17/110: List of all the Negroes on the Rozelle Plantation at the entry of Major Garth and his wife, now Mrs
Hamilton, to the estate (after 1738).

AA/DC17/113: List of Negroes and Stock upon the Pemberton
Valley plantation (1 January 1756).

AA/DC17/113: Letters which contain references to the slave
insurrection and rebellion on a neighbouring plantation,
giving details of events, including the slaughter of whites,
destruction, mood of the people and also the general consequences and effect on work on their own plantations
(February 1760–24 August 1760).

AA/DC17/V8, 15 May 1795–29 December 1797, Book of letters written by Alexander West Hamilton from the Pemberton Valley Plantation in Jamaica. His letters are addressed to Thomas Blane, Hugh Hamilton, John Hamilton and David MacDowall Grant. The letters concern business to do with the Pemberton Valley Plantation and mentions poor sugar crops and slave insurrection.

AA/DC17/2, 1832–1845, Correspondence and accounts of Archibald Hamilton of Rozelle. Includes material on the Pemberton Valley estate, Jamaica. Includes:

1832–44, Correspondence between Alexander (Sandy) Hamilton and his brother Archibald regarding Pemberton Valley. Includes references to estate profits and labour shortages following the end of slavery.

1834, John Hamilton, Archibald's brother, concerning family matters and Pemberton Valley. References also to the ending of slavery and the introduction of a transitional apprenticeship labour system.

AA/DC17/7, 1821–1847, Miscellaneous correspondence of Archibald Hamilton. Includes financial and personal interests, Royal Navy and Christ Church appointments. Also included is a large section containing material on personal and family matters, RN and Christ Church hospital appointments.

AA/DC17/9, 1821 & 1838, John Hamilton to Archibald Hamilton concerning the Pemberton Valley estate.

AA/DC17/12, 1821, Pemberton Valley estate accounts.

1821–42, Lists of company ships showing destination, tonnage, owners, principal officers etc and time of coming afloat. Shows Montgomerie Hamilton as being in command of the *Dunina*.

1821, 9 July, A list of company ships abroad, at home and in construction.

AA/DC17/113 1719–1861, Large bundle of correspondence, both business and personal, accounts, reports, printed adverts etc covering a wide range of subjects, which can be generally divided as follows:

1735–60, Plantations. Correspondence and accounts of the Pemberton Valley and Rozelle Plantations in Jamaica. Includes legal documents relating to the dispute over ownership.

1740s–50s, Letters referring to the need for more enslaved workers, their purchase and prices, and also the extension of Pemberton Valley lands, details of hurricane damage and miscellaneous business.

1749, 2 July, Letter, intrigue concerning the governor of Jamaica, Edward Trelawny.

1756, 1 Jan, List of Negroes and Stock upon the Pemberton Valley plantation.

1760, 16 Feb, Letters which contain references to the slave insurrection.

1760, 20 Apr, Rebellion on a neighbouring plantation, giving details.

1760, 2 June, Events, including the slaughter of whites, destruction, mood.

1760, 24 Aug, The people and also the consequences in general.

1761, June, Effect on enslaved workers on the Hamiltons' plantations.

Ayrshire Kirk Sessions:

A few cases from the hundreds in the church records for Maybole old parish church between 1777 and 1813. CH2/809/8. For comparison, I consulted CH2/8252/2, CH2/73/1, CH2/261/1/1, CH12/572/6/1/1, CH2/81/7, CH2/104/2, CH2/751/14, CH2/772/3, CH2/531/7, all available from Ayrshire Archives.

Luath Press Limited

committed to publishing well written books worth reading

LUATH PRESS takes its name from Robert Burns, whose little collie Luath (*Gael.*, swift or nimble) tripped up Jean Armour at a wedding and gave him the chance to speak to the woman who was to be his wife and the abiding love of his life. Burns called one of the 'Twa Dogs' Luath after Cuchullin's hunting dog in Ossian's *Fingal*.

Luath Press was established in 1981 in the heart of Burns country, and is now based a few steps up the road from Burns' first lodgings on Edinburgh's Royal Mile. Luath offers you distinctive writing with a hint of unexpected pleasures.

Most bookshops in the UK, the US, Canada, Australia, New Zealand and parts of Europe, either carry our books in stock or can order them for you. To order direct from us, please send a £sterling cheque, postal order, international money order or your credit card details (number, address of cardholder and expiry date) to us at the address below. Please add post and packing as follows: UK – £1.00 per delivery address; overseas surface mail – £2.50 per delivery address; overseas airmail – £3.50 for the first book to each delivery address, plus £1.00 for each additional book by airmail to the same address. If your order is a gift, we will happily enclose your card or message at no extra charge.

Luath Press Limited
543/2 Castlehill
The Royal Mile
Edinburgh EH1 2ND
Scotland
Telephone: +44 (0)131 225 4326 (24 hours)
email: sales@luath. co.uk
Website: www. luath.co.uk